Sumerian Grammar

Handbook of Oriental Studies
Handbuch der Orientalistik

Section One
THE NEAR MIDDLE EAST

EDITED BY
H. Altenmüller
B. Hrouda
B. A. Levine
R. S. O'Fahey
K. R. Beenhof
C. H. M. Versteegh

Volume Seventy-One

SUMERIAN GRAMMAR

Sumerian Grammar

Dietz Otto Edzard

SBL

Society of Biblical Literature
Atlanta

SUMERIAN GRAMMAR

This edition published under license from Koninklijke Brill NV,
Leiden, The Netherlands by the Society of Biblical Literature.

Library of Congress Cataloging-in-Publication Data

Edzard, Dietz Otto.
Sumerian grammar / by Dietz Otto Edzard.
p. cm.
Originally published : Boston : Brill, 2003. (Handbuch der Orientalistik. Erste Abteilung, Nahe und der Mittlere Osten ; 71. Bd.)
Includes bibliographical references and index.
ISBN-13: 978-1-58983-252-7 (paper binding : alk. paper)
ISBN-10: 1-58983-252-3 (paper binding : alk. paper)
1. Sumerian language–Grammar. I. Title.

PJ4013.E38 2006
499'.955–dc22 2006026259

Printed in the United States of America
on acid-free paper

CONTENTS

Preface xi
Abbreviations xiii

Chapter One The Sumerian Language 1
1.1. General Characteristics 1
1.2. The (hopeless) question of the linguistic affiliation of Sumerian 2
1.3. The linguistic environment of Sumerian 3

Chapter Two How we read Sumerian 7
2.1. General 7
2.2. Spelling of Sumerian 8
2.2.1. Classification of cuneograms 8
2.2.2. Combination of cuneograms; spelling proper 10
2.2.3. Evolution of Sumerian spelling 10

Chapter Three Minimalia of Sumerian phonology and syllabic structure 13
3.1. Phonology 13
3.1.1. Vowels 13
3.1.2. Consonants 14
3.2. Syllable structure 22

Chapter Four The "word" in Sumerian, parts of speech 23
4.1. "Word" 23
4.2. Parts of speech 23

Chapter Five Substantives 29
5.1. General 29
5.2. Possession 29
5.3. Number 31
5.4. Case 33
5.4.1. Notes on the phonetic and spelling behaviour of the case particles 35
5.4.2. Notes on the individual case particles 35
5.4.2.1. Absolutive 35
5.4.2.2. Ergative 35

5.4.2.3. Genitive 36
5.4.2.4. Locative 39
5.4.2.5. Dative 40
5.4.2.6. Comitative 40
5.4.2.7. Ablative-instrumental 41
5.4.2.8. Terminative 42
5.4.2.9. Directive 43
5.4.2.10. Equative 44
5.4.2.11. Recapitulation of the case particles 44

Chapter Six Adjectives 47

Chapter Seven Determination, specification: demonstrative particles 49
7.1. -ne(n) 49
7.2. -bi 50
7.3. -e(?) 50
7.4. -ri(?) 50
7.5. -še 51
7.6. Recapitulation 51

Chapter Eight Overview of the sequence of particles for possession, number and case 53

Chapter Nine Pronouns 55
9.1. Personal pronouns 55
9.2. Possessive pronouns 56
9.3. Demonstrative pronouns 57
9.3.1. ur_5 57
9.3.2. ne-e(n) 57
9.4. Interrogative pronouns 57
9.5. Alleged pronouns 58

Chapter Ten Numerals 61
10.1. General 61
10.2. Cardinal numbers 61
10.3. Ordinal numbers 66
10.4. Fraction and measure terminology 67
10.5. Distributional relations of numbers 67

Chapter Eleven Adverbs 69

Chapter Twelve The verb 71
12.1. Preliminaries 71
12.2. *ḫamṭu* and *marû* 73
12.3. Plural verbs 74
12.4. Verbal base *ḫamṭu/marû*/sg./pl. grids 74
12.5. Sorts of plurality (*ḫamṭu* reduplication) 79
12.6. Note on verbal reduplication 80
12.7. Conjugation 81
12.7.1. Conjugation pattern 1: Intransitive (and passive) 81
12.7.1.1. The verb me 82
12.7.2. Conjugation pattern 2a: Transitive 83
12.7.3. Conjugation pattern 2b: Transitive 87
12.7.4. Prefixless finite verbal forms 90
12.7.5. Was Sumerian a language with "split ergativity"? 90
12.8. Dimensional indicators 92
12.8.1: 1–26. Non-ventive indicators 94
12.8.2: 27–62. Ventive indicators 103
12.8.3. Dimensional indicators without reference to a person? 109
12.9. Prefixed indicator [e, i] 109
12.10. Prefixed indicator [a(l)] 111
12.11–12. Modal and connecting indicators 112
12.11. Modal indicators 113
12.11.1. Indicative 113
12.11.2. Negative indicative 113
12.11.2.1. Suffixed -nu 114
12.11.2.2. [nu] as a separate verbal base 115
12.11.3. Cohortative 115
12.11.4. Negative cohortative 116
12.11.5. Precative 116
12.11.6. Vetitive (negative precative) 117
12.11.7. Affirmative 1 117
12.11.8. Negative affirmative 118
12.11.9. Prohibitive 118
12.11.10. Affirmative 2 119
12.11.11. Affirmative 3 120
12.11.12. Frustrative 120

12.12. Connecting indicators 121
12.12.1. Prospective 121
12.12.1.1. A precedes B 122
12.12.1.2. Polite imperative 122
12.12.2. Connecting indicator [inga] 123
12.12.2.1. [inga] 124
12.12.2.2. [nu-nga] 124
12.12.2.3. [ga-nga] 124
12.12.2.4. [he-nga] 125
12.12.2.5. [na-nga] 125
12.12.2.6. [ši-nga] 125
12.12.2.7. [nuš-inga] 126
12.12.2.8. 'Irregular' [inga-na] 126
12.12.2.9. Summary of [inga] 127
12.13. Imperative 127
12.13.1. Unextended imperative 128
12.13.2. Extended imperative 129
12.14. Non-finite verbal forms 130
12.14.1. B-[Ø], B-B-[Ø]: unextended bases 131
12.14.2. B-[a], B-[ed], with or without copula 132
12.14.2.1. B-[a], mes-Ane-pada construction 132
12.14.2.1.1. B-[a] 132
12.14.2.1.2. mes-Ane-pada construction 133
12.14.2.2. B-[ed], B-[edam] 134
12.14.2.2.1. B-[ed] 134
12.44.2.2.2. B-[ed + copula] 134
12.14.3. B-[ede], B-[eda], B-[ada] 134
12.14.3.1. B-[ede] 135
12.14.3.2. B-[eda] 136
12.14.3.3. B-[ada] 136
12.14.4. Conjugated participle or "pronominal conjugation" 137
12.14.4.1. 1st sg. *ḫamṭu* 138
12.14.4.2. 2nd sg. *ḫamṭu* 138
12.14.4.3. 3rd sg. person class *ḫamṭu* 139
12.14.4.4. 3rd sg. non-person class *ḫamṭu* 139
12.14.4.5. 3rd pl. person class *ḫamṭu* 139
12.14.4.6. 1st sg. *marû* 139

12.14.4.7. 2nd sg. *marû* 139
12.14.4.8. 3rd sg. person-class *marû* 140
12.14.4.9. 3rd sg. non-person class *marû* 140
12.14.4.10. 3rd pl. person-class *marû* 140
12.14.4.11. Irregular behaviour of the verb ĝen/du 140
12.14.4.12. deli-ĝu$_{10}$-ne etc. 141
12.14.4.13. Conjugated participles: open questions 141
12.15. Compound verbs 142
12.15.1. Compound verbs: free formations 143
12.15.1.1. Extended nominal element 145
12.15.1.2. šu ti/te(-ĝ) and other compound verbs and the special behaviour of their "objects" 145
12.15.1.3. Complete incorporation of the nominal element 147
12.15.2. Compound verbs with a verbalizer 148
12.15.2.1. Clear cases of verbalization 148
12.15.2.2. Verbalization no longer recognizable to us 149
12.15.3. Difficult case: artificial splits? 149
12.16. Nominalization of finite verbal forms 150
12.16.1. The nominalized phrase is in the absolutive 151
12.16.2. The nominalized phrase is in the genitive 152
12.16.3. The nominalized phrase is in the locative 152
12.16.4. The nominalized phrase is in the ablative 153
12.16.5. The nominalized phrase is in the terminative 154
12.16.6. The nominalized phrase is in the equative 154
12.16.7. Nominalized phrase with a possessive particle 154

CHAPTER THIRTEEN Post-nominal and/or post-verbal particles other than case particles (5.4) 157
13.1. [(e)še] 157
13.2. [ĝešen] ([ĝišen]) 158

13.3. [nanna] 158
13.4. [šuba] 159
13.5. [ri] 160

Chapter Fourteen Conjunctions and subjunctions 161
14.1. Conjunctions 161
14.1.1. [u] 161
14.1.2. [ma] 162
14.2. Subjunctions 162
14.2.1. [uda] 162
14.2.2. [tukumbi] 163
14.2.3. [ena] 164
14.2.4. [mu] 164
14.2.5. [iginzu] 165

Chapter Fifteen Exclamations 167
15.1. [a] 167
15.2. [alala] 167
15.3. [alulu] 167
15.4. [allili] 168
15.5. [aua] 168
15.6. [ellu, elala, ilu, ilulamma] 168
15.7. [gana] 168
15.8. [heam] 168
15.9. [inu] 169
15.10. [i Utu] 169
15.11. [mel(i)ea] 169
15.12. [ua] 170
15.13. [ulili] 170

Chapter Sixteen Emesal 171
Chapter Seventeen The Sumero-Akkadian linguistic area 173
Chapter Eighteen Summary—and what is still missing? 179
Bibliography 181
Index 187

PREFACE

The present Sumerian Grammar with which the Publisher Brill kindly entrusted the author is essentially based on introductory classes of Sumerian offered at the Institut für Assyriologie und Hethitologie of Munich University over the last twenty years, as well as on a two semester course on "Geschichte der sumerischen Sprache" (winter 1996/97 and summer 1997). Part of the "History" was also presented in lectures at the University of London and at Oxford University between October 15 and November 5, 1998. While offering my own personal ideas—some of which will no doubt be considered highly subjective—I have tried to discuss, or at least quote, differing opinions as often as possible.

In order to avoid footnotes, the main text has been interspersed with numerous "notes" where secondary comments and explanations are to be found.

As a non-English speaker, I was in need of someone to correct my grammar, style, spelling, and punctuation. Nicholas Postgate of Trinity College, Cambridge University, proved to be the ideal adviser, himself not unfamiliar with the problems of Sumerian grammar. He not only offered innumerable corrections but quite often also guidance, by pointing out that an argument was unclear, that a description was lacking evidence, or even that some paragraph was misplaced. These corrections were made partly by mail and to a considerable degree during a three day stay by the author at Trinity College and at the home of the Postgates. For all this, my most sincere gratitude is due to Nicholas.

The author gratefully acknowledges that he made frequent use of Steve Tinney's lexical "Index to the Secondary Literature. A collated list of indexes and glossaries to the secondary literature concerning the Sumerian Language" (Philadelphia 1993 ff.).

The Publishing House Brill and their Editors, Mevr. Tanja Cowall and Mevr. Patricia Radder, have been extremely patient with the author's self-indulgent interpretation of the deadline originally set for the publication of the book. They are, therefore, entitled to my heartfelt gratitude.

Frau Ursula Hellwag MA of Munich most kindly took upon herself the trouble to compose the final draft of the manuscript which the author, unused to the world of computers, had typed on his beloved “Olympia”.

München, December 2002

ABBREVIATIONS

AfO	= Archiv für Orientforschung, Berlin, 1923 ff.
AHw.	= W. von Soden, Akkadisches Handwörterbuch, 1959–1981.
AIUON	= Annali dell 'Istituto Universitario Orientale di Napoli, sezione linguistica, 1959 ff.
Ali Letters	= F. A. Ali, Sumerian Letters: Two Collections from the Old Babylonian Schools. (diss. Univ. of Pennsylvania, 1964).
AOAT	= Alter Orient und Altes Testament, 1969 ff.
ARET	= Archivi reali di Ebla, Testi, 1985 ff.
ARM	= Archives royales de Mari, 1950 ff.
ARN	= M. Çığ/H. Kızılyay/F. R. Kraus, Altbabylonische Rechtsurkunden aus Nippur, 1952.
AS	= Assyriological Studies, 1931 ff.
ASJ	= Acta Sumerologica, 1979 ff.
AWL	= J. Bauer, Altsumerische Wirtschaftstexte aus Lagasch (= StudPohl 9, 1972).
Bau B	= CT 36, 40 = ETCSL 4.02.2.
BWL	= W. G. Lambert, Babylonian Wisdom Literature, 1959.
CAD	= The Assyrian Dictionary of the University of Chicago, 1956 ff.
CIRPL	= E. Sollberger, Corpus des inscriptions “royales” présargoniques de Lagaš, 1956.
CLAM	= M. E. Cohen, The Canonical Lamentations of Ancient Mesopotamia, 1988.
Copper and Silver	= Disputation, see ETCSL 5.3.6.
Curse Akkade	= J. S. Cooper, The Curse of Agade, 1983; = ETCSL 2.1.5.
Diri	= lexical series diri SI.A *siāku* = (*w*)*atru*.
DP	= M. F. Alotte de la Fuyë, Documents présargoniques, 1908–1920.
Ean.	= Eanatum in CIRPL.
EG	= The Epic of Gilgameš.

ELA	= Enmerkar and the Lord of Aratta (S. Cohen, 1973); = ETCSL 1.8.2.3.
En. I	= Enanatum I in CIRPL.
Enlil and Ninlil 2	= Enlil and Sud; = ETCSL 1.2.2.
EnmEns.	= Enmerkar and Ensuḫkešedana, A. Berlin 1979; = ETCSL 1.8.2.4.
Ent.	= Entemena (Enmetena) in CIRPL.
Enz.	= Enentarzi in CIRPL.
Farmer's Instructions	= M. Civil, Aula Orientalis, Suppl. 5, 1984; = ETCSL 5.6.3.
Father and Son	= Å. Sjöberg, JCS 25 (1973) 105–169; = ETCSL 5.1.2.
Forde Nebraska	= N. W. Forde, Nebraska Cuneiform Texts of the Sumerian Ur III Dynasty, 1967.
GEN	= Gilgameš, Enkidu and the Nether World; = ETCSL 1.8.1.4.
Gilgameš and Agga	= D. Katz, Gilgamesh and Akka, 1993; = ETCSL 1.8.1.1.
Gilgameš, Enkidu and the Netherworld s. GEN	
Gilgameš und Huwawa A	= D. O. Edzard, ZA 80 (1990) 165–203; id., ZA 81 (1991) 165–233; = ETCSL 1.8.1.5.
Gilgameš and Huwawa B	= D. O. Edzard, Bayer. Akad. der Wiss., Phil.-Hist. Klasse, Sitzungsbericht 1993/4; = ETCSL 1.8.1.5.1.
Gungunum	= D. R. Frayne, RIME 4 (1990) 114 ff.
HSAO	= Heidelberger Studien zum Alten Orient, 1967 ff.
HSM	= Harvard Semitic Museum (tablet signature).
HSS	= Harvard Semitic Studies, 1912 ff.
Inanna/Enki	= G. Farber-Flügge, Der Mythos "Inanna und Enki" unter besonderer Berücksichtigung der Liste der me (= StudPohl 10, 1973); = ETCSL 1.3.1.
Inanna's Descent	= W. R. Sladek, Inanna's Descent to the Nether World (diss. Baltimore, 1974); = ETCSL 1.4.1.
Innin šag.	= Å. W. Sjöberg, in-nin-šà-gur$_4$-ra. A Hymn to the Goddess Inanna by the en-Priestess

Enḫeduanna, ZA 65 (1975) 161–253; = ETCSL 4.07.3.

Iraq = (journal) Iraq, 1934 ff.

ITT = Inventaires des Tablettes de Tello, 1910–1921.

Jaques = M. Jaques, Le vocabulaire des sentiments dans les textes sumériens (diss. Univ. de Genève n.d. [1999]).

JCS = Journal of Cuneiform Studies, 1947 ff.

JNES = Journal of Near Eastern Studies, 1942 ff.

Keš Hymn = G. B. Gragg, The Keš Temple Hymn, in: Å. W. Sjöberg, The Collection of the Sumerian Temple Hymns (= TCS 3, 1969) 157–188; = ETCSL 4.80.2.

LamSumUr = P. Michalowski, The Lamentation over the Destruction of Sumer and Ur (= MesCiv. 1, 1989); = ETCSL 2.2.3.

Lament of Ur = S. N. Kramer, Lamentation over the Destruction of Ur (= AS 12, 1940); = ETCSL 2.2.2.

LamUr I s. Lament of Ur.

Lugal = J. van Dijk, LUGAL UD ME-LÁM-bi NIR-GÁL, 1983; = ETCSL 1.6.2.

Lugalbanda I s. C. Wilcke, RIA 7 (1987–90) 121–125; ETCSL 1.8.2.1.

Lugalbanda II s. C. Wilcke, ibid., 125–129; ETCSL 1.8.2.2.

Lugalbanda and Enm. see Lugalbanda I.

MAD = Materials for the Assyrian Dictionary, 1952 ff.

Martu A = A. Falkenstein, SGL I (1959) 120–140; = ETCSL 4.12.1.

MBI = G. A. Barton, Miscellaneous Babylonian Inscriptions I, 1918.

MCS = Manchester Cuneiform Studies, 1951 ff.

MDP = Mémoires de la Délégation en Perse, 1900 ff.

MEE = Materiali epigrafici di Ebla, 1979 ff.

MSL = Materialien zum sumerischen Lexikon/Materials for the Sumerian Lexicon, 1937 ff.

Nanna's Journey = A. J. Ferrara, Nanna-Suen's Journey to Nippur (= StudPohl SM 2, 1973); = ETCSL 1.5.1.

NATN = D. I. Owen, Neo-Sumerian Archival Texts primarily from Nippur, 1982.

NBGT = Neo-Babylonian Grammatical Texts, in: MSL 4 (1956) 129 ff.

NG = A. Falkenstein, Die neusumerischen Gerichtsurkunden (= Bayer. Akademie der Wiss., Philos.-hist. Klasse, Abhandl. NF 39, 40, 44, 1956–1957).
Nik. = M. V. Nikolskij, Drevnosti Vostočnyja III/2, 1908.
Ninmešara = A. Zgoll, Der Rechtsfall der En-hedu-Ana im Lied nin-me-šara (= AOAT 246, 1997).
Ninurta G = M. E. Cohen 1975 (see bibl.); = ETCSL 4.27.07.
NRVN = M. Çığ/H. Kızılyay, Neusumerische Rechts- und Verwaltungsurkunden aus Nippur, 1965.
NS = Neue Serie, New Series, Nova Series.
NS = Neo-Sumerian.
OB = Old Babylonian.
OBGT = Old Babylonian Grammatical Texts, in: MSL 4 (1956) 46 ff.
OLZ = Orientalistische Literaturzeitung, 1898 ff.
Or. = Orientalia (NS), 1932 ff.
OrSuec. = Orientalia Suecana, 1952 ff.
OS = Old Sumerian.
PBS = University of Pennsylvania, Publications of the Babylonian Section, 1911 ff.
PN = Personal Name.
PSD = The Sumerian Dictionary of the University Museum of the University of Pennsylvania, 1984 ff.
RA = Revue d'assyriologie et d'archéologie orientale, 1886 ff.
RGTC = Répertoire géographique des textes cunéiformes, 1974 ff.
RIME = The Royal Inscriptions of Mesopotamia, Early Periods, 1990 ff.
Rīm-Sin D = D. Charpin, Le clergé d'Ur au siècle d'Hammurabi, 1986, 282–86; = ETCSL 2.6.9.4.
RIA = Reallexikon der Assyriologie (und Vorderasiatischen Archäologie), 1928 ff.
RSO = Rivista degli Studi Orientali, 1907 ff.
SBH = G. Reisner, Sumerisch-babylonische Hymnen . . ., 1896.
Schooldays = S. N. Kramer, JAOS 69 (1949) 199–215; = ETCSL 5.1.1.
Scribe and Son see Father and Son.
Sin-kāšid = D. R. Frayne, RIME 4, 440–64.
SKIZ = W. H. Ph. Römer, Sumerischen "Königshymnen" der Isin-Zeit, 1965.
SLTNi. = S. N. Kramer, Sumerian Literary Texts from Nippur, 1944.

S – O – V	= Subject – Object – Verb.
SP	= Series Prior.
SP	= E. I. Gordon, Sumerian Proverbs, 1959.
SR	= D. O. Edzard, Sumerische Rechtsurkunden des III. Jahrtausends . . . (= Bayer. Akademie der Wissenschaften, Abhandlung NF 67, 1968).
Stat.	= Statue.
SRT	= E. Chiera, Sumerian Religious Texts, 1924.
StudPohl	= Studia Pohl, 1967 ff.
STVC	= E. Chiera, Sumerian Texts of Varied Contents (= OIP 16, 1934).
Šulgi A	= Klein 1981, 167–217; = ETCSL 2.4.2.01.
Šulgi B	= G. R. Castellino, (StudSem. 42, 1972); = ETCSL 2.4.2.02.
Šulgi D	= Klein 1981, 50–123; = ETCSL 2.4.2.04.
Šulgi F	= M. G. Hall, A Study of the Sumerian Moon-God . . . (diss. Philadelphia, 1985); = ETCSL 2.4.2.06.
Šulgi X	= Klein 1981, 124–66; = ETCSL 2.4.2.24.
TCL	= Textes cunéiformes du Louvre, 1910 ff.
TCS	= Texts from Cuneiforms Sources, 1966 ff.
Three Men of Adab	= Alster 1981–1983; = ETCSL 5.6.5.
TIM	= Texts in the Iraq Museum, 1964 ff.
TLB	= Tabulae Cuneiformes a F. M. Th. de Liagre Böhl collectae, 1954 ff.
TM	= Tell Mardikh (Ebla) (tablet signature).
TMH (NF)	= Texte und Materialien der Frau Professor Hilprecht Collection . . ., 1932–1934; NF = 1937, 1961 ff.
TrDr.	= H. de Genouillac, La trouvaille de Dréhem, 1911.
TSŠ	= R. Jestin, Tablettes sumériennes de Šuruppak . . . , 1937.
TUT	= G. Reisner, Tempelurkunden aus Telloh, 1901.
UET	= Ur Excavations, Textes, 1928 ff.
Ukg.	= Urukagina (Erikagina) in CIRPL.
Ur Lament see Lement of Ur.	
Ur-Namma Code	= Wilcke 2002.

Ur-Namma's Death	=	E. Flückiger-Hawker, Urnamma of Ur in Sumerian Literary Tradition (= OBO 166, 1999), 93–182; = ETCSL 2.4.1.1.
Ur-Ninurta	=	D. R. Frayne, RIME 4 (1990) 64–68.
VS	=	Vorderasiatische Schriftdenkmäler der (königlichen) Museen zu Berlin, 1907 ff.
WO	=	Die Welt des Orients, 1947 ff.
WF	=	A. Deimel, Wirtschaftstexte aus Fara (= WVDOG 45, 1924).
WVDOG	=	Wissenschaftliche Veröffentlichungen der Deutschen Orient-Gesellschaft, 1900 ff.
YOS	=	Yale Oriental Series, Babylonian Texts, 1915 ff.
ZA	=	Zeitschrift für Assyriologie und verwandte Gebiete, 1886–1938, or: und Vorderasiatische Archäologie, 1939 ff.

CHAPTER ONE

THE SUMERIAN LANGUAGE

Für Olympia, die mir seit 1954 alle meine Arbeiten geschrieben hat und die mir auf drei Kontinenten gefolgt ist.

1.1. General Characteristics

Sumerian was called eme-ki-en-gi-ra "tongue of Kiengir (Sumer)" or eme-gi_7(-r) in Sumerian proper and *lišān Šumeri(m)* "tongue of Šumeru" in Akkadian.

The replacing of [š] by [s] in most modern languages (but not Russian) has its analogue in the change of [š] for [s] in names of the Hebrew bible.

Sumerian is characterized by the interaction of a word base (nominal, verbal, other) which may be invariable or subject to variation (e.g., change of vowel, reduction, extension), and an intricate system of prefixed and suffixed morphemes. The word base itself is impenetrable by other morphemes. Unlike Semitic, no infixes occur. Cf. ha-ma-ab-šúm-mu [ha-m+a-b-šum-e] "he should give it to me" (WO 8, 173: 11b2): precative-to-me-it-base give-ergative (3rd person sing. person class). The number of prefixed morphemes varies between zero and six for the verb, zero and one for the noun; the number of suffixed morphemes between zero and three for the verb, zero and three for the noun. Words of considerable length may be built up that way, e.g., hu-mu-na-ni-ib-gi_4-gi_4 "let him return it to him there" (6 syllables, not comparable, however, with Akkadian *ittanablakkatūnikkunūšim* "they will, over and again, revolt against you", 10 syllables).

In both strings of morphemes, prefixed or suffixed, the sequence of the individual elements is unchangeable. The morphemes are mostly monofunctional, as is the rule in agglutinating languages, and very rarely multifunctional as the morphemes of Semitic or Indo-European.

Instead of gender, Sumerian distinguishes a "person" and a "non-person" class. The case system includes an ergative, and the verbal inflection is characterized by ergativity (whether there was, or evolved, "split ergativity" is still a matter of debate—see below 12.7.5). There is well developed, but far from perfect, concord between dimensional suffixes of the noun and dimensional indicators prefixed to the verb, e.g., DN-ra object mu-na(-n)-řú "*to* god NN, object, he-built-*to*-him".

As for number, singular and non-singular may be opposed; there are different ways to express plurality.

The general word order of Sumerian is S – O – V, unless some part of speech is taken to the front for focus.

The nominal or verbal base is the essential carrier of meaning, and only bases are listed as entries in the lexical lists. Occasionally, meaning is modified by the occurrence of a "frozen" morpheme. Also, the composition of two (rarely more) nominal word bases may lead to a new meaning beyond the sum of the meanings of the individual parts of the compound, e.g., é-gal "house big" = "palace" (Akk. *ēkallu*) or má-tur "boat small", a special type of boat (Akk. *maturru*).

In the light of these general aspects, Sumerian may be compared to such languages as Georgian, Basque, or Itelmen and many others. Such comparison is, however, purely structural and of no consequence for the question of the linguistic affiliation of Sumerian.

1.2. The (hopeless) question of the linguistic affiliation of Sumerian

Scholars have wasted much effort looking for living cognates of ancient Sumerian, not realizing that the problem is practically insoluble for the following reasons:

Sumerian must have separated from a hypothetical language family of which it was part in the middle or late fourth millennium B.C. at the latest. We know next to nothing about the sound and structure of Sumerian before the middle of the third millennium. Thus there is a gap of at least two thousand years between that time and the oldest reconstructible form of any of the languages which have been compared to Sumerian (e.g., Turkish, Hungarian, Sino-Tibetan).

Efforts to find cognates have been exclusively based on the sound of individual words. Yet according to W. Deeters (1963, 76) who discussed the problem of Basque-Caucasian affinities, any words in languages A and B that sound alike today are more likely to be unrelated than related because they are the product of phonetic evolution over several millennia—not to mention the possible diachronical change of meaning. While according to Deeters, if contemporaneous language X were really a descendant from a language Y, related to *Proto-Sumerian more than five or six millennia ago, the sound structure and vocabulary of that hypothetical language Y are liable to have become altered beyond recognition.

The only essay going beyond the comparison of Sumerian and another language by way of vocabulary is G. Steiner's "Sumerisch und Elamisch: Typologische Parallelen", ASJ 12 (1990) 143–76.

Steiner stresses structural similarities in the case system, pronominal system, verb ("intransitiv-passivische Verbalauffassung"), word order (S – O – V), nominalization of the verbal complex, and in his summary he arrives at the cautious statement that "diese beiden Sprachen trotz ihrer sehr unterschiedlichen morphologischen Struktur zu einer 'Sprachgruppe' zusammengefaßt werden können". An essential difference between Sumerian and Elamite is, however, the fact that the Sumerian verb base is, as a rule, embedded in a string of prefixes and suffixes whereas Elamite almost exclusively uses only suffixes.

In any case, even if Sumerian and Elamite were really (remote) relatives, the general problem of the linguistic affinity of Sumerian would remain unresolved.

1.3. The linguistic environment of Sumerian

From since at least the end of the fourth millennium, Sumerians were neighbours of the Elamites in Elam and of Semites, both sedentary and nomadic, in Mesopotamia proper. Any attempt at extending this picture must rest on speculation for lack of solid proof. The earliest evidence for the Elamite language stems from clay tablets with "Proto-Elamite" script whose find spots extend as far as Tepe Yaḥyā, ca 900 km ESE of Susa (corresponding to the distance between Uruk and Damascus as the crow flies). Although the "Proto-Elamite" script has not yet been convincingly deciphered, it seems plausible to assume that it was a predecessor of the Elamite linear script of the Akkade period which has been shown to represent the Elamite language.

It cannot be excluded that, within Mesopotamia proper, Sumerian had neighbours who spoke a language—or languages—that were, step by step, superseded by Sumerian, but which left their traces in Sumerian proper names (gods, places) and vocabulary. Thus, e.g., divine names such as Nanše or Ĝatumdu, goddesses at home in the Ĝirsu/Lagaš region, may belong to a substratum, or adstratum, because these names defy all efforts to explain them by way of Sumerian etymology. Our judgement in this matter is, however, highly subjective because we know nothing of the early history of Sumerian and its sound structure. In fact, our first tentative identification of Sumerian "sound" hardly goes farther back than 24th century B.C., and the publication of the Ebla glosses for Sumerian lexical items brought more than one surprise.

For some time, a "monosyllabic myth" has been popular among Sumerologists, relegating words of more than one syllable to a "Proto-Euphratian" substratum.

Cf., e.g., B. Landsberger 1944, apud A. Salonen 1968, 31.

See, however, the very sobering discussion of G. Rubio 1999, 1–16, "On the alleged 'pre-Sumerian' substratum" where the author arrives at the conclusion (p. 11), "Thus, there is no monolithic substratum that would have left, in a sort of primeval age, its vestiges in Sumerian lexicon. All one can detect is a complex and fuzzy web of borrowings whose directions are frequently difficult to determine".

Nanše and Ĝatumdu (and others) may be pre-Sumerian names, as may many place names. But we have no means at our disposal to prove such a supposition. It is a well known fact that proper names are specially prone to changes of all kind (slurring, abbreviation, deformation by analogy, popular etymology).

Hurrians—with a language of their own—first appear in cuneiform sources toward the end of the third millennium B.C. They most probably never were immediate neighbours of the Sumerians, and so direct language contact can be excluded, at least during the centuries before the Third Dynasty of Ur.

In general, it may be said that the Mesopotamian plain was not conducive to a great variety of languages, as against Iran, Anatolia or the Caucasus which, until our days, has been a veritable language museum.

As a consequence of early close contacts between Sumerians and Semites, a situation arose which greatly stimulated mutual influences. Sumerian was heading for a Sumero-Akkadian "linguistic area"—

and so was Akkadian. Quite a few occurrences of apparent "de-Sumerization" or Akkadization of the language have led some scholars to the opinion that Sumerian had ceased to be a living spoken language as early as the end of the third millennium. The "areal" situation will be discussed more in detail below in Chapter 17.

CHAPTER TWO

HOW WE READ SUMERIAN

2.1. General

One may say that we see Sumerian through an Akkadian glass darkly, because the values ("Lautwerte") of nearly all signs used in the Sumerian syllabaries of different places and periods have been identified by way of Akkadian syllabic spellings or—additionally—from the so-called tu-ta-ti syllabaries. Since Akkadian did not express in its explanatory glosses more than four vowel phonemes, each short or long, i.e., [a, ā, e, ē, i, ī, u, ū], we are restricted to that set also for Sumerian. Whilst, as regards vowel quantity, some arguments may be adduced for the existence of an opposition between short and long vowels [v : v̄], no means have so far been found to achieve a precise reconstruction of Sumerian vowel qualities. The minimal set would be A, E/I, U, with A and U clearly distinguished in spelling while for E/I very often there is the same ambivalence as in Akkadian spelling.

Note: A. Poebel suggested the existence of Akkadian [o] (AS 9, 1939, 116 f. with fnn. 1 and 1(!)), followed by St. Lieberman "The Phoneme /o/ in Sumerian" (Fs. T. B. Jones [1977] 21–28, = AOAT 203) and Aa. Westenholz who extended the evidence for "The Phoneme /o/ in Akkadian" (ZA 81 [1991] 10–19).

Being unable, however, to reconstruct Sumerian [o] from spelling or spelling variants, we disregard it throughout the present grammar.

Spelling variants in parallel texts (synchronic or diachronic) sometimes prove a precious source for phonology, as do scribal "errors".

Apart from lexical glosses, an important source for the sounds of Sumerian are loanwords in Akkadian and in a restricted number of case sign names: kar > *kārum* (not **karrum*) "quay, mooring place" points to a long [ā] in kar, i.e., [kār], whereas é-gal > *ēkallum* (not *ēkālum) suggests short [a] in gal, i.e., *[kal]. The sign name of HI, DÙG is du-ú-gu [dūgu], not *du-ug-gu *[duggu] which makes us prefer a long [ū] in Sumerian dùg, du_{10}(-g), i.e., [dūg]. See more in detail below, 3.1.

Just as for the vowels, the identification of Sumerian consonants depends essentially on Akkadian evidence: glosses in syllabaries and vocabularies, the behaviour of loanwords and, partly again, sign names. The reconstruction of the hypothetical inventory of Sumerian consonantal phonemes is, however, much more difficult than in the case of the vowels. Comparison of *ēkallu* (é-gal) "palace" (above) and *unetukku* (ù-ne-e-dug$_4$) "letter" show that, at least in our Latin transliterations, unvoiced stops (K, T) in the Akkadian loanwords correspond to voiced stops (G, D) in our rendering of the Sumerian basic expressions. This difference in our transliteration is due to the fact that the oldest Akkadian syllabary known at present, Proto-Ea (MSL 14 [1979] 3–81), offers voiced instead of unvoiced stops: du-ú: KA (p. 44:308), ga-la: GAL (p. 50:471).

The complicated phonetic relation between Sumerian and Akkadian consonants (again: as we transliterate them) has given rise to much speculation as to whether there was a double or a triple set of stops in Sumerian: D : T or D : T_1 : T_2, etc., the unvoiced part being either a single phoneme or split into two, e.g., simple and post-glottalized (T, T'). This question will be discussed in more detail, and with tables, below pp. 15 f.

2.2. Spelling of Sumerian

2.2.1. *Classification of cuneograms*

Sumerian is written, in its "classical" form of the Gudea and Ur III period, by means of five classes of cuneiform signs. This distinction is not, though, visible, but only based on context.

a) Logograms or word signs, expressing a nominal or verbal word base, e.g., lú "person", mu "name", "year", dùg "good", "sweet (said of water)", -zu "your" (sing.), ba "to attribute".

b) Syllabograms or syllabic signs, used to convey a sound only, without primary reference to meaning, e.g., ba- (verbal prefix), mu- (verbal prefix), -ke$_4$ (nominal suffix, comprising the final [k] of the genitive morpheme [ak] and the [e] of the ergative case); gu-za "chair".

c) Phonetic indicators, a sub-class of (b), i.e., syllabograms used to specify the reading of a single sign (or of a sign group). So, in GIŠ.TÚG.PI = ĝéštug, the signs GIŠ und TÚG yield the reading of PI [ĝeštug], namely ĝéštug. It is a matter of convention whether we transliterate GIŠ.TÚG.PI as ĝéštug or as $^{\text{giš-túg}}$ĝeštug with two phonetic indicators raised.

d) Signs for number or the combined notation of measuring unit +

number, e.g., min "two", banmin "two ban" = 2 × 1 bán = 2 × 10 sila (1 sila = about 1 litre).

e) Determinatives: these are signs which precede or follow words or names in order to specify them as belonging to semantic groups. Determinatives can be proven not to have been pronounced (although doubt may exist in specific instances), and they are raised in our transliteration: AN.EN.LÍL = ^{d}En-líl "the god Enlil"; EN.LÍL.KI = EN.LÍL^{ki} = Nibru^{ki} "the city Nippur" (Enlil's main cult centre). The determinatives are:

AN (or DIĜIR), preceding divine names; abbreviated as raised ^{d} for d(eus), d(ea).

KI (ki "place, earth"), following place names, e.g., Unug^{ki} "Uruk".

ÍD (íd "river, canal"), preceding names of rivers or main canals, e.g., ^{íd}Idigina "Tigris"; but note íd-éren-na "army canal" where íd is part of the name.

ĜEŠ (ĝeš "wood, tree"), preceding terms for wooden objects or names of trees, e.g., ^{ĝeš}banšur = *paššūru* "table", ^{ĝeš}al = *allu* "hoe". The Akkadian loanwords clearly show that ĜEŠ cannot be part of the word. But note in contrast ĝeš-ùr "beam" with the Akkadian loanword form *gušūru* showing that ĝeš is part of the word.

URUDU (erida, eridu, urudu "copper"), preceding terms of metals and metal objects, e.g., ^{urudu}za-rí-in (*zarinnu*) (mediocre quality of metal, mainly of copper).

DUG (dug "vessel"), preceding terms of earthenware, e.g., ^{dug}a-da = gur$_5$ = *adagurru* (vessel with pointed bottom).

KU$_6$ (ku$_6$ "fish"), following the names of fish, e.g., suhur-máš^{ku_6} = *suḫurmāšu* "goat-fish" (mythological being), "capricorn" (constellation).

MUŠEN (mušen "bird"), following the names of birds, e.g., tu^{mušen} "pigeon".

LÚ (lú "person"), preceding names of some (male) professions, e.g., ^{lú}nu-kiri$_6$ = *nukaribbu* "gardener".

SAR (sar "vegetable"), following the names of garden plants, e.g., šúm^{sar} = *šūmu* "garlic".

Ú (ú "grass", "plant"), preceding names of plants, e.g., ^{ú}búr-da = *urnû* "mint"(?).

GI (gi "reed"), preceding reeds and objects made of reed, e.g., ^{gi}pisan = *pis/šannu* "box", "container", also determined by ^{ĝeš}.

NA$_4$ (na$_4$ "stone"), preceding names of stones and stone objects, e.g., ^{na_4}nunuz = *erimmatu* (egg-stone, a bead).

TÚG (túg "textile, garment"), preceding names of cloth or garments, e.g., ^{túg}NÍG.LÁM = *lamḫuššû*, (a long or knee-length skirt).

KUŠ (kuš "skin, hide, leather"), preceding leather objects, e.g., ^{kuš}lu-úb = *luppu* "(leather) bag".

ŠE (še "barley") and ZÍD (zíd "flour") are occasionally used as determinatives for types of grain or flour respectively.

Whereas the use of some determinatives is rather consistent and more or less predictable (at least from the Akkade period onward), this does not apply to others. To the first category belong ^{d}, ^{ki}, ^{ĝeš}, ^{mušen}, ^{ku_6}.

To resume the five sign classes, we have to stress once more that their distinction is nearly exclusively based on context: ba or mu may belong to (a) or (b), ĝeš to (a), (c), or (e). Even number signs (d) are not exempt from ambiguity, because, e.g., EŠ (3 × U) may mean "thirty" (d), but also be used as a syllabogram (b) in (mainly Old Bab.) -me-eš [meš]; note also i (= ia = 5 × AŠ) or àš (= 6 × DIŠ).

2.2.2. *Combination of cuneograms; spelling proper*

In "standard" (Ur III, Old Bab.) Sumerian spelling, the nominal or verbal base is frequently noted by a logogram (type a), whereas accompanying (prefixed or suffixed) morphemes are expressed by syllabograms (see 2.2.1, type b), e.g., al-tuš "he was sitting there" where prefix al- is a syllabogram, base tuš a logogram.

A special feature of Sumerian spelling is the "repetition" of the final consonant of a logogram by the initial consonant of a following syllabogram to indicate simply the addition of a vowel. So, "in Ur", [Urim-a] is not spelled *Úrim^{ki}-a, but Úrim^{ki}-ma. The [m] of the syllabogram [ma] is redundant, the sign conveying simply the [a] of the locative case. Here there is no reason to suppose consonantal length. The phenomenon is purely orthographic.

Note: This way of spelling has, occasionally, found its way into Akkadian. When, in Old Akk. or Old Bab., the scribe turned the verbal form *i-din* [iddin] "he gave" into ventive [iddinam] "he gave (it) to me", he wrote *i-din-nam*. See F. R. Kraus, RSO 32 (1957) 103–108.

We traditionally read the main temple complex of Uruk, É-an-na "House of Heaven/An", as Eanna where Sumerian spelling is reflected in our Latin transcription. There is, in fact, no reason to read -nn-. Eana would correspond to what is meant in Sumerian.

2.2.3. *Evolution of Sumerian spelling*

The progress achieved during a period of at least one millennium may be roughly described as a continuous advance towards phonetic exactitude, i.e., the exact rendering of every spoken syllable. Writing Sumerian started from only noting bases, numerals, and combinations of numbers + measure.

This "nuclear" writing (Th. Jacobsen, ZA 52 [1957] 91 ff. fn. 1) still disregarded any additional morphemes (nominal and verbal prefixes and suffixes). Phonetic abstraction (writing, e.g., gi both for "reed" and the syllables [gi, ge] and, in slightly varied form (GI-gunû) for the notion of "return" [ge_4]) opened the way for noting syllables of the types [V], [CV], [VC], [CVC]; see 2.2.1, type b. "Syllabaries" (= inventories of syllabograms) came into being. Some syllabograms were freely applicable, i.e., they could occur in any position of a word (initial, medial, final) whereas others were of restricted use; éš is mainly used, in Ur III and early Old Bab., to denote the 3rd p. pl. suffix on certain verbal forms.

Note: Neither Sumerian nor Akkadian syllabaries offer a clear 1 : 1 relation of signs and sounds. On the one hand, one sign may denote different syllables, e.g., NE = ne, dè, bí, and on the other hand, identical or minimally different syllable-sounds could be noted by different signs, e.g., [aš] = aš or áš, [en] = en or èn (LI).

One of the main problems was the notation of syllable-closing consonants in syllables of the type CVC. Here, the inventory was insufficient (signs like bam, mag, nal, etc. were never created). At first, a syllable-closing consonant was just disregarded, e.g., ba-ug_7-ge "they died" stood for [ba'ugeš, ba-u-geš]. With lugal-me, only context could show whether lugal-me(š) "they are kings" or lugal-me(n) "I am/you are king" was meant. Until Ur III, and partly still in OB, the person or non-person class ergative or absolutive markers -n- or -b-, placed immediately before the verbal base, were left unnoted, because they always were found in a close syllable; mu-na-řú "he/she built for him/her" stood for [mu-na-n-řú]. Therefore, reconstruction of a given verbal form often depends on our—subjective—interpretation.

The decisive invention to remedy the situation was made by a scribe—or scribal school—of pre-Sargonic times, who combined CV_1 + V_1C to denote CV_1C, e.g., mu-un for [mun]. The Akkadian rather than Sumerian scribal world must be credited with this invention—unique in the world history of writing—because in Akkadian with its frequent three-consonantal roots non-notation of a syllable-closing consonant would have led to much more ambiguity than in Sumerian.

CHAPTER THREE

MINIMALIA OF SUMERIAN PHONOLOGY AND SYLLABIC STRUCTURE

3.1. Phonology

3.1.1. *Vowels*

[a]: al (Akk. *allu*) "hoe"
gag (Akk. *kakku*) "peg, nail", "club, weapon"
gala (Akk. *kalû*) "singer (in cult), cantor"
bárag (Akk. *parakku*) "dais"
(hé-)ĝál (Akk. *he(n)gallu*) "let it be" = "abundance"

[ā]: kār (Akk. *kāru*) "quay, mooring wall, harbour"
nār (Akk. *nāru*, Ass. *nuāru*) "singer, musician"
ān (Akk. *ānu*) "sky, heaven", "God of Heaven"

[e]: mušen, *mu-še-en-nu* [mušennu] "bird", sign name for HU, MUŠEN

[ē]: ēn (Akk. *ēnu*) "en priest"

[i]: apin (Akk. *epinnu*) "plough"
bukin (Akk. *bukinnu*) "trough"
sikil, in šúm-sikil (Akk. *šumsikillu*) "garlic"

[ī]: kīd (Akk. *kītu*) "reed mat"

[u]: dub (Akk. *ṭuppu*) "tablet"
huš, *ḫu-uš-šu* [*ḫuššu*], sign name for HUŠ

[ū]: nūn, $^{d}E_4$-nun-na (Akk. **E/Anūnakū*)

Note: Not ^{d}A.NUN.NA = **Anunnakū*; the Old Bab. contracted form Enukkū can be explained only as the product of -n(a)k- > -kk-, and not of *-nn(a)k- > -kk-.

būr (Akk. *pūru*) "(watertight) vessel"

The question of Akkadian (Old Akk. and Old Bab.) [o] and [ō] has been discussed by Westenholz (see above 2.1 note).

The existence of an (original) diphthong [ay] in Sumerian may be inferred from the Hebrew loan form of Akkadian *ēkallu* (< é-gal): *hēḵal* <**haykal* (also Arabic *haykal* "temple, structure"). The Sumerian word for "father", OS A (as in A-kur-gal "the father is the great mountain"), OB a-a or a-ya (cf. PSD A/1, 32 ff.), leads one to suppose the form

[ay], [aya] (only the first, however, being a diphthong strictly speaking). The minimal inventory of Sumerian vocalic phonemes would then read: a, ā; e, ē; i, ī; u, ū; (o, ō)

Two notes are, however, needed with regard to our reconstruction:

(a) It is not always clear, from the spelling, whether [e] or [i] was intended. In the (non-standard) spelling of a curse formula (copy of a Šulgi inscription), en hé-a "whether he can be an en" is replaced by in he-a (TIM 9, 35:19). We are often at a loss whether we should transliterate NI = ni or né, BI = bi or bé.
(b) Instead of a quantitative opposition short: long, there may have been an opposition of open and closed vowels (such as is the case in modern German).

Ideas of how Sumerian should be pronounced certainly changed diachronically among the learned community of scribes. So, e.g., KU = dab_5 ("to seize") is glossed da-ab in Proto-Ea 19 (MSL 14, 30), but di-ib in Ea I 156 (MSL 14, 184), yielding our transliteration díb. Cf. correspondingly, PA = sàg ("to strike"), glossed sà-ag in Proto-Ea 490 (MSL 14, 51), but s[i]-ig in Ea I 298 (MSL 14, 191).

It is not clear to the author how this change of vowel came about.

3.1.2. *Consonants*

When trying to establish the (minimal) set of Sumerian consonantal phonemes, we will once more base ourselves on loanwords in Akkadian and on sign-names as the most reliable sources.

For stops (labial, dental, velar), there are three possible types of relation between a Sumerian word (as rendered in the transliteration we derive from Proto-Ea and later lexical sources) and the corresponding Akkadian loanword:

a) labial stops

a1) P' : P	apin	: *epinnu* "seeder plough"
	pisan	: *pis/šannu* "box"
a2) B : P	barag	: *parakku* "dais"
	bala	: *palû* "term of office"
	dub	: *ṭuppu* "tablet"

Note: For P' etc. see Gelb 1961², 39 (below).

a3) B : B   not attested

b) dental stops

b1) T' : T	not attested		
b2) D : T	du	:	*tuppu* "tablet"
	kid	:	*kītu* "reed mat"
	ù-ne(-e)-dug$_4$	:	*unetukku* "letter"
b3) D : D	é-duru$_5$(A)	:	*edurû* "village"
	saĝ-dili	:	SAG-*di-lu-û* "(single head =) bachelor"

c) velar stops

c1) K' : K	kar	:	*kāru* "quay"
	kiri$_6$	:	*kirû* "palm grove"
	kid	:	*kītu* "reed mat"
c2) G : K	gala	:	*kalû* "cantor"
	engar	:	*ikkaru* "tenant farmer"
	é-gal	:	*ēkallu* "palace"
	barag	:	*parakku* "dais"
	ù-ne(-e)-dug$_4$	:	*unetukku* "letter"
c3) G : G	ga-na	:	*gana* "hey, now then"
	aga	:	*agû* "tiara"

Gelb 1961^{2}, 39 dealt with the relation of Sumerian stops and Akkadian spelling before, in, and after the Old Bab. period. He started from a binary system, b/p : p', d/t : t', g/k : k', assuming an original opposition of indiscriminate voiced/unvoiced versus unvoiced post-glottalized stops. Gelb supposed a "sound shift" to have taken place in Old Bab., and he visualized his theory in a chart:

Before Old Bab.			Old Bab.	Old Bab. and Later	
Written	Phoneme	Sound	Sound Shift	Phoneme	Sound
BA	b/p	p	p > b	b	b
PA	p'	p'	p' > p	p	p
DA	d/t	t	t > d	d	d
TA	t'	t'	t' > t	t	t
GA	g/k	k	k > g	g	g
KA	k'	k'	k' > k	k	k

Gelb's chart does not take into account the more complicated, triple, relations revealed by Sumerian words and their loans in Akkadian. While we will not be able definitely to prove our theory, we may at least point to the fact that a triple (or even more ample) set of stops is well attested in world languages, e.g., unvoiced : voiced : unvoiced post-glottalized/unvoiced velarized; or unvoiced unaspirated : voiced unaspirated : unvoiced aspirated. We will only give two examples:

1) Akkadian: p/b/-; t/d/Ṭ; k/g/ḳ (Q).
   Here, Ṭ and Q cannot be defined more closely, because we are unable to say whether Ṭ and ḳ/Q were post-glottalized stops (as in modern Ethiopic languages) or velarized stops (as in Arabic).
2) Georgian: p/b/p'; t/d/t'; k/g/k'.
   p', t', k' are here post-glottalized stops.

For a more than quadruple set, cf. Sanskrit p/ph/b/bh; t/th/d/dh; k/kh/g/gh; with additionals cerebral stops ṭ/ṭh/ḍ/ḍh.

Despite this demonstration of possibilities, we have to admit that most aspects of the phonetics and phonology of Sumerian stops remain subject to doubt.

Apart from stops, we depend to a very high degree on Akkadian evidence for the other phonemes. What is offered below may only be part of a more developed system.

There are three nasals: labial [m], dental [n], and palatal(?) [ĝ]:

m:	zà-mi	: *sammû* ("praise") "harp"
	lu-lim	: *lulīmu* "stag" (Kulturwort?)
n:	na-r̂ú-a	: *narû* "erected stone" (with inscription), "stele"
	ù-ne(-e)-dug$_4$	: *unetukku* "letter"
	eren	: *erēnu* "cedar" (Kulturwort)

Note: As for final [M] and [N], the loanword evidence is sometimes in contradiction with Sumerian spelling and/or lexical glosses. In spite of ezeN : *isinnu* "festival", the Ur III genitive of ezeN is indicated by -(m)a; cf. níĝ-ezeN-ma "festival accessories". AN is used both for the name of the "sky (god)", An, genitive an-na, and for the copula, -am$_6$, spelled A.AN = àm from Sargonic times onward (A.AN being contracted from contextual -a'am = nominalizer -a + copula [m]).

ĝ: The transliteration of this phoneme was first proposed by J. Krecher, HSAO 1 (1967) 87 fn.*, and further by him in Fs. L. Matouš II (1978) 7–73: "Das sumerische Phonem ĝ". Its spelling characteristics are mainly use of the syllabograms GÁ (ĝá, ĝe$_{26}$), ÁG (áĝ), MI (ĝi$_{6}$). Sumerian loanwords in Akkadian often reflect [ĝ] by spelling -n- or -ng- (see below). Moreover, there is a [ĝ]: [M] correspondence in Emesal words, e.g., ĝá-ra "to me" : Ma-ra; ĝál "exist" : Ma-al.

[ĝ] occurs in all three positions of the words: initial, medial, final, thus behaving in complete accordance with other consonantal phonemes.

ĝuruš "adult male" : Ebla sign name *nu-rí-šúm* (MEE 3 [1981] 198: 46)

daĝal "wide", glossed da-ĝál

balaĝ "lyre(?)" : *balangu, balaggu*

hur-saĝ "mountain range" : *ḫuršānu*

Besides [ĝ], there also is the combination [ĝ+g], and there may have been a difference between [ĝ] and [ĝg] or [ĝĝ] comparable to that between English singer and finger.

Cf. engar "tenant farmer", glossed en-ga-ar, Akkad. *ikkaru*; nan = gar "carpenter", glossed na(-an)-ga-ar, Akkad. *nangāru, naggāru*, where the gloss each time has GA = *ga*.

The identification of [ĝ] as a palatal nasal would logically complete a nasal series m, n, x (= ĝ).

A different description was offered by Th. Jacobsen, ZA 52 (1957) 92 f.: "a nasalized velar pronounced with rounded lips (nasalized labio-velar), approximately c̃$_{w}$".

There are two liquids: [l] and [r]; they are, once more, seen through Akkadian "glasses". Both occur in all three positions.

l:	lú-u$_{18}$-lu	: *lullû* "man"
	la-ha-an	: *laḫannu* "bottle"
	bala	: *palû* "term of office"
	kisal	: *kisallu* "court (primarily of a temple)"
	hé-ĝál	: *he(n)gallu* "abundance"

As for final [l], classical Sumerian spelling distinguishes between continuation with -la or—more rarely—-lá, e.g.:

ĝál-la	gibil-lá (also -la); see Krecher 1966, 113 with fnn. 328 f.
lugal-la	
lul-la	líl-lá
si-il-la	(šu-)pe-el-lá (also -la); see Attinger 1993, 710–14.

sikil-la
šul-la
til-la

If in view of this distribution one might be tempted to posit two kinds of [l] : [l_1] and [l_2], it must be admitted, on the other hand, that there is no counterpart in the [e] sector: when sikil or líl are continued by [e], spelling is in both cases [LI] = -le, e.g., dEn-líl-le "Enlil" (ergative).

An as yet unsolved problem of Sumerian phonetics is found in the variation of initial [NU] with [Lu] or [La]. The Ebla spelling of lugal "(big person =) king" is nu-gal ARET 5, 24 ii a; iii 1–5; iv 1–3 paralleled by lugal in 24 i a, ii 1–4, iii 1–4; 26 i a. The negative prefix nu- has a variant la- before prefix ba- (and, secondarily, li- before bí-). The Akkadian loan of nu-banda "foreman" is *laputtû* (*luputtû*) with oldest attestation in Old Bab. (CAD L 98 c 2')

r: rab : *rappu* "clamp"
barag : *parakku* "dais"
kar : *kāru* "quay"

Note: Apart from *rappu*, Sumerian loanwords beginning with r- are probably absent in Akkadian (cf. Edzard, ZA 90 [2000] 292 with fn. 2).

A Sumerian phoneme to be distinguished from [r] has been supposed to exist first by Th. Jacobsen, ZA 52 (1957) 93 fn. 1 (d), and then by J. Bauer, "Zum/dr/-Phonem im Sumerischen", WO 8 (1975) 1–9; the ensuing discussion has been summarized by J. Black, RA 84 (1990) 108 f., 111, and note, with more literature, Attinger 1993, 143. The argument is the presence of spelling (or glossation) variants with either D or R-syllabograms, e.g., na-RÚ-a "implanted stone" = "stele", with Akkadian loanword *narû*, but na-DI-a TIM 9, 35:2, 12 (cf. CAD N/1, 364 lex.).

The symbol [r̂] has been introduced (in order not to confuse it with Czech ř), but—in contrast to [ĝ], no general agreement has so far been found: is it a single phoneme or rather a consonantal cluster (DR)? We tentatively adopt [r̂]:

r̂: r̂ú "to implant, build" (formerly separated as dù and r̂ú).
kur̂$_5$(TAR) "to separate"

The (original) existence of a phoneme (or of two phonemes?) [H] in Sumerian may, again, be inferred for various reasons. [H] is here used as a symbol rather than an exactly defined sound, but [h] has a good chance.

a) é-gal, *ēkallu*, "palace" is reflected by hkl in Ugaritic and by *hēḵal* in Hebrew (see also above 3.1.1). This leads us to suppose an original *hē or *hay for Sumerian "house". In Mesopotamian Old Akkadian É = *ʾà* is found for Semitic [ḥ] (I. J. Gelb, MAD 2^2 [1961] 88 f.), in Ebla both for [h] and [ḥ] (M. Krebernik, ZA 72 [1982] 220 f.).
b) The Hebrew name of the Tigris, quite evidently a Mesopotamian loan, is *Ḥiddeqel* with initial [ḥ], whereas we only know an Akkadian form Idiglat. The town ^{d}ÍD^{ki}, *I-da*^{ki} (Old Bab.), URU *I-di* (Middle Bab.) (RGTC 2 104 f.; 3, 135 f.), classical Is, still exists as modern Hīt on the Euphrates. Apparently, initial [h] survived in the modern name. Whatever the etymology of the name, there is some chance that Sumerian "river" originally sounded [hid].
c) The Akkadian syllabogram *ú* is used, in Ugaritic, for [hu] as in Ú-PI = *hu-wa* "he" in a Sumero-Akkadian-Hurrian-Ugaritic quadrilingual lexical text: J. Nougayrol, Ugaritica 5 (1968) 245: no. 137 ii 28'. This usage of Ú for [hu] probably goes back to the spelling of Amorite PNs (cf. M. P. Streck 2000, 241), and it may reflect Sumerian [Hu] for ú "grass".
d) Sumerian nominal and verbal bases ending (at least in our transliteration) in a vowel absorb a following -e (of the ergative), -e(-ne) (personal pl.), or -e-dè (verbal suffix), sometimes noting a plene vowel instead of [e]: ama-a "mother" (ergative) instead of *ama-e; lú-ù "person" (erg.), ama-ne "mothers", ugula-ne "overseers". There are, however, cases where this rule does not hold: gala-e-ne "cantors", ì-lá-e(-ne) "he (they) will pay" (note the unconventional spelling i-la-i in Mari, ARM 8, 48:9).

When Irikagina of Lagaš contrasts the "women of the past" (munus-u_4-bi-ta-ke_4-ne) with the "present/nowadays women" (munus-u_4-da-e-ne) (Ukg. 6 iii 20' and 23'), we have a regular genitive compound in the first case: [munus-ubita-(a)k-ene], but an adjectival compound in the second case: [munus-uda-ene], lit. "women-(in the day =)today-pl.]".

Here, u_4-da (locative) is used like an adjective. After the locative [uda], the [e] of [ene] is not absorbed or elided. This can only mean that there was some kind of hiatus between the locative designation [a] and the pers. pl. ending [ene]: [munus-uda'ene].

This admittedly slender evidence may lead to the conclusion that after a vowel the [e] of certain morphemes was not absorbed or elided, if there was a "barrier", audible, but not visible in our transliterations. We propose to note that supposed barrier by [H]: galaH-ene, ì-láH-e, munus-udaH-ene.

Akkadian preserved the common Semitic unvoiced velar fricative [ḫ], as in *a-ḫu-um* [aḫum] "brother". We transliterate [h] in Sumerian whenever words are glossed by syllabograms ḫa, ḫé, ḫi, ḫu, aḫ/iḫ, úḫ, disregarding the crescent below the [ḫ]. Still, we may be sure that the [ḫ] of the Akkadian loanword in Sumerian, *puḫrum* (*pu-úḫ-ru-um*) "assembly" was pronounced like, or very close to, Akkadian [ḫ]. We may, furthermore, rely, as usual, on Sumerian loanwords in Akkadian, where Sumerian [h] is rendered by Akkadian [ḫ]:

hur-saĝ : *ḫuršānu* "mountain range"
he-ĝál : *ḫe(n)gallu* "abundance"
bahar : *paḫāru, paḫḫāru* "potter" (the *-ḫḫ-* of Akkadian is due to the assimilation of the word to the Akkadian pattern *parrās-* (cf. Arabic *faḫḫār*)
ki-mah : *kimāḫu, kimaḫḫu* "(greatest place =) grave"

These correspondences do not imply, however, that in all Sumerian occurences our transliterated [h] was identical in sound (or close to it) with Akkadian [ḫ]. There may have been voiced and unvoiced variants which escape us.

We will be brief on Sumerian sibilants, because this group of sounds is already difficult for us to define in Akkadian, where we have no exact idea about the identity (and possible diachronic change) of [z, s, ṣ, š, ś]. It is all the more difficult even to approximate the Sumerian values.

Z: zà-mi : *sammû* "lyre"
ezen : *isinnu* "festival"
a-zu : *asû* "physician"
S: kisal : *kisallu* "courtyard"

ús	: *ūsu* "guideline, behaviour"
hur-saĝ	: *ḫuršānu* "mountain range"
saĝĝa	: *šangû* "main temple administrator"
énsi(-k)	: *iššiakku* "city ruler, governor" (the Akkadian *-akku* ending is most probably due to the restitution of the Sumerian genitive particle [ak]; see also below nu-èš : *nêšakku*)
dub-sar	: *tupšarru* "scribe"
šà-tam	: *šatammu* "temple administrator"
nu-èš	: *nêšakku* (a high-ranked priest) (for the Akkadian ending *-akku* see above, énsi(-k)

The rather complicated correspondences between Sumerian forms and their rendering in Akkadian loanwords reminds us of the stops:

z : z		d : d
z : s	and	d : t
s : s		t : t

The evidence becomes even more difficult to judge because of word-initial or word-medial correspondence s : š as in hur-saĝ : *ḫuršānu*. From this, A. Falkenstein, ZA 42 (1934) 152–54, had concluded there had been (diachronically) different "Lehnwortschichten", and he also noted, p. 153, fn. 2, cases where word-initial sibilants of identical words were registered with [s] or [š] by scribes. Later, in 1959, he proposed the existence of Sumerian [ś] in order to explain "irregular" sibilant correspondences (1959, 24).

If accepted this would yield this tentative chart of Sumerian consonantal phonemes:

p'	p	b	m				
t'	t	d	n	l	(l_2)	r	r̂
k'	k	g	ĝ				
š	(ś?)						
	s	z					
*H	h						

Our transliteration in this grammar will, however, follow traditional values and will not note p', t', or k'.

3.2. Syllable structure

Here again we are dependent on Akkadian, because we are only able to reach Sumerian syllabograms through their Akkadian pronunciation. As a Semitic language has no initial consonantal clusters (tra-, stra-), word-internal clusters of more than two consonants (-astra-, -abstra-) or word-final clusters of two or more consonants (-art, -arst, -arbst) and, consequently, there are no syllabograms serving comparable purposes, we cannot identify Sumerian syllables with a structure differing from Akkadian. Therefore, while we may ask whether Sumerian syllables of the type bra-, pli-, sku-, -arp, -urps actually existed, there is no way to prove them.

Note: A. Falkenstein, starting from the assumption that the verbal prefix ba- can be segmentized as b+a-, concluded that, by analogy, ba-ra- might have been a spelling for intended *b+ra-, i.e. [bra], see 1949, 190; 1950, 185 with fn. 2. This assumption has been refuted by J. N. Postgate, JCS 26 (1974) 18.

Taking our transliteration at face value, Sumerian had the following types of syllables:

V:	e.g.,	a
CV:	e.g.,	ba, ri, ru
VC:	e.g.,	ab, eš, uĝ
CVC:	e.g.,	bar, min, mun

Note: The Ur III unorthodox spelling nam-bi-ri (NRVN I 4:4; see also 2:4 f.) stands for expected *nam-(é)ri(m) [namri] and suggests a pronunciation [nambri] with [b] as a glide between [m] and [r]. We are reminded of comparable glides (between a nasal and a liquid) in Greek an-d-rós (genitive of ἀνήρ "man"), French (and English) hum-b-le, etc.

So, even if a Sumerian internal cluster -mbr- may have occurred in spoken language, it was—until proof of the contrary—a secondary phonetic phenomenon.

It goes without saying that in the spoken language there must have been free variants of pronountiation, depending on speed, with all such universal features as slurring, elision, assimilation, dissimilation.

CHAPTER FOUR

THE "WORD" IN SUMERIAN, PARTS OF SPEECH

We will try to define Sumerian parts of speech not by applying classical models, but by observing the morpho-syntactic behaviour of Sumerian "words".

4.1. "Word"

A "word" in Sumerian is an entity that can convey meaning on its own without anything spoken before or after. In é-šè "towards the house", é is a word whereas -šè, the terminative postposition, is not. We define [še] as a nominal particle.

In ì-ĝál "it is there/available", ĝál "to exist" may occur independently, but the prefixed element ì- may not. We define [i] as a verbal particle.

Thirdly, in é-zu "your house", -zu "your" (sg.) does not qualify as a "word", because to the question "whose house is this, mine or yours?" the answer cannot be *-ĝu$_{10}$ or *-zu, but only ĝá(-a)-kam, za(-a)-kam "it is (of me =) mine", "it is (of you =) yours". [ĝu], [zu] and others are connectible with both a nominal and a verbal base. We define them as common particles.

Note: I owe the distinction of nominal, verbal, and common particles to G. B. Milner, Fijian Grammar (1956) 130 f. (M. uses "general" instead of "common".)

The Sumero-Akkadian lexicographers were apparently aware of the idea "word". Their lexical entries exactly correspond to our idea of a "word" (or of a compound); it is only in the grammatical series (OBGT, NBGT) that we see entries which we would define as "particles" (or rather syllables through which a morpheme boundary ran, e.g., un, an, in, en listed to denote consonantal preverbal -n-).

4.2. Parts of speech

We may distinguish eight parts of speech: (1) nouns, (2) pronouns, (3) numerals, (4) verbs, (5) adverbs, (6) exclamations, (7) subjunctions, conjunctions, (8) interrogations. All these occur as "words" (see our definition above) and may be found as entries in lexical texts. (1) to (4) may be combined with bound particles (prefixes, suffixes): nominal, verbal, and common. (5) to (8) do not combine with particles. (1) to (3) may be opposed to (4) as nonverbal to verbal categories.

Parts of speech can be identified exclusively on context. There is no way to tell by the form of the base alone whether we are faced with a noun (dur, tur), a verb (gur), or some other part of speech.

A further subdivision of (1) nouns into (1a) substantives and (1b) adjectives is not unproblematic. On the one hand, sikil "pure" cannot form a plural *sikil-e-ne "the pure ones" whereas it may be followed by the plural of the copula: sikil-me-eš "they are pure". For "the pure ones" a nominal head would be needed: lú-sikil-e-ne "the pure persons". On the other hand, sikil following a nominal head, e.g., ki-sikil "(pure place =) girl, young woman" behaves exactly like an apposition and, as such, may take on all nominal particles.

For practical reasons, we will make the distinction between substantives and adjectives. As a guide-line of high antiquity we may again take the fact that certain Sumerian nouns are entered in lexical lists as Akkadian substantives while others are rendered by Akkadian adjectives. In Akkadian itself, the differentiation of substantives and adjectives is unproblematic on both morphological and syntactical grounds.

(1a) The substantive has the following grammatical categories: class (person, non-person), number (singular, non-singular, plural, collective, detailed, etc.), case (absolutive, ergative, genitive, dative, locative, ablative, comitative, terminative, directive, equative), possession singular: 1st, 2nd, 3rd person: person and non-person class; plural: 1st, 2nd, 3rd person: person class only.

These grammatical categories—apart from class—are realized by the suffixation of particles.

The substantive may form part of quite intricate appositional and genitive constructions. It may be followed by adjectives. Some substantives may be repeated ("reduplicated", e.g., énsi-énsi "all of the city rulers"), but we cannot as yet establish whether reduplication was open to any substantive or subject to restrictions.

Substantives and adjectives may take the prefixed particle nam-, serving to express an abstract concept: nar "musician", nam-nar "music", mah "very big", nam-mah "greatness".

(1b) The adjective rarely occurs on its own. It is usually connected with a (preceding—rarely following) substantive. Adjectives may serve as the base of adverbs, e.g., dirig-bi "(its excessive =) excessively". A few adjectives which express dimension take a reduplicated form when the preceding substantive is meant to be in the plural, e.g., diĝir-gal-gal(-e-ne) "the great gods" (see also 5.3.7).

Note: This usage has been imitated in Akkadian where an equally restricted class of adjectives expressing dimension has bases with a lengthened middle radical, e.g., *ilū rabbûtu* "the great gods" (Reiner 1966, 64).

Note: There is a conspicuous similarity between Akkadian nominal formations in -*ūtu* which express both the masc. plural of adjectives (e.g., *damqūtu* "good ones") and an abstract notion (e.g., *ṣīrūtu* "majesty", or *šarrūtu* "kingship"), and Sumerian formations with nam- (e.g., nam-mah "greatness", nam-lugal "kingship"). This similarity has most probably to be seen as another symptom of a Sumero-Akkadian linguistic area.

When an adjective is attached to a substantive, all suffixed particles pertaining to the substantive are placed after the following adjective so that one might argue, formally, that the adjective behaves like a substantive. In reality, however, the whole complex (substantive + adjective) has been substantivized.

Adjectives, like substantives, may take the prefixed particle nam-, e.g., nam-mah "quality of being the greatest" (but it is not yet known how far this was a productive feature); cf. p. 24 bottom.

Thomsen 1984, 64 f., quotes Gragg 1968, 9 who considers adjectives as a sub-class of the verb. In fact, adjectival bases can often be turned into verbal bases, but this can hardly be stated as a general overriding rule.

Black 2003.

(2) Pronouns have the categories of person (1st, 2nd, 3rd), class (person, non-person), number (sg., pl.), and case.

(2.1) Personal pronouns: As 1st and 2nd persons can, by nature, only be person class (unless non-person class becomes a "person" in a literary context), the differentiation of person : non-person is restricted to the 3rd person; moreover, it does not operate in the 3rd pl., where only person class occurs.

As for case, personal pronouns have a restricted system of case inflection as compared with substantives: absolutive and ergative are identical in form; there is no ablative or directive.

We do not include as parts of speech the bound forms of personal pronouns in their quality of possessors; cf. below 5.2.

We may include, among pronouns, the question words "who",

"what", because the answer may not only be a substantive (who: my father), but also a person (who: me, you). Sumerian, like most of the world's languages, distinguishes "who" (a-ba) and "what" (a-na).

The system of deictic pronouns is still poorly explored in Sumerian. Bound forms (suffixed particles) are not included here; see below 7.

(3) Numerals. Cardinal numerals are written in the sexagesimal system (see below, 10.2) following the item counted. In this respect, they resemble adjectives, and as with adjectives if a complex of substantive + cardinal number is provided with a suffixed particle, it is shifted from the substantive to the numeral, the whole complex, substantive + numeral, being turned into one noun.

Numerals occur in the genitive, after a substantive, in order to denote ordinal numbers: mu-3-kam "(it is the year of three =) third year".

(4) The verb is the most complex part of speech in Sumerian. It has an extremely variable set of prefixed particles as well as a number of suffixed particles. The verbal base in itself may be subject to variation.

The verb may express the following categories: person, class, number, action, direction, tense/aspect, mood.

Except for lexical lists where the (simple or reduplicated) verbal base is regularly equated with Akkadian infinitives, the verbal base extremely rarely occurs alone, without any prefixed or suffixed particles.

A verb(al complex) may be turned into a noun, i.e., be nominalized, by the addition of the suffixed particle [a] (see 12.16). Such a newly created noun may then be subject to nominal inflection (receiving suffixed case particles). Nominalized verbal complexes frequently have to be rendered by English dependent clauses. The very productive system of Akkadian (nominal) infinitive constructions may be seen as an Akkadian share in the Sumero-Akkadian linguistic area (see 17).

(5) Adverbs. Words which describe in a more precise way the idea contained in a verb are traditionally defined as adverbs: "he arrived", "he recently arrived". In Akkadian, this category is usually formed with an adjective as base + the ending *-iš*, e.g., *eššu* "new", *eššiš* "anew", *damqu* "good", *damqiš* "nicely". This way of forming adverbs has two Sumerian counterparts:

gibil-bi "(its new =) anew",
zi-dè-eš [zid-eš] = zi(d) "true" with the adverbiative particle [eš] (Attinger 1993, 253–56), "truly", "in a sincere, reliable way".

Note: The obvious similarity of Sumerian [eš] and Akkadian [iš] may not be due to pure chance. Was the Sumerian adverbiative a loan from Akkadian?

Less frequently, -bi + šè (or -éš?) are combined: mah-bi-ŠÈ "in a most exalted way"; gibil-bi-ŠÈ "anew".

Cf. Thomsen 1984, 66 f.

The adverb being already a derived form, it is frozen in itself and not subject to further change.

(6) Exclamations. They express joy, fear, pain, surprise, doubt, etc. i (^{d}Utu) "woe (o Sungod)", u_8-ú-a [way] "alas, woe", a-la-la "hey", and others.

Here also belong the expressions for "yes", hé-àm (lit. "let it be") and "no", in-nu (where the negative particle [nu], given the status of a base, is preceded by the neutral motion particle [i]).

(7) Because Sumerian mainly uses nominalized verbal phrases (to which postpositions may be added—see 12.16) instead of subordinate clauses, it essentially lacks subjunctions and conjunctions. Note ì-gi-in-zu "as if", tukumbi "if" (for which Old Sum. has [uda], see 14.2.1).

As a conjunction, ù "and" has been borrowed from Akkadian [wa, u].

Note: Borrowing "and" is well known in agglutinating languages: ve (Arabic wa) in Turkish, ja (Old Germanic jah) in Finnish, eta in Basque. But Sumerian u only occurs to connect phrases, not parts of speech; insofar it is not a replacement of Sumerian -bi(-da) which may connect parts of speech (see hereafter).

As a replacement for a conjunction, -bi or -bi-da is attested: áb amar-bi-da "the cow (with its =) and the calf";

^{d}Nin-ĝir-su, ^{d}Šára-bi(-r) "to Ningirsu and Šara" Ent 28/29 i 5–6 (see 5.4.2.6. b).

(8) Interrogations. We can only partly translate into Sumerian the famous hexameter quis quid ubi quibus auxiliis cur quomodo quando. For "who" and "what" see 9.4; "where" is me-a; "why" is a-na-aš (-àm) [anaš'am] "for what (is it)?".

[J. Black, Sumerian lexical categories, ZA 92 (2002) 60–77, came to the author's attention only after the preceding chapter had been written.]

CHAPTER FIVE

SUBSTANTIVES

5.1. General

Sumerian substantives lack gender, but are strictly divided into two classes: person and non-person. A. Falkenstein used "Personen- und Sachklasse", M.-L. Thomsen "animate and inanimate". We follow Attinger because animals (unless they are personified in literary context) are "animate", but "non-person", and they are not "Sachen".

The form of the substantive does not betray its class. It is shown by agreement: lugal-a-ni "his owner" (said of a slave), lugal-bi "its owner" (said of a garden). Only person class substantives may take the ergative plural (-e)-ne or form a dative; only non-person substantives may form an ablative. Class is also expressed in verbal morphology.

With a limited number of substantives, gender (masc., fem.) is expressed lexically: ninta "male", munus "woman"; ses "brother", $nin_{(9)}$ "sister"; anše "male donkey", éme(ANŠE.MÍ) "jenny", etc.

Apart from class, the categories of substantives are possession, number, and case: ses-$\hat{g}u_{10}$-(e)ne-da "with my brothers" where the particles serving the respective functions occur in a predictable and invariable order.

5.2. Possession

Ownership of something or someone by something or someone is expressed by a set of suffixed particles, closest in rank to the owner (substantive, nominal compound, or nominalized verbal form in -a). No distinction is made between alienable and inalienable possession (sa$\hat{g}$-$\hat{g}u_{10}$ "my head", a-šà-$\hat{g}u_{10}$ "my field") or, in the 1st person pl., between the categories inclusive ("ours" = "mine and yours present") and exclusive ("ours" = "mine and yours absent", "mine and theirs"). For the independent personal pronouns see 10.

For reasons of morphological behaviour we have dissociated possessive particles from free personal pronouns.

Note: Jacobsen 1965, 100[19] had proposed to see a distinction between "inclusive" and "exclusive" in such forms as ga-an-ši-su$_8$-dè-en "let us proceed toward it" (!) (incl.) and ga-ba-ab-túm-mu-dè "let us carry (him) off" (excl.), but his examples do not fit the general definition of these two pronominal categories.
Note: Kienast 1980, 54, explained each possessive particle as "enttontes Enklitikon" (following Falkenstein 1959, 33): 1st sg. *-ĝa would become -ĝu (under the influence of the preceding consonant), and -ĝu would, then, have engendered 2nd sg. -zu. Falkenstein's explanation of lugal-ani as "König er" (for "his king") cannot be proven (see also 9.2).

There are three persons each in sg. and pl.; the 3rd sg. distinguishes person and non-person class. All other persons are restricted to person class.

1st	sg.		-ĝu$_{10}$(MU)
2nd	sg.		-zu
3rd	sg.	person	(-a)-ni
3rd	sg.	non-person	-bi
1st	pl.		-me
2nd	pl.		-zu-ne-ne
3rd	pl.		(-a)-ne-ne

While there are clear morphological sg.: pl. relations in 2nd and 3rd persons, 1st sg. and 1st pl. are not related (nor are they in Akkadian) because "ours" cannot be *"mine + mine", but only "mine + yours" or "mine + his/hers/its".

Morphological behaviour:

1st sg.	is -ĝá in gen. and loc.
2nd sg.	is -za in gen. and loc.
3rd sg.	p. -a-ni follows a consonant, -ni follows a vowel. (-a)-ni is (-a)-na in gen. and loc.
3rd sg.	non-p. is -ba or -bi-a in gen. and loc.
1st to 3rd pl.:	with -me, -zu-ne-ne, (-a)-ne-ne, no overriding of final -e by -a of gen. takes place.

Note: 1st to 3rd sg. differ from nouns ending in a vowel. Whereas in ab-ba-eri-(a)ke$_4$-ne "city elders" the [a] of [ak] is elided, with the possessive particles sg. it is their final vowel that yields—at least graphically—to the [a] of genitive [a(k)] or of locative.

When the possessor is another noun, use of a genitive compound is made whereby the relation between possessor and possessed depends on meaning: ká-é-gal-la(-k) "the gate (possessed) of the palace (possessor)"; but lugal-Unu^{ki}-ga(-k) "the king (possessor) of Uruk (possessed)". Much more rarely, the inverted genitive construction is used: é-a(k) lugal-bi "of the house, its (king =) owner".

5.3. Number

Sumerian number differs fundamentally from that in Akkadian where practically all substantives may form a plural and a restricted number may form a dual. Sumerian has no dual (but cf. note to 5.3.5).

5.3.1.

A plural properly speaking (implying two or more counted objects) and marked by a special suffixed particle is restricted to person class: [(e)ne] with the distribution [ene] after consonant, including [H], and [ne] after vowels. The first [e] thus behaves like the [e] of the ergative or directive case particle: lugal-e-ne "kings", galaH-e-ne "cantors", ugula-ne "overseers".

Orthographically, the first [e] may be contained in a Ce syllabogram, e.g., diĝir-ré-ne (OS), diĝir-re-e-ne (OB), ab-ba-eri-ke_4-ne "city elders".

If the substantive is extended by an adjective, an apposition or by another noun in the genitive, [ene] follows the extended complex: diĝir-gal-gal-e-ne "the great gods", ama-a-a-An-na-ke_4-ne "the mothers and fathers of An".

5.3.2.

Plurality may be expressed by reduplication of the nominal base: a-gàr-a-gàr "fields", ĝiš-gi-ĝiš-gi "cane-brakes", bára-bára-Ki-en-gi énsi-kur-kur-ra(-k) "the (daises =) rulers of Sumer, the city-rulers of the other lands", gur_7-gur_7 "(many) piles of grain/silos".

Reduplication here, apparently, serves the need to express the idea of plural where the simple sg. base which may sometimes also function to express a collective (see 5.3.8) would lack clarity.

Reduplication very rarely occurs with extended nouns: ses-gal-ses-gal "(elder brothers =) school elders".

It is not known to us whether reduplication of substantives may sometimes have resulted in variant pronunciation, as it did with, e.g., deli "one", deli-deli > de/idli "single ones".

5.3.3.

A rare type of partial reduplication is ku-li-li "mutual friends", probably to be compared to Akkadian *itbāru* "mutual friends" as against *ebrū* "friends".

5.3.4.

dedli (see also 5.3.2. end) indicates a detailed plurality: kišib-dedli "the individual sealed documents", bàd-dedli-gal-gal "the individual big fortresses".

Note: dedli is closer in rank to the substantive than the regular adjective. dedli may be followed by [(e)ne]: lú-dedli-ne "the individual persons".

5.3.5.

hi-a "mixed" indicates a plurality of heterogeneous items: túg-hi-a "diverse textiles", u_8-udu-hi-a "sheep".

Note: J. Krecher, OLZ 73 (1978) 28 with fn. 2, referred to hi-a indicating a duality through mention of only one member: mer-hi-a "(the diverse south (-winds) =) north and south". This is reminiscent of Arabic *al-Furātān* "(the two Euphrates =) E. and Tigris", *al-qamarān* "(the two moons =) sun and moon".

5.3.6.

The exact quantity may be expressed by a cardinal number following a substantive. Here, no extra plural word or particle is needed: me-$umun_7$ "the seven ordinances", é-ninnû "Fifty Houses", Niĝirsu's temple complex and ziggurat at Ĝirsu, *lugal-ussu "eight kings".

Note: Texts frequently write 8 lugal instead of lugal 8. The inverted notation has been borrowed from accountancy texts where figures, for the sake of visual clarity are noted at the beginning of a line, and so written exactly one below the other.

5.3.7.

A few adjectives appear in reduplicated form when the preceding substantive is plural: diĝir-gal-gal "the great gods"; na_4-di_4(TUR)-di_4 "small stones".

Here, one is reminded of the Akkadian pl. form of some adjectives: *rabbûtu, ṣeḫḫerūtu, arrakūtu.* For more discussion, see above 4.2.1(b).

Note: Against Falkenstein 1949, 72, Thomsen 1984, 65, supposes that the reduplication of adjectives could express superlatives. However, in the case of na_4-gal-

gal na$_4$-di$_4$-di$_4$ there is hardly the idea of "biggest, smallest stones", but simply "big, small stones". Moreover, as gal-gal, di$_4$-di$_4$ virtually only occur when the noun is plural, there is no reason to assume a superlative, or elative, function.

5.3.8.

Finally, plurality may be present in a simple unextended substantive with collective meaning: ku$_6$, udu, túg are "fish", "sheep (and goats)", "textiles/garments".

5.3.9.

Summing up, we may state that number in Sumerian nouns and adjectives has a totally different significance from that in Akkadian: apart from an opposition singular : plural, we see different non-numerical notions such as totality, collectivity, detailed quantities, mixed quantities.

5.4. Case

Sumerian has ten cases: (1) absolutive, (2) ergative, (3) genitive, (4) locative, (5) dative, (6) comitative, (7) ablative(-instrumental), (8) terminative, (9) directive, (10) equative. A second locative is only attested with the verb; see 12.8.1.26.

Of these, ergative (2) and directive (9) are identical in spelling, and their original identity has often been suggested; cf. 5.4.9.

For (4) to (9) our enumeration corresponds to the sequence of the directional prefixed particles of the verb.

Cases (4), (5) and (7) to (9) may be summarized as directional. The equative (10) stands apart: it is restricted to sg. and it may override any of the cases (4) to (9), so that ses-gin$_7$ not only means "like a brother", but also, e.g., "as with a brother", depending on context.

Note: to some degree this feature of (10) is shared by Akkadian: *kīma eleppim* "like a boat" may also mean "as in a boat"; cf. also Turkish hasta gibi ona bakmıştı "he looked at him as (at a sick person =) if he were a sick person".

	"king"	"mother"	"tree"	"city"	"your mother"	"his/her tablet"	"kings"	"mothers"
(1) abs.	lugal	ama	ĝeš	eri	ama-zu	dub-ba-ni	—	—
(2) erg.	lugal-e	ama	ĝeš-e	eri	ama-zu	dub-ba-ni	lugal-e-ne	ama-ne
(3) gen.	lugal-la(-k)	ama(-k)	ĝeš-a(k)	eri(-k)	ama-za(-k)	dub-ba-na(-k)	lugal-e-ne(-k)	ama-ne(-k)
(4) loc.	(—)	—	ĝeš-a	eri-a	—	dub-ba-na	—	—
(5) dat.	lugal-ra	ama-r(a)	—	—	ama-zu-r(a)	—	lugal-e-ne-r(a)	ama-ne-r(a)
(6) com.	lugal-da	ama-da	ĝeš-da	eri-da	ama-zu-da	dub-ba-ni-da	lugal-e-ne-da	ama-ne-da
(7) abl.	—	—	ĝeš-ta	eri-ta	—	dub-ba-ni-ta	—	—
(8) term.	lugal-šè	ama-šè	ĝeš-šè	eri-šè	ama-zu-šè	dub-ba-ni-šè	lugal-e-ne-šè	ama-ne-šè
(9) dir.	(cf. 2)	(cf. 2)	ĝeš-e	eri	(cf. 2)	dub-ba-ni	(cf. 2)	(cf. 2)
(10) equ.	lugal-gin_7	ama-gin_7	ĝeš-gin_7	eri-gin_7	ama-zu-gin_7	dub-ba-ni-gin_7	—	—

5.4.1. *Preliminary notes on the phonetic and spelling behaviour of the case particles*

In general, a number of (a) phonotactic and (b) spelling rules apply when case particles are added to a noun. For [e] of the ergative or directive see 5.4.2.2 and 5.4.2.9. For the extremely complicated behaviour of the genitive case particle [ak] see 5.4.2.3. Case particles consisting of a vowel ([e], [a]) or beginning with a vowel ([ak]) may be written either with a vowel sign or with a syllabogram CV, representing both the consonant belonging to the preceding—nominal or verbal—base and the vowel of the respective case particle, e.g., kur-ra [kur-a] "in the foreign country". For more details, see the paragraphs on the individual case particles.

5.4.2. *Notes on the individual case particles*

5.4.2.1. *Absolutive*

The absolutive which is unmarked denotes—in our modern interpretation—both the 'subject' of an intransitive verbal form and the 'object' of a transitive verbal form. In Sumerian "father (absolutive) sleeps" and "mother (ergative) cooks dinner (absolutive)", father and dinner are in the identical unmarked case.

The absolutive being the unextended form is the form cited in lexical lists. Absolutive is also used, as a vocative, for calling a god, person, or animal. Nominal pl. in [(e)ne] does not occur with absolutive.

5.4.2.2. *Ergative*

The ergative marks the subject of a transitive ('object'-taking) verbal form. Its usage is consistent in classical Sumerian, and it is only under 2nd millennium Akkadian influence that absolutive and ergative may be used "incorrectly".

The [e] of the ergative (as well as the directive—see 5.4.2.9) is not graphically shown when the preceding substantive ends in a vowel. It is either disregarded in spelling or replaced by a "plene" vowel sign, corresponding to the last vowel of the preceding noun: ama or ama-a "mother", lú or lú-ù "person". It is unknown whether the "plene" vowel sign served (a) to indicate a pronunciation of a single vowel different from the absolutive form, e.g., amâ instead of ama, or (b) to denote a syllable to be pronounced separately, e.g., ama'a, or whether it was (c) a mere visual mark for guiding the reader without relevance for pronunciation. (a) appears to be the most plausible option.

Apart from -e, the ergative (or directive) may be noted by -Ce, e.g., ^{d}En-líl-le [Enlil-e].

While it is still disputed whether the Sumerian verb is construed in pure or in "split" ergativity (cf. the discussion in 12.7.5), it must be stressed that, judging by the distribution of absolutive and ergative in classical Sumerian syntax, there is no "split" whatsoever in the nominal part of Sumerian SOV phrases.

Note: The question which verbs were actually considered transitive or intransitive is often difficult to answer, the more so as the modern interpreter cannot help being influenced by his or her native language. Sumerian "to enter" (ku$_4$-r/ku$_4$-ku$_4$) is introduced by the ergative as if it were "to make an entry". In English, "to enter", may be used both as a transitive and an intransitive verb, whereas in German there is a strict distinction between "eintreten" (intr.) and "eintreten lassen, hinein bringen, etc." (trans.).

When the head of a genitival (regens-rectum) compound, e.g., lugal-kur-kur-ra(-k) "king of all countries", is in the ergative, the particle -e is shifted from the regens to the end of the rectum: lugal-kur-kur-ra-ke$_4$ instead of *lugal-e kur-kur-ra.

Note: The syllabogram KID, in our transliteration -ke$_4$, is, strangely enough, not attested in the series Proto-Ea; cf. MSL 14, 41:243–254: gi-i (var. ge-e, g[i$_4$-. . .]), su-úh, li-il. Therefore, some scholars in the past preferred -gé instead of -ke$_4$ which has been inferred from our idea of the grammatical structure.

-ke$_4$ may, however, be proven by spelling variants. Cf. SRT 11:68 sipa ^{d}Ur-^{d}Namma-ke$_4$ "the shepherd Ur-Namma" paralleled by TCL 15, 38:10 si-pa Ur-^{d}Na-ma-KI, and see Å. Sjöberg, OrSuec. 10 (1961) 11; or Ninmešara 116 ki su-ub ma-ra(-ab)-AG-ne//-a$_5$(AG)-ke$_4$-ne "they kiss the ground before you".

A reading -gé (instead of -ke$_4$) would contradict the fact that nouns ending in -g and prolonged by [e] are regularly spelled -ge or -ge$_4$, but not *-gé.

For the homophony and—probably—common origin of ergative and directive (see also 5.4.2.9) cf. Steiner 1976.

5.4.2.3. *Genitive*

The genitive is the most complicated of the case particles, both in morphology and in syntax. Starting from the basic morpheme [ak] we can note four allomorphs:

(a) [ak] in the position -C-ak-V, e.g., lugal-Úrim^{ki}-ma-ke$_4$ "the king of Ur" (erg.).

(b) [k] between -V and -V, e.g., ab-ba-eri-ke$_4$-ne "the city elders" (erg.).
(c) [a(k)] between -C and -Ø, e.g., lugal-Úrim^{ki}-ma(-k) "the king of Ur" (absol.).
(d) [(V)(k)] between -V and -Ø, e.g., ab-ba-eri(-k) "the city elder" (absol.).

There are four exceptions from the above rule (b): When -ĝu$_{10}$ "my" (see 5.2) -zu "yours", (-a)-ni "his/hers", or -bi "its" (non-p. class) stand in the genitive, the final [u] or [i] is overlaid by the [a(k)] of genitive or by the [a] of locative, yielding -ĝá, -za, (-a)-na, -ba.

Note: Pronouns, cross-linguistically, exhibit peculiarities of their own: in morphology, plural formation, and other respects.

As regards the allomorphs (c) [a(k)] and (d) [(k)], it remains unknown what happened, phonetically speaking, to the final [k] of the genitive morpheme.

That it did not disappear totally becomes clear from the OS spelling rule for the dative case particle [r(a)]. It is not noted in writing after a preceding vowel, e.g., ^{d}Nanna(-r) "to the Moongod", because syllable-closing consonants were still (mostly) disregarded in spelling up till and during Ur III. [ra] is noted after a consonant, e.g., ^{d}En-líl-ra "to Enlil" and also after [a(k)], e.g., ^{d}Nin-ĝír-su(-k)-ra. Quite apparently, there was not one syllable *[sur], but two, [su(k)-ra].

Also, Sumerian loanwords in Akkadian resulting from genitival compounds, display an ending -Vkku, e.g., áb-zà-mi(-(a)k) "cow (as part) of the lyre" > *apsamikku*, a geometrical shape, most probably "trapezium".

With a genitival compound X-Y-a(k) any possessive, number, or case particle pertaining to X has to follow the whole compound, e.g., lugal-Úrim^{ki}-ma(-k)-da "with the king of Ur"; cf. already above, ad 5.4.2.2 (ergative).

However, either X or Y of the compound may be extended by the addition of adjectives or of another dependent substantive (the latter again to be put in the genitive). This results in an intricate, but logical, genitive "algebra":

(a) X (= A-B) – Y-a(k): ur-saĝ-kal-ga—^{d}En-líl-lá(-k) "the mighty warrior of Enlil".
(b) X – Y (= A-B)-a(k): eri-bar—abul-tur-ra(-k) "suburb of the small city-gate".

(c) X (= A-B-a(k)) – Y -a(k): ab-ba-eri(-k)—Unug^{ki}-ga-ke$_4$-ne "the city elders of Uruk".
(d) X – Y (= A-B-ak) -a(k): saĝĝa-^{d}Nin-ĝír-su-ka(-k) "the temple administrator of the Lord-of-Ĝirsu".

Probably for reasons of euphony, no more than two genitive particles were allowed on a string, even if three or more genitival relationships are involved.

What is more, in X – Y -a(k), both X and Y may be extended by appositions: X_1 = X_2 – Y -a(k) or X – Y_1 = Y_2 -a(k). In such cases the string of noun + apposition(s) functions like a simple noun so that there will be no further consequence for the genitive "algebra". Cf. for X_1 = X_2, ^{d}Nin-ĝír-su(-k) ur-saĝ-kal-ga—^{d}En-líl-lá(-k)-ra "to N., mighty warrior of Enlil". Here, Ningirsu(k) and mighty warrior are in apposition.

For Y_1 = Y_2: suhuš-an-ki(-k) "the foundations of Heaven (and) Earth", where an-ki "Heaven and Earth" represent a string (though additive instead of appositive).

Possessive particles may equally be incorporated. In X – Y-a(k), both X and Y may carry a possessive particle:

ká—é-gal-la(-k)-ĝu$_{10}$ "my (gate of the palace =) palace gate".
ká—é-gal-la-ka-ni "his (gate of the palace =) palace gate".
Here possession applies to the whole compound.
Contrast ká—é-gal-ĝá(-k) "the gate of my palace".
ká—é-gal-la-na(-k) "the gate of his palace".
Here only Y (the rectum) is marked by a possessive particle.

OB scribes sometimes became confused with their more elaborate constructions: bàd-gal-[BÀ]D^{ki} eri-nam-ŠAGIN(-a(k))-nam-dumu-naka-ni "the great wall of Der, the city of governorship (nam-ŠAGIN) of his (son-ship =) state of crown-prince", i.e., ". . . of the city where he had been governor when he was still a crown-prince".

Here, X = bàd-gal and Y = the city-name with a complicated string of apposition and genitives: A_1-A_2(-ak)—B-ak. The possessive particle -ani "his" should also have been in the genitive, -a-na. We may understand the scribe's 'mistake' by re-translating the whole complex into Akkadian: **dūram rabiam ša Der āl šakkanakkūtim ša mārūti-šu* the last *-šu* of which was mechanically rendered by the scribe by Sumerian -a-ni.

Apart from the X-Y-a(k) syntagma with a bound genitive, there is free, unbound, genitive with no regens expressed occurring much more rarely, at least in the documentation of historical times: ĝá (-a)-kam, za(-a)-kam "it is of me, you" = "it is mine, yours"; An-na-kam "it is of An (or: of heaven)". A free genitive may also appear as a rectum before its regens: In such cases, the regens has to refer back to the rectum by adding a possessive particle sharing the class (person or non-person) of the rectum: é-a(-k) lugal-bi "of the house, its owner" = "the owner of the house".

Note: This construction represents a universal type. Whether it was more frequent—or even predominant—in prehistoric Sumerian cannot be said.
Note: It is generally difficult to find etymologies for case particles (but see 5.4.2.6 for the comitative). Th. Jacobsen, "Notes on the Sumerian genitive", JNES 32 (1973) 161–66, made a tentative proposal to connect genitive [ak] with the verb ak *"to gather" and to explain (p. 166) é-lú-ak "from 'house gathering in the man', i.e., connecting with him, to 'house of the man'". In his last paragraph, though, Jacobsen mentions the possibility of an underlying "verb ak of not recoverable specific meaning".
G. Zólyomi, "Genitive constructions in Sumerian", JCS 48 (1996) 31–47.

5.4.2.4. *Locative*

The locative is rendered by -(C)a. We presented an argument for an original form [aH] (above 3.1.2), but we cannot determine the vowel quantity: -a(H) or -ā(H). Locative -a, like the [a] of genitive [ak] supersedes the final vowel of the possessive particles of the sg.: -ĝu$_{10}$, -zu, -a-ni, -bi : -ĝá, -za, -a-na, -ba.

Note: Besides u$_4$-ba "at (its day =) that time", there also is u$_4$-bi-a (Akkadian *in ūmišu*). The distinction of the two temporal adverb and the reason for the—uncontracted—u$_4$-bi-a are not yet clear, but note below, 7.2.

The main function of the locative is to indicate rest and arrest at a goal, not movement toward or into something (which would rather be rendered by the terminative, see 5.4.2.8); there is no insistence on direct contact (for which see directive, 5.4.2.9).

eri-me-a "in our city"; an-ki-a "in heaven (and) on earth".

As in many languages, local rest may be transferred to the temporal sphere: šà-mu-ba-ka "(in the middle of =) during that year"; u$_4$-bi-a "at that time".

The locative, as is evident from its functions, is essentially restricted to the non-person class, and as such it stands in complementary distribution with the dative (see 5.4.2.5), which is exclusively used with nouns of the person class. It does not occur with pl. [(e)ne].

Note: Ali Letter B 2:1 lugal-ĝá (instead of lugal-ĝu$_{10}$-ra) "to my lord", quoted in Thomsen 1984, 98, is an exception to the above stated rule of complementary distribution.

5.4.2.5. *Dative*

The dative case particle [ra] has the allomorphs [ra] and [r] where the original distribution was probably between [ra] after a consonant (including -H and genitive -a(k)) and [r] after a vowel. In OS, no dative is marked graphically when the preceding noun ends in a vowel (see above 5.4.2.3). In NS and OB Sumerian both -V-Vr and -V-ra occur. Cf. lugal-/nin-a-ni-ir "to his/her lord/lady", ubiquitous in royal inscriptions, as against lugal-ĝu$_{10}$-ra "to my lord" in the opening of letters.

Note: Cf. Michalowski 1993 nos. 87–92, 94 Na-ni(-r) "to Nani", but 93 Na-ni-ra. Rarely lugal-ĝu$_{10}$-úr, ^{d}Nanna-ar "to my lord", "to the Moongod".

Cases where, after a vowel, -ra is written instead of -Vr, may either be regarded as purely orthographical variants or as some kind of grammatical hyper-correction.

Dative -r(a) with person class nouns almost always stands in complementary distribution with locative -a, occuring with non-person class nouns.

Note: Zólyomi 1999 proposed a complementary distribution of personal dative and "inanimate" directive in the prefixed string of verbal directional particles.

As for the relationship between case particles and verbal dimensional prefix particles, the case of the concord of -r(a) and verbal infixed -na- "to him/her" is one of the most clearly marked.

The function of dative -r(a) is, generally, to indicate that an action or state is in a person's favour; that speech is addressed to a person; or that a certain state of mind (e.g., love, hatred) is felt towards a person.

5.4.2.6. *Comitative*

The comitative is expressed by [da]. There is no restriction to either person or non-person class. The general function is to express company, doing something or being with someone or something; being in someone's neighbourhood; mental and intellectual participation; ability to do something. The particle may, originally, have been identical with the noun da "side"; but this cannot be proved.

an-da gú-lá-a "(hang the neck with =) embracing heaven" (said of the height of a building).

ama-a [d]umu-da gù n[u]-mu(-n)-da(-n)-dé "a mother did not (talk with =) nag her child" Gudea Cyl. A xiii 3.

Commodity (grain, silver) PN$_1$ (ergative) PN$_2$-da an-da-tuku "PN$_1$ (creditor) (has with =) is owed by PN$_2$ (debtor)" NRVN I 61:7, and often in pre-Sargonic and Ur III debt documents (for the verbal prefix a(l)- see 12.10).

An ^{d}Inana-da húl-a-e "An, rejoicing over Inana" Inana and Ebih 61.

Note: For var. see Jaques n.d. II 216.

bala-nam-lugal-la-ĝá 3 še:gur-ta . . . kù-babbar 1 gín-e hé-eb-da (-n)-sa$_{10}$ "during my royal office one shekel of silver (bought with it =) could buy three kor of barley each" Sin-kāšid 13:11–19, and see nos. 8, 10, etc. (RIME 4, 460).

There are two special functions of the comitative:

(a) Our idea of "without" is expressed by X-da nu-me-a "not being with X", e.g., ĝá-da nu-me-a "not being with me" = "without me" in the sense of "without my permission"; cf. the PN Nin-da-nu-me-a "Without the Lady?", being a hypothetical question, to be continued by something like "is there anything possible?" (e.g., Struve 1984, 138).

Note: In early OS, the PN Diĝir-da-nu-me-a is noted as Diĝir-nu-me, e.g., WF p. 26* n.v. "^{d}Nu-me".

Note: A similar idea underlies English "with-out", Russian vne "in not", or German children's "mit ohne" for "ohne".

(b) áb amar-bi-da "the cow with its calf" expresses an idea closely related to, or even identical with, "the cow and (the) calf" (note the interchangeability of "chicken with/and rice"). Sumerian lacks a word for "and" and, at the latest in NS, borrowed Akkadian ù.

Note: For the X Y-bi-da construction cf. Turkish Leyla ile Mecnun "with L., M." = "Mecnun and Leyla". For the borrowing of "and" see above 4.2 (7).

The combination -bi-da has a variant -bi which also occurs in lexical lists (cf. bi = ù MSL 4, 195:159; bi = *ù, qa-*[*du*] MSL 4, 175:215 (NBGT); bi, bi-da = *ù* MSL 4, 137:203 f. (NBGT).

OS Ent. 28–29 i 5–6 ^{d}Nin-ĝír-su ^{d}Šara-bi(-r) "to Ninĝirsu and Šara".

Poebel 1923, 147 f.

5.4.2.7. *Ablative-instrumental*

The ablative-instrumental case particle is expressed by [ta] which, at least in our Latin transliteration, is phonologically clearly differentiated from comitative [da]. It only occurs with non-person class nouns and, therefore, cannot occur with pl. [(e)ne].

Its functions are to indicate the starting point from which someone or something comes from or by means of which (instrumentally) something is realized or manufactured (cf. French produire qc. à partir de qc.).

an-gal-ta ki-gal-šè "from the great Above to the great Below" Inana's Descent 1.

The local aspect was easily transferred to the temporal: u_4-bi-ta "from that day" = "since that time".

^{geš}tukul-kal-ga ^{d}En-líl-le mu-na(-n)-šúm-ma-ta "with the mighty weapon which Enlil had entrusted to him".

The ablative, placed after a nominalized phrase, serves to express what is a temporal subordinate clause in Akkadian: saĝ-ki-gíd-da-^{d}En-líl-lá-ke_4 Kiš^{ki} gu_4-an-na-gin_7 im-ug_5-ga-ta "after Enlil's frown had killed Kiš like the bull of Heaven" Curse of Akkade 1.

Note: Or "as by means of the Bull of Heaven"; see above 5.4 for the equative overriding other cases.

Ablative -ta cannot be applied to person class nouns so that where "from (a person)" is needed the circumpositional version ki-N-a(k)-ta, lit. "from the place of N", is often used. Cf. the ubiquitous ki-PN_1(-ak)-ta PN_2 (erg.) šu ba-an-ti "PN_2 received (object) from PN_1".

A special function of -ta is to indicate distribution, such a quantity "each": see, e.g., Sin-kāšid 13:11–19, above 5.4.2.6.

5.4.2.8. *Terminative*

The terminative case particle owes its designation to its main function: to indicate that someone or something reaches a goal.

It is usually written with the syllabogram šè, but sometimes as -Vš. It is unknown how the pronunciation of šè differed from [še] in še(-ga) "favoured".

Note: We owe to Attinger 1993, 253–56, the strict distinction between the "terminative" case particle and the adverbial particle [eš(e)], for which he proposed "adverbiative" ("adverbiatif"). A common origin of both particles is not improbable.

Note that Proto-Ea (MSL 14, 33:61) with e-še ÉŠ (var. še, ši) is inconsistent as is Ea I (MSL 14, 186:180–182) which by offering the equivalences e-eš = *a-na*, še-e = *ki-ma*, and e-eš = *eb-lu*, at least to our modern interpretation, seems to have switched "terminative" (e-eš = *a-na*) and "adverbiative" (še-e = *ki-ma*).

The original distribution of the allomorphs [še] and [š] most probably has its counterpart in dative [ra] and [r] (see 5.4.2.4), -šè would then have stood after a consonant, whereas -š (either written or latent) would be found after a vowel. However, as regards the allomorph [š], either spelling is inconsistent or our present understanding is still inadequate. In the ubiquitous dedicatory formula "for his/her life", the spelling is consistently nam-ti-la-ni-ŠÈ and never *-ni-iš oder *-ni-eš. Either there were two syllables [niše] or -ni-ŠÈ stood for one syllable [niš].

Falkenstein 1949, 113 f., referred to the spelling saĝ-biš(PEŠ) "to its head" Gudea Cyl. B ii 18 with contrasting saĝ-bi-ŠÈ in Cyl. A iv 11, and see Falkenstein 1949, 30.

The terminative is most obviously opposed to the ablative in such phrases as an-gal-ta ki-gal-šè (see 5.4.2.7) or Úrim^{ki}-ta Nibru^{ki}-šè "from Ur to Nippur".

Local use is, again, transferred to temporal: u_4-ul-lí-a-šè "until (those days =) all future".

Moreover, the terminative may be used to indicate abstract ways of reasoning: cause, reason, purpose. Cf. mu-bi-šè "(to its name =) therefore"; a-na-aš(-àm) "for what is it" = "why"; níĝ-ba-aš "as (the purpose of) a present".

The terminative, set after a nominalized verbal phrase (whether introduced by u_4 or not) serves to express what is a subordinate temporal clause in Akkadian (with *adi*): "until . . .".

Both the terminative and adverbiative particles have to be kept separate from the quotation particle [eše] which the Gudea corpus equally spell -ÉŠ (in OB e-še). Cf. below 13.1.

5.4.2.9. *Directive*

The directive (locative-terminative) case particle [e] was, most probably, identical in sound with the ergative [e] and because both particles share the same spelling and phonotactic behaviour, the origin of the ergative particle has been sought in the directive. See above 5.4.2.2.

Be that as it may, by the time we have some insight into the phonetic realities hidden behind Sumerian spelling habits, both cases have clearly established themselves as separate entities and, most tellingly, the concord of the two case particles with verbal prefix particles is also different. Cf. Gudea Cyl. A iv 4: kar-Niĝin^{ki}-na-ke_4 (dir.) má (absol.) bí(-n)-ús "he (= Gudea, erg.) had the boat moor at the quay of N.".

The main function of the directive is to express movement arriving (into contact with) an object, or position adjacent to (in contact with) an object.

The directive is mainly used with nouns of the non-person class, and it is only rarely found with person class, e.g., ama dumu-ni [dumu-(a)ni-e] níĝ nu-ma-ni-ra [nu-mma-ni-n-ra] "no mother beat her child", lit. "let something hit at her child" Gudea Cyl. A xiii 3.

We may try to visualize the directional functions of locative, terminative, and directive in the following graphs:

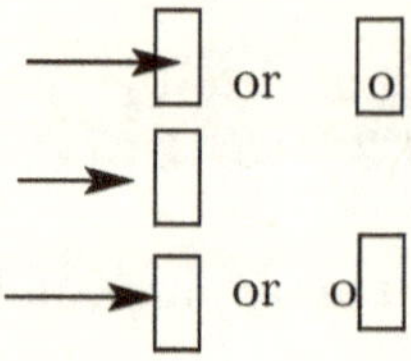

Locative: motion into, position inside.

Terminative: motion towards.

Directive: motion arriving at, position next to.

5.4.2.10. *Equative*

Noun + -gin$_7$(GIM) formations may be taken as cases because the particle has the same position as the case particles for ergative through directive. Equative stands apart, however, in that it may, virtually, contain the notion expressed by a dimensional case (cf. above, 5.1 and see 5.4.2.7 end).

The equative expresses comparison and corresponds to Akkadian *kīma* (which may equally imply a dimensional case). Equative may be used with nouns of both classes: person or non-person, but it is not attested with plural.

GIM = gin$_7$ shares with some substantives the -m/n variant of its final consonant. In Proto-Ea 530 (MSL 14, 53), GIM/DÍM is glossed gi-in, ge-en, and gi-im. When -GIM is followed by the copula [am] the spelling is GIM-nam, thus clearly leading to -gin$_7$-nam.

Note, however, ur$_5$-GIM-ma-àm in Lugalbanda and Enm. 163 (cf. Thomsen 1984, 109 [249]) where -ma- has been confirmed by collation (Wilcke 1969, 107, note to line 163).

It cannot be excluded that the variant form GIM = gim was influenced by the [m] of Akkadian *kīma*.

Note: For the PN A-ba-DN/ses-ĝu$_{10}$-GIM, there are variant spellings with -KI and -KID = -gé). The first var., A-ba-^{d}En-líl-KI (YOS 4, 302:27) may be dismissed as a simple case of dittography: line 28 offers šà-EN.LÍL.KI "in Nippur". For A-ba-ses-ĝu$_{10}$-gé see ITT 4, 7450:8.

5.4.2.11. *Recapitulation of the case particles*

The addition of case particles 2 and 4 to 10 is mutually exclusive, this also being the reason for the non-existence of such expressions as *lugal-ra-gin$_7$ "like for a king".

Note: a-ab-ba-sig-ta-ta "from the Lower Sea" in Lugal-zagesi 1 ii 4–5 (Steible 1982/II 317) is no exception to the rule because -ta is added to a frozen expression, sig-ta "from-below" = "lower". See the discussion by Wilcke 1990, 471–475, who also offers comparable examples for . . . -ta-(a)k and . . . -ta-šè.

On the other hand, any of the case particles 2 to 10 may be added to genitive (3) [(a)(k)], yielding the sequences [ake], [aka(k)], [aka], [a(k)ra], [a(k)da], [a(k)ta], [a(k)še], [ake], [a(k)gin].

The case system is more restricted in the plural of person class where as well as the locative (4) and the ablative (7), which are incompatible with person class, the absolutive (1) and equative (10) are unrepresented.

CHAPTER SIX

ADJECTIVES

Adjectives accompany substantives which they qualify; or, as a predicate, they occur with the verbal copula: udug-hul "evil demon"; é-gibil "new house".

Once a substantive + adjective compound has been formed it is impenetrable and any particle has to follow the complex as a whole: ses-gal-ra "to the (big brother =) school overseer".

An apparent exception occurs when a substantive is followed by the individualizing plural element didli (see 5.3.4). Here, dedli virtually also functions as an adjective as it is in origin, but it is closer to the substantive: bàd-dedli-gal-gal "the individual big fortresses".

There has been much debate on whether adjectives should be considered a part of speech of their own (cf. 4.2. (1b)). Gragg 1968, 91, proposed to classify them as a sub-category of the verb, by which he is—tentatively—followed by Thomsen 1984, 64. Attinger 1993, 148 f., distinguishes between primary and secondary adjectives, the criterion being whether or not they may be provided with the suffixed particle [a]. Krecher 1978, 376–403 (esp. 382–85), had proposed determinant force to -a: zi(-d) "true", zi-da "right (not left)". Formally, zi-da is indistinguishable from du_{11}-ga "said", i.e., the so-called *ḫamṭu* participle of the verb (see 12.14.2). Krecher's study was taken up by Klein 1993, 81–98, "The suffix of determination /a/".

We owe to Black 2003 the first extensive study of the Sumerian adjective, and he offers morphological and syntactical criteria for the identification of adjectives. Much of the following is based on his study.

The respective criteria are not applicable to each and every adjective, but rather apply in a variety of situations: ability to reduplicate (shared with substantives and verbs); suffix -a (shared with the *ḫamṭu* participle of the verb); negation with nu- (shared with verbs); position after a substantive; "nominal predicate of copular clauses".

Black sees no "watertight" category of adjective and, therefore, submits 'adjectives' to scrutiny in terms of both their formation and semantic type (dimension, physical property, colour, human propensity, age, value, speed, uncertain).

In view of the Sumero-Akkadian linguistic area (see 17) and the bilingual lexical entries, we might, however, venture a rather pragmatic approach: what did the scribes, in their Akkadian translations, consider as adjectives (for in Akkadian, the adjective as a part of speech is not contested)? Their approach was probably very close to ours.

The adjective occurs in simple form: mu-gibil "new year", udug-hul "evil demon", kisal-mah "greatest (= main) court".

It occurs in reduplication: na_4-gal-gal "big stones", me-^{d}kal-^{d}kal "highly valued rites".

Note: For reduplicated adjectives as a means to express the pl. of the preceding substantive see 5.3.7.

A special feature is the reduplication of some adjectives denoting colours: bar_6-bar_6 "white", from Ur III on spelled by single UD, but pronounced babbar; sig_7-sig_7 "green".

An adjective occurs as a base + particle -a: á-zi-da "right (arm =) side" (see Krecher 1978, above); kaš níĝ-du_{10}-ga "(beer, good thing =) beer of specially good quality".

Note: níĝ-du_{10}-ga = **dummuqu* "improved"; is there a correspondence with D-stem ("quttulu") adjectives of Akkadian? (J. N. Postgate)

There is a considerable number of compound nouns which Black treats, according to their syntactical position, as extended adjectives; we quote only three examples from Black's catalogue: á-ĝál "(strength available =) strong", ní-tuku "(having awe =) reverent"; gal-zu "(knowing great =) skilful".

For the adjective as a base for adverbial expressions see ch. 11.

CHAPTER SEVEN

DETERMINATION, SPECIFICATION: DEMONSTRATIVE PARTICLES

Certain particles suffixed to a substantive may serve to mark it as something set apart. These particles have traditionally been treated as dependent forms of the demonstrative pronoun.

See Falkenstein 1949, 55 f.; 1959, 34; Thomsen 1984, 80–82; Attinger 1993, 175 f.

As with possession (see 5.2) we prefer to separate "pronouns" as independent words from particles attached to a noun. In the case of determination or specification there is another reason to keep demonstrative pronouns and demonstrative particles separated. Whereas free ne(n) "this" only occurs as non-person class, dependent -ne(n) may refer to substantives of both the person and non-person classes.

There are five particles to be discussed: -ne(n), -bi, -e, -ri, and -še. The evidence for some of these is not uncontroversial, partly because of orthographical ambiguity or scarcity of references.

7.1. *-ne(n)*

-ne(n): u_4-ne-na "on this very day" Gudea Stat. B ix 7.

Note: For this passage Falkenstein 1949, 55 fn. 8, had a translation "an diesem seinen Tag", combining a demonstrative and a possessive particle. Thomsen 1984, 80, has "on this day".

u_4-ne máš-ĝi$_6$-ka "on that day, in a night time vision" Gudea Cyl. A i 17.

Note: Pace Edzard 1997, 69, who reads u_4-dè. A sequence directive [e] and locative [a] for describing the time of the day would, however, be quite unusual. u_4-ne is virtually in the locative, too, but the case particle [a] is only noted at the end of the string.

lú-ne is so far only attested in lexical context: lú-ne-da = *itti annîm* "with this one" OBGT I 307 (MSL 4, 48); ki-lú-ne(-k)-ta = *itti annîm* ibid. 308, and see lines 309–341.

Note: It is hard for modern grammarians to judge whether these examples should be considered—at least partly—as a learned exercise or as a reflex of late OB spoken Sumerian. Already ibid. lines 309 f. lú-ne-da-me-eš, lú-ne-me-eš-da = *itti annûtim* raise our suspicion, because the pl. of the copula, me-eš "they are", is mechanically inserted to express nominal, not verbal, plurality. On the other hand, most of the sg. examples meet the standards we are setting for "our" Sumerian grammar.

7.2. *-bi*

-bi is most probably identical with the possessive particle of the 3rd sg. non-person class, and one easily sees a transition in meaning from "its, relating to something" to "that", "the aforementioned".

u_4-bi-a "(in its day =) at that time", sometimes referring to primordial days.

u_4-bi-a already in Ukg. 4 ii 4 = 5 ii 5. The distribution of u_4-bi-a and u_4-ba (cf. 5.2) is not yet clear. Was the [i] of demonstrative [bi] not overridden by the locative case particle [a] as was the [i] of possessive [bi]? In that case one would, perhaps, have to distinguish between [biH] and [bi].

7.3. *-e(?)*

It is difficult to establish the separate existence of a demonstrative particle [e], since it would be identical in spelling with the ergative and directive case particles.

Gudea Stat. B vii 49–53 is often quoted: alan-e ù kù-nu za-gìn nu-ga-àm [nu-(i)nga-am] ù erida-nu ù nagga-nu sipar-nu kiĝ-ĝá lú nu-ba-ĝá-ĝá "for the/this statue nobody was supposed to apply in work silver or lapis lazuli, or copper or tin or bronze". Here, it is not clear at all whether alan-e is "statue + demonstrative particle" or simply the directive case ("to apply in work material to the statue").

-e is attested in lexical context: lú-e-ra, lú-e-me-eš-a OBGT I 326 f. (MSL 4, 49).

For the second form, cf. the note at the end of 7.1.

Woods 2003, sees the demonstrative -e as the origin of the ergative case particle. See also Yoshikawa, end of 7.4.

7.4. *-ri(?)*

With -ri it is uncertain whether it should be considered a demonstrative or an adjective meaning "far away, remote"; cf. CAD N/2, 186 *nesû* adj. lex. for Nabnītu X 36 (MSL 16, 118: IX (= X) 36 where it is read dal) and Aa II/7: 11' (MSL 14, 293: ri-i = *né-su-ú*).

-ri is mainly found in the phrase u_4-/ĝi$_6$-/mu-ri(-a) "in those days/nights/years" when the poet refers to beginning in primordial time; cf. already OS TSŠ 79 i 1–5 (UD.GAL.NUN text). -ri-a may be analysed either as [ri] + locative case particle -a or as [ri] + -a of *ḫamṭu* participle, with the locative not further noted in spelling.

Note: Shaffer 1963, 122, referred to SBH no. 4:162 f. etc. u_4-RI-LI-na (= *ina ūmē ullūti* "in those days") and he preferred reading u_4-re-èn-na instead of u_4-dal-le-na, from which Attinger 1993, 176, deduces a pair "-re/i, -re-èn". The topic must be left to further research.

Note: Yoshikawa 1993, 185–92, tried to show there was a "Spatial Deictic System in Sumerian", with -e "something in the space which is close to the speaker and addressee" and -ri "something which is remote from the space occupied by the speaker or addressee". Yoshikawa essentially bases himself on lexical texts, not on context examples.

7.5. *-še(?)*

-še occurs in lú-še in Gilgameš and Agga 69–71, 91–92 referring to Gilgameš seen on the Uruk city wall by beleaguering Agga. Jacobsen 1965, 177 fn. 55, tentatively proposed "anyone from here" basing himself on NGBT II i 11–15 (MSL 4, 158 f.) where, however, only line 11 [lú-š]e = *animmamû* can be restored more or less reliably. Katz 1993, 43, 45 offers "that person"; Römer 1980 lines 91 f. lú-še "der Mann da".

So, due to the extreme scarcity of attestation, -še is not a certain candidate for inclusion among the demonstrative particles.

7.6. *Recapitulation*

To sum up, out of the five elements discussed here, -ne(n), -bi, -e, -ri, and -še, only two: -ne(n) and -bi, may be convincingly classified as demonstrative particles.

CHAPTER EIGHT

RESUMING THE SEQUENCE OF PARTICLES FOR POSSESSION, NUMBER AND CASE

In Sumerian ses-ĝu$_{10}$-(e)ne-r(a) "to my brothers" exhibits a sequence possessive—number—case whose particles cannot switch in rank one with another.

Note: Demonstrative particles (see 7) are not included here. They most probably share the rank with possession.

For the sake of comparison, examples are given for Turkish, Mongolian, Hungarian, and Finnish:

Turkish: kardeş-ler-im-e "to my brothers" (brother—pl.—poss.—case).
Mongolian: (minu) aqa-nar-dur "to (my) brothers" (brother—pl.—case).
Hungarian: barát-a-im-nak "to my brothers" (brother—pl.—poss.—case).
Finnish: talo-i-ssa-ni "in my houses" (house—pl.—case—poss.).

These few examples may show that there is no "universal" rule, in agglutinative languages, for the hierarchy of the suffixed morphemes used to express possession, number, and case.

CHAPTER NINE

PRONOUNS

9.1. Personal pronouns

The system is still incomplete for us in the 1st and 2nd pl. This corresponds to the strange fact that many inflected forms of the verb in the 1st and 2nd pl. cannot be safely reconstructed and/or, when they occur in different manuscripts of OB literary texts, present incongruous variants.

1st sg. ĝá-e (or contracted $ĝe_{24}$-e)
2nd sg. za-e (but note contracted NS zé)
3rd sg. person cl. OS a-ne, NS, OB e-ne

3rd sg. non-person class: no independent pronoun is safely attested although one would expect it, given the existence of possessive -bi. ur_5 "this, that" may be considered a substitute. ur_5, however, does not seem to occur alone, only in combination with case particles and/or the copula: ur_5-gin_7 "like this", ur_5-šè-àm "for this (purpose)".

Note to 1st and 2nd sg.: It is hard to ascertain the exact phonetic nature of these pronouns. The dative forms ĝá-ra, za-ra may point to bases [ĝa], [za]. But regressive assimilation is equally possible. Moreover, [ĝe] → [ĝara], [ze] → [zara] would not be inconceivable. Cf. modern Turkish ben, sen with datives bana, sana.

1st pl. me, secondarily me-en-dè-en

Note: me = *ni-i-nu* is clearly offered by Proto-Ea vocabulary 71:5 (MSL 14, 19), and there is no need to attribute me of Proto-Ea to the possessive particles, -me "our" (see 5.2). Admittedly, however, independent me "we" is so far unattested in context, but the chances of meeting such a me are—statistically—quite small, because the personal pronouns only occur when emphasis is needed.

The lexical equation me-da-nu = *i-na ba-l*[*u-ni*] "without us" OBGT I (vii) 484 (MSL 4, 53) is obviously derived from me "we".

The (secondary) form me-en-dè-en looks identical to the inflected copula, "we are": [me-(e)nden]. For me-en-dè(-n) in OB literary context, cf. Lam. Ur and Sumer 240.

2nd pl. me-en-zé-en, za-e-me-en-zé-en
Attested lexically only.

Note: me-en-zé-en looks identical to the inflected copula, "you are": [me-(e)nzen]. By analogy with the relation -zu : -zu-ne-ne in the set of possessive particles, a form *za-ne(-ne) might be reconstructed, because "you" (pl.) often is "thou + pl.". For secondary pronouns of the 1st and 2nd pl. cf., e.g., Spanish nosotros, vosotros, or French nous autres (français) "we (French)".

3rd pl. person class a-ne-ne (OS, NS), e-ne-ne (OB).

Here, the relation between 3rd sg. and pl. clearly is one of a private opposition: "they" = "he/she + pl.", [ane-(e)ne], [ene-(e)ne].

As in many languages, Sumerian personal pronouns have a reduced declension pattern, compared to that of the substantive. There is just one form, at least judging by orthography, for absolutive and ergative; then there are genitive, dative, comitative, and equative. Locative and ablative are not to be expected because they only occur with non-person class. Terminative is so far unattested, and directive, if it existed, would have been identical in spelling with the ergative.

As with substantives, an ablative can, however, be constructed with the help of the circumpositional syntagma ki- . . . -ta. So ki-zu-ta "from your place" would equal "from you" (cf. 5.4.2.7 end).

The free genitive ĝá(-a)-kam, za(-a)-kam "it is (of me, you =) mine, yours" functions as a free possessive pronoun (see 9.2).

Dative: ĝá(-a)-ra, ĝá(-a)-ar, zá(-a)-ra, e-ne-ra, e-ne-er "to me, you, him/her".

Comitative: ĝá-e-da-nu-me-a "not being with me" = "without me", "without my permission" (cf. 5.4.2.6).

Equative: ĝá-e-gin$_7$-nam "it is like me".

Note: We do not quote the rich lexical evidence for 1st to 3rd pl. pronouns, as offered in OBGT I 376–556 (MSL 4, 50–54), because much of the Babylonian scribe's interpretation looks dubious in the light of modern scholarship. Compare e-ne-ne-ra and e-ne-ne-er (ibid. 554 and 556) both of which we would translate as "to them" [enene-r(a)], but are rendered by *šu-nu-ti* and *e-li-šu-nu* respectively.

9.2. Possessive pronouns

Strictly speaking, these exist only in the form of the genitive of the personal pronoun combined with the copula, e.g., ĝá(-a)-kam "it is (of me =) mine".

We have treated the possessive particles by themselves under "possession" (see 5.2). While the morphological relation between those particles and the free forms is obvious, it is still difficult to explain the origin of the possessive particles unless we move back into prehistory (cf. Poebel 1923, 76).

At any rate, the high antiquity of possessive particles is suggested by the fact that of the categories of possession, number, and case particles, the possessive particles rank closest to the substantive (see above ch. 8).

9.3. Demonstrative pronouns

The Sumerian system is more difficult to describe and define than the very clearly developed system of Akkadian demonstrative pronouns.

There are, so far, only two words known that would deserve the definition of (independent) demonstrative pronouns:

9.3.1. ur_5

ur_5 (already mentioned 9.1): ur_5 hé-na-nam(-ma-àm) "let it really be this", ur_5-gin_7 "like this", ur_5-ra-ke_4-éš "therefore" (lit. [ur-ak] as a free genitive, with the adverbiative particle [eš(e)]).

ur_5 is restricted to the non-person class and has, therefore, been considered a substitute for the—non-existing—personal pronoun, 3rd sg. non-person class.

9.3.2. *ne-e(n)*

ne-e(n) is equally restricted to the non-person class, at least as far as it occurs independently.

ĝá-e za-kam ne-e a-na-àm ì-til-l[e] "I am yours, this—what is it?—will (live =) stay" Innin šag. 246 (ZA 65, 198).

lú gùd-ĝá ne-en ba-e(-a)-AG-a "you, the person (who) did this to my nest" Lugalb. 105, and see Wilcke 1969, 164.

ne nam-[di]-dEn-líl-lá "this is [a judgement] of Enlil" Ur III PN, NG no. 40:9, reflected by ne-en-nam di-ku_5-dNanna-kam = *annûm dīnu ša Sin* "as (regards) this, it is a judgement of the Moongod" van Dijk 1953, 129:42 f. (PBS 10/1, 1 iv 18).

9.4. Interrogative pronouns

Here, the universal pair "who" and "what" prevails, the first [aba] asking about someone of the person class, the second [ana] about something of the non-person class. The opposition b : n (instead of *n : b) is surprising, at least if one expects a morphological correspondence between interrogative and personal pronouns as, e.g., in Latin quis : is, quid : id or German wer : er, was : das.

For a-ba, ergative a-ba-a is attested, and both a-ba and a-na, like 3rd person class pronoun e-ne, may be combined with the copula -àm. Generally speaking, the restrictions as to the affixation of case particles affecting the personal pronouns apply equally to the interrogative pronouns (see 9.1).

There is no adjectival interrogative, as a possible correspondence to Akkadian *ajjû, ajjītu* "which". For na-me "any one" see 9.5.2.

Note: CAD A/1, 234 *ajû* lex., quotes a late reference where na-me is rendered by *ajjû* "which"; here, however, the Sumerian text has the well-known syntagma na-me + negated verb, perhaps as a question, so that the Akkadian translation "which one" would actually render "(has) no one".

9.5. Alleged pronouns

9.5.1. *Reflexive pronoun?*

The Sumerian base ní-(te-) serves to express, along with possessive particles, notions which we are used to translate by "myself", etc. i.e., by a reflexive pronoun: šám-ní-te-na "purchase price of himself" (= for his own person) NG no. 38:7; ní-zu-šè ĝéštu-zu "to yourself your ear!" (= "be aware of yourself") Angim 81, and see more examples in Thomsen 1984, 78 f.

There seems to have been a general distribution rule: ní-te-V versus ní-C, i.e., ní-ĝu$_{10}$/-zu versus ní-te(-a)-ni, ní-te(-a)-ne-ne for "my/your/itself", "him/herself, themselves". But note ní-te-ĝu$_{10}$-šè "to myself" UET 6/2, 144:36 f., quoted by Attinger 1993, 174.

NS or OB ní-te is preceded by OS ME-te, most probably to be read ni$_x$-te (Attinger 1993, 174): Nite(TE:ME)-ga-i "Let me praise (my)self" DP 73 ii 2 (PN).

For bilingual contexts where ní-te = *ramanu* see CAD R 117 lex.

ní-(te-) + possessive particle is a nominal phrase not different from, e.g., saĝ + poss. particle, and therefore, strictly speaking, ní-(te-) cannot be considered a "pronoun". One would rather associate ní-(te) with parts of the body.

Alster 1974, 178–80; Cavigneaux 1978, 177–85; Thomsen 1984, 78 f.; Attinger 1993, 174 f. with more lit.

9.5.2. *Indefinite pronoun?*

na-me is found both as a substantive and as an adjectival base, independent of person or non-person class. In the majority of references it occurs along with a negative verbal form, so that it means either (positive) "any (one)" or (negative) "no (one)".

lú-na-me, níĝ-na-me, u_4-na-me "anyone", "anything", "any (day =) time"; na-me nu-kúr-ru "nobody will alter it" SKIZ 83 i 15.

Note: In the last example as in parallel cases, na-me may be an abbreviated form of lú-na-me.

[me] of na-me should at least until we have better knowledge not be associated with the verbal base me "to be".

Thomsen 1984, 78; Attinger 1993, 174.

CHAPTER TEN

NUMERALS

10.1. General

The Sumerian language had a "sexagesimal" system in which numeration proceeded in alternating steps of 10 and 6: 1–10, 10–60, 60–600, 600–3600, 3600–36000, 36000–216000. With sixty as the "hundred", Sumerian numeration had the enormous advantage of being able to divide by 3 or 6 without leaving a remainder. The sexagesimal system has left its traces in our modern divisions of the hour or of the compass. It permeates the metrological systems of the Ancient Near East.

Powell 1971; 1989.

Since cardinal and ordinal numbers, including fractions, as well as notations of length, surface, volume, capacity, and weight are next to exclusively written with number signs, we are poorly informed on the pronunciation and the morpho-syntactical behaviour of numbers in Sumerian. To what degree were numbers subject to case inflection? If 600 was pronounced ĝeš-u "sixty ten", i.e., "ten (times) sixty", what was the pronunciation of "sixty (plus) ten", i.e., 70? Was there a difference of stress or some other means of intonation, e.g., *[ĝéš(d)u] versus [ĝeš(d)ú]?

Syntactically, persons or things counted were followed, not preceded, by numerals so that the position of a numeral corresponds to that of an adjective. For—purely graphic—exceptions to this rule see 5.3.6, note.

10.2. Cardinal numbers

The oldest pronunciation guide for the Sumerian cardinal numbers 2 to 10 is an exercise tablet from Ebla: TM 75.G. 2198: Edzard 1980; 2003b.

Ebla	later tradition
1. (slanted vertical wedge)	aš, deli, diš ($ge_{(4)}$)
2. mì-nu [min]	min
3. $iš_{11}$-ša-am [iš/eš + copula]	$eš_5$
4. li-mu [lim(m)u]	limmu
5. i [ia]	ía
6. A-šu [Aš]	àš
7. ù-mi-nu [umin]	$umun_5$, imin
8. ù-sa-am [us + copula]	ussu
9. ì-li-mu [ilim(m)u]	ilimmu
10. u_9-wa-mu [*haw(?) + copula]	u

Diakonoff 1983, 83–93, cf. G. Pettinato, AIUON 41 (1981) 141–43 ("inspired" by Edzard 1980).

Notes on the individual numbers 1 to 10:

For 1 and the following cardinal numbers, the most exhaustive treatment still is that by Powell 1971, 13 ff.

1: for deli (di-li, de-e-li, du-li), aš and diš so far only an approximate distribution pattern can be offered:

deli is "single, unique" (*wēdum*); cf. lú-saĝ-deli, glossed *sagdilû* "(person, single head =) bachelor". Reduplicated deli: dedli indicates detailed plurality (see 5.3.4). AŠ-ni "he/she all alone" is read deli-ni or aš(a)-ni by individual authors. The OS PN [Ašani "he alone"] is spelled A-$ša_4$(DU)-ni (DP 125 iv 6), or $Aš_x$(GE_{23})-$ša_4$-ni (DP 124 iv 2; 126 iv 3).

See J. Bauer, RA 64 (1970) 188, partly corrected by J. N. Postgate, AfO 24 (1973) 77.

However, deli-du-ni "he is coming alone" might also be proposed. AŠ(deli)-diĝir-re-ne "the only one of the gods" VS 10, 199 iii 4 (cf. Falkenstein 1959, 66). A similar uncertainty is found with the epithet of the Moongod, ^{d}AŠ-im_4/im-bar_6-bar_6/babbar (discussed by M. Krebernik, RlA 8, 362 f. § 2.3; there is no var. "áš").

It is difficult to differentiate aš from deli. If 6 really were 5+1, Ebla A-šu might be explained as *[ia+aš]. This is, however, quite uncertain.

diš may have been the regular counting word ("one, two, three"), not bound to either person or non-person class. bandiš "1 seah" (followed by banmin), munus diš-àm "there was a (certain) woman" Gudea Cyl. A iv 23. There is, however, no lexical correspondence diš = *ištēn*, and, strangely enough, diš is not found in Proto-Ea.

For the Emesal form [did] see Schretter 1990, 164 f.

2: It is unclear whether Ebla mì-nu stands for [min] (which we adopted) or for bi-syllabic [minu]. Ebla spelling does not yet clearly denote syllable-closing consonants and often resorts to CV(-C) or CV-C(V). Note, however, that 4 li-mu definitely stands for the bi-syllabic numeral.

Apart from min, there is tab "double, parallel". tab and min are combined in gú-tab-min-bi "its two parallel banks".

3: Ebla $iš_{11}$-ša-am can only be explained as 3 [iš] or [eš] + copula [am]; note also the copula in Ebla 8 and 10.

4: Ebla li-mu may stand for single or lengthened [m]. Post-Eblaic lexical glosses note lim-mu, rarely LAM-mu. For níĝ-úr-limmu "(thing four limbs =) quadrupeds" an emesal writing has ne-mu-li-mu (TCL 15, 3:4; Falkenstein, ZA 53 [1959] 101 fn. 34).

5: Ebla i is ambiguous as it may stand for [ya] or [yi] (cf. Krebernik, ZA 72 [1982] 191). i early found its way into Sumerian and Akkadian syllabaries. Powell 1971, 35 pointed to the OS spelling šu-IÁ for šu-i "barber". 5 is part of numerals 7 and 9; see below.

6: Ebla A-šu (for the -u ending see above 2) is graphically as ambiguous as is Ebla 5. A may stand for [a, ay, aw, ya] (Krebernik, ZA 72 [1982] 180 f.).

6 has been analysed as 5+1 by analogy with the evident cases of 5+2 and 5+4. So, *ia+aš "5+1" might have yielded [ya'aš], [yāš]. The post-Eblaic gloss a-áš may, but does not have to, stand for [āš]; a in a-áš may also be taken as a simple vocalic indicator: ^{a}áš. If 6 really were a compound of 5+1, then the element "1" could only be [aš] and not [diš].

7: Ebla ù-mi-nu (for the ending -u see above 2) does not display the expected form 5+2 because of its Anlaut [u]. This, however, is most probably due to anology with the Anlaut of following 8, [us] or [us(s)a]. Later, [umin] turned into [umun]. The etymologically "correct" imin, used by most Assyriologists, is not attested at all in lexical glosses, but occurs in sign-names; see Powell 1971,40; Gong 2000, 139.

Note: Rhyme and assonance are universally attested in neighbouring digits: cf. Latin quattuor, quinque, Turkish altı, yedi, sekiz, dokuz, Finnish yksi, kaksi, viisi, kuusi, or, most noteworthy, Slavic 9 whose initial n- turned into d- by analogy with 10, e.g., Russian dev'at', des'at'.

8: Ebla ù-sa-am, i.e., [us + copula] or [us(s)a + copula], is definitely not *5+3, as is still assumed in Thomsen 1984, 82 who derives "ussu < *iá+eš$_5$ (5+3)".

Powell 1971, 37 with fn. 2 and 38 fnn. 1–4 (with previous literature) already clearly dismissed the 5+3 theory.

For the difficulties we encounter with the exact form of 8, see Powell 1971, 41 f.

9: Ebla ì-li-mu offers the earliest and clearest example of a Sumerian digit compound 5+n. Note, however, that the first element, 5, is spelled NI = ì and not I as with 5. Maybe ì (versus I) noted a reduced form of 5 in the compound.

10: Ebla U$_9$-PI-mu is difficult to "normalize". Anlaut U$_9$ with values [ha] or [ḫa] (cf. Edzard 1980, 126) would be compatible with two of the five glosses preserved for U "ten": u$_4$, ú, a, hu-u, ha-a (Powell 1971, 43 f.). Since there is no trace of [m] in later glosses, Ebla -mu may be again part of the copula [am]: *ha-wa-m(u), leaving us with *haw+am. *[haw], in the course of time, may have turned into *[hō] *[hū].

At this juncture it must be remembered that U, in earlier OB Akkadian spelling, was used to indicate [o], as Poebel 1939, 116 f. and Westenholz 1991 have shown.

No evidence is so far available for the pronunciation of numbers 11 to 19. We may guess at juxtaposition of 10 + digit with possible reduction or contraction in the compounds.

20: [niš], [neš]. For lexical evidence see Powell 1971, 48; CAD E 367 *ešrā* lex. No references are available before the 1st mill.

30: [uš(u)]. Powell 1971, 48; CAD Š/1, 234 *šalāšā* lex. No references are available before the 1st mill.

Note: In view of 50 = 40 + 10, one might venture an evolution *niš-u 20+10 > *(n)ušu. But an independent word is possible as well. For independent 30 cf., e.g., Turkish otuz.

40: [nimin], [nīn]: Powell 1971, 48, CAD E 255 *erbā* lex. No references are available before the 1st mill.

[nimin], glossed ni-mìn, ni-mi-in, ni-in, may be explained as a reduced form of *[niš-min] "two twenties".

50: [ninnû], Powell 1971, 49; CAD Ḫ, 81 *ḫamšā* lex.

[ninnû], glossed ni-/ni-in-/nin-nu-u is a short form for *[ni(š)min-u] "forty + ten". No references are available before the 1st mill.

Note: ninnû (not "ninnu", pace Edzard 1997 passim in "Eninnu") is certainly a far shot from the contemporary—and virtually unknown—pronunciation of Nin-Ĝirsu's ziggurat complex at Ĝirsu, é-ninnû "50 houses" during the 24th to 21st centuries B.C.

60: [ĝeš(d)]. The reading of 60 was definitely settled by Steinkeller 1979, 176–87. For lex. evidence see Powell 1971, 50–53; CAD Š/3, 380 *šuši* lex.

Whereas multiples of 60 have been glossed, e.g., 120 = ĝeš-min, we do not know how 61, 62 etc. were pronounced. It is hardly possible in a society permeated with calculation and accountancy, that 62 *ĝeš+min "sixty (plus) two" and *ĝéš-min "two sixties" should have been homophonous.

600: [ĝeš(d)u] "ten sixties". Again, we may ask how 600 was distinguished in fast speech from 60 + 10 = 70.

Akkadian had an individual word for 600, *nēru* of unknown origin, remembered by Greek νῆρος.

600 became a new basic number so that 1200 was *ĝeš(d)u-min "two six-hundreds".

Note: Let it be asked how 2002 (3 × 600 + 3 × 60 + 22) was pronounced. Was it something close to *[ĝeš(d)u-eš ĝeš-eš niš-min]?

3600: [šar] šár "circle" represents both the concrete figure and the "myriad". It was borrowed by Akkadian as *šār* and, finally, by Greek as σάρος. See Powell 1971, 78; CAD Š/2, 36.

36,000: [šaru] is spelled ŠÁR × U until at least Ur III and later on ŠÁR.U.

Unlike 600, 36,000 has not become a new basic number. 72,000 is šár-niš "twenty 3600" and not *"two 36,000". 180,000 is šár-ninnû "fifty 3600". See Powell 1971, 73–77.

216,000: [šarĝeš(d)] = "sixty 3600, also šár-gal "big 3600". [šarĝeš(d)] is written ŠÁR × ĜÉŠ or ŠÁR × U-gunû until Ur III and later on ŠÁR.ĜÉŠ. See Powell 1971, 73–78.

The highest number attested is 216,000 × 60 = 12,960,000, šár-gal-šu-nu-tag-ga "big 3600 that has not been touched". See Powell 1971, 76–78.

In practice, šár-gal occurs in Ur III administrative documents with the count of reed-bundles; cf., e.g., šár-gal, 4 ŠÁR × U, 2 šár 4 600, 7 60, 27 = 216,000 + 144,000 + 7200 + 2400 + 420 + 27 = 367,647 gi-sa "reed-bundles" P. Artzi/S. Lewy, Atiqot 4 (1965) no. 8 iv 3 = 10–11.

Note: It is interesting to note the increase of the number 3600 –> 36,000 –> 216,000 in royal inscriptions from Ĝirsu in the phrase "when god's hands seized (the ruler) from among n people": [šà-l]ú-šár-ta (Enmetena, CIRPL Ent. 32 i 2''), šà-lú-ŠÁR × U-ta (Erikagina, CIRPL Ukg. 4/5 vii 18), šá-lú-ŠÁR × U-*gunû*-ta (Gudea, Stat. B iii 10). It would, of course, be absurd to refer this diachronic increase of symbolic figures to a corresponding growth of the population.

Sumerian numerals, as to be expected, had special forms in Emesal. Emesal voc. III 131–133 (MSL 4, 39) notes [did], [imma] and [ammuš] for "1, 2, 3"; for [muš] "60" see ibid. 134–138. More details in Powell 1971, 51–53; Schretter 1990, 154 ff. nos. 53, 70, 71, 190, 331, 395, 397.

A peculiar system, rising in groups of three, for 1 to 7 is found in the (reconstructed) series me-er-ga "1", TAKA "2", peš "3"; peš-bala "beyond three" "4", peš-bala-ge$_4$ "beyond three + one" "5", peš-bala-ge$_4$-ge$_4$ "beyond three + one + one" "6", peš-peš-ge$_4$ "three three one" "7": NBGT IV 33, 41–45 (MSL 4, 164 f.), and see Powell 1971, 28–32 with lit. Origin (and application) of this system are still unknown.

10.3. Ordinal numbers

In principle, cardinal numbers may also function as ordinal numbers, cf. Gudea Cyl. A xxi 1 é-a(k) sá-min-nam nam-mi(-n)-sì "(Gudea) verily laid the second square (of the ziggurat)", followed by sá-eš$_5$-àm (xxi 5) up to sá-umun$_7$ (xxi 11).

Note: For purely rhythmical reasons, one-syllable numbers are followed by the copula [am], two-syllable numbers are not (see W. Heimpel, Or. 39 [1970] 492–95). For the general interpretation (as against Edzard 1997, 82) see C. Suter, ZA 87 (1997) 1–10.

A secondary means to form ordinal numbers was to put the number in the genitive followed by the copula [am]: u_4-2-kam [u(d)-min-ak-am] "it is of day two" = "the second day". This construction, already towards the end of the OS period, was extended by the addition of a second genitive case particle so that, practically, [(a)kama(k)] became the ending to mark an ordinal number. Cf. the locative u_4-$umun_7$-kam-ma-ka "on the seventh day" Gudea Cyl. A xxiii 4. Since the number sign is never explicitly followed by the [a] of the genitive, it is possible that the ordinal number ending was in fact [kama(k)] and not [(a)kama(k)].

For an OB sequence "first" to "seventh" cf. Gilg. and Huwawa A 37–43 diš-àm, min-/$eš_5$-/$limmu_5$-/ía-/àš-/$umun_7$-kam-ma, referring to "the first (demon)" etc.

10.4. Fraction and measure terminology

For the extremely diversified Sumerian system of fractions and measurements, see Powell 1971, 84–248, and 1989 throughout.

10.5. Distributional relations of numbers

For expressing "each", the (measure +) number are followed by the ablative case particle, e.g., gín-7-ta "(rings of) 7 shekels each"; to -ta, the copula [am] may still be added: -ta-àm.

Poebel 1923, 113–14.

munus-u_4-bi-ta-ke_4-ne ninta-2-ta ì(-n)-tuku-am_6 "the women of yore took two men each" (CIRPL Ukg. 6 iii' 20'–22').

10.6. Multiplication

For "times", a-rá "course" is placed before the numeral: a-rá-3(-kam) "three times".

Poebel 1923, 114–16.

Note: Semantically, cf. gang, gång in Scandinavian languages.

CHAPTER ELEVEN

ADVERBS

We here restricted the term "adverb" to derivations from adjectives or non-finite verbal forms in -a (*ḫamṭu* participles), Attinger's "adverbes de manière" (1993, 168–70), excluding expressions indicating modality or time, Attinger's "adverbes de modalité et de temps" (1993, 170); see below 14.2.5. Most of the "adverbes de manière" correspond to Akkadian adverbs in *-iš*, e.g., *damqiš* "in a good way".

For literature see Attinger 1993, 168–70; see also above 4.2.(5).

Formally, there are three types of adverbs: a) R-bi, b) R-bi-eš(e), c) R-eš(e).

a) šúr-bi = *ezziš* "furiously", mah-bi = *ṣīriš* "in a magnificent way" (CAD Ṣ 207), gal-bi "greatly", and see Attinger 1993, 169 (b) for many more examples ("type très productif").

b) gibil-bi-eš/-éš "anew". This is type (a) with the addition of the adverbiative ending.

c) zi-dè-eš/-éš(-e/-šè), i.e., [zid-eš(e)] "in a true, correct, righteous way".

According to Attinger, this type, combined with adjectives, is "peu productif".

[eš(e)] may, on the other hand, also be combined with substantives, yielding a "type très productif" (Attinger 1993, 168); cf. only šul-le-éš "in the manner of a strong young man", u_4-dè-eš/-éš(e), i.e., [ud-eš(e)] "like daylight".

CHAPTER TWELVE

THE VERB

12.1. Preliminaries

Describing the Sumerian verb is the most difficult part for the grammarian. One still admires A. Poebel's work of 1923 who practically "conquered the unconquerable" with his Grundzüge der sumerischen Grammatik. Since Poebel, Sumerian grammars, partly for the language as a whole, partly for chosen sectors, but always with the focus on the verb, have appeared in a considerable number and in chronological density: Deimel 1924, ^{2}1939; Jestin 1943, 1946, 1951; Falkenstein 1949, 1950, 1959; Sollberger 1952; Römer 1982; Thomsen 1984; Jacobsen 1956, 1965, 1988; Black 1984, ^{2}1991; Attinger 1993; Edzard 1995; Kaneva 1996.

The Sumerian verb consists of a base, e.g., gu_7 "to eat", and a series of prefixed and/or suffixed particles. The base is quoted in lexical texts and is regularly translated by an Akkadian infinitive (gu_7 = *akālu*). One may distinguish between finite verbs, expressing person, and non-finite verbs: infinitives, participles, or the base alone.

The base is impenetrable, i.e., no infixes may be inserted such as *-t(a)-* or *-ta(n)-* in Akkadian. The base is either invariable in form or subject to variation, e.g., extended or reduced form, reduplication (full or partial), 'Ablaut', or heteronymy, e.g., è/è-d, gi_4/gi_4-gi_4, ĝar/ĝá-ĝá, ti/te-ĝ, dug_4/e.

Frequently the same spelling is used for two variants, e.g., naĝ(NAG) "to drink", has to be read na_8-na_8(NAG.NAG) when reduplicated. But in quite a few cases one cannot be certain whether B (= base) has but one reading or two.

Note: A specially ambiguous sign is DU which, as a verbal base, may be read (depending on context) du, ĝen "to go", gub "to stand", "put", túm, de_6 "to bring", rá, not to mention the different readings of reduplicated DU.DU or $\frac{\text{DU}}{\text{DU}}$.

Variants of the base of a given verb may concern the categories *ḫamṭu* and *marû* and/or singular and plural.

For the sake of clarity we introduce, for verbal bases, grids with horizontal and vertical divisions, into which the varying forms of the base can be entered (as far as they are already known):

	sg.	pl.
ḫ.		
m.		

For details on the categories *ḫamṭu* and *marû* see 12.2.

The surrounding (i.e., prefixed and suffixed) verbal particles present an enormous variety, and they may be classified, in diminishing distance, or rank, from the base:

a) the particle [ed], suffixed, compatible only with the *marû* base.

b) ergative and absolutive markers, both prefixed and suffixed.

c) prefixed markers of dimensional reference, ranked in the sequence (from right to left) locative 2, directive, terminative, ablative(-instrumental), comitative, dative, locative. These partly have person or non-person reference. The first-to-the-left of these, moreover, may imply motion or absence of motion.

d) prefixed markers of connection, negation, and of diverse positive or negative modalities.

e) and f) nominalizer [a] and copula [am], both suffixed.

Whereas the variation of the string of suffixed particles is limited, the "prefix string" offers an astounding number of variants, since up to 5 particles may appear in a row, e.g., enim hu-mu-na-ni-ib-ge_4-ge_4 [hu-mu-na-ni-b-gege] "the word—verily—ventive—dative (to him/her)—directive/causative—absolutive (it)—make return (*marû* base)—(ergative: he/she)" = "he/she verily answers him/her thereupon".

Heimpel, in his 1974 count of OB "prefix chain" variants, added up to 1264; this figure may now easily be raised to about 1300–1400. For the pre-Ur III period Heimpel offered 122, for the Gudea corpus 154 "prefix chains".

Note: For the sake of comparison, compare the "prefix chains" in modern Basque (Guipuzcoan), a language structurally comparable to Sumerian: 537 Variants are listed in J. L. Mendizabal, La lengua vasca, ^{2}1959 [Buenos Aires] 353–69.

Let it be borne in mind, however, that in modern French, if we arrange all possible combinations of bound elements je with me, te, le, la, nous, vous, les, lui, leur, en, y, each in the positive and negative, e.g., je te le dis etc., we arrive at about 80 forms. In fact, je-ne-lui-en-ai-rien-dit "I did not tell him/her anything about it" is as complex a verbal form as many in Sumerian.

12.2. *Ḫamṭu* and *Marû*

These Akkadian adjectives meaning, "quick" and "fat, slow" respectively, were used as grammatical terms by the compilers of bilingual lexical lists. They have been the cause of lengthy learned debates, since Yoshikawa 1968.

ḫamṭu (*ḫanṭu*) or *marû* is found as an addition to the Akkadian translation of a Sumerian (verbal) entry, e.g.,

igi-zu = *uddû ḫanṭu*, igi-zu-zu = II *marû*

"to mark, indicate (when *ḫ*.)", to mark, indicate (when *m*.)"

Edzard 1971, 209–12, gave a survey of the successive efforts of scholars to explain *ḫ*. and *m*. from 1885–1968; the discussion between 1971 and 1984 has been summarized by Thomsen 1984, 115–23; thereafter, Black [2]1991, 99–119; Lambert 1991, 7–9, brought arguments that *ḫ*. and *m*., found in the right hand Akkadian column of lexical lists referred to the left hand, Sumerian, column (and not to the right hand col., as Steiner 1981, 1–14, as well as Jacobsen 1988, 173, had seen it).

See now also Attinger 1993, 185–87, and Krecher 1995, 142 with fn. 1, with more lit.

If *ḫamṭu* and *marû* refer to the Sumerian verbal base, they cannot in all cases be describing its form. For while, e.g., igi-zu is, in fact, "quick (short)" as opposed to igi-zu-zu, "slow (long)", ĝen "to go" (*ḫ*.) versus du (*m*.) presents no such opposition. The same formal dilemma we would encounter in Akkadian where, e.g., *iprus* : *iparras* would correspond to "short" : "long" whereas *īkul* : *ikkal, išīm* : *išām* would not.

Be that as it may, Krecher's decisive argument (1995, 142) was that the references "*ḫ*. and *m*." in the right, Akkadian, column should be seen in the same way as the reference EME.SAL, which can only refer the Sumerian expression given in the left, Sumerian, column.

It has in fact proved practical to apply the terms *ḫamṭu* and *marû* to those complementary variants of the Sumerian verbal base, occurring in two different, transitive, conjugation patterns: "preterite" in-ĝar "he set (something)" and "present" ib-ĝá-ĝá "he sets/will set it"; and to two non-finite uses of the verbal base: ĝar-ra [ĝar-a] "set" (past participle) and ĝá-ĝá-(d) [ĝa-ĝa-ed] "setting" (present participle).

We will, therefore, retain those two terms both for different verbal bases and for the conjugation patterns in which they occur.

Note: The two conjugation patterns have, alternatively, been named "Präteritum": "Präsens-Futur" (Poebel 1923; Falkenstein 1949–50; Römer 1982, 55 f.); "achevé":

"inachevé" (Jestin 1943, 209); "perfective" : "imperfective" (Steinkeller 1979, 54; Jacobsen 1988, 174 with fn. 15); "standard construction" : "secondary construction" (Black [2]1991, passim and spec. 130 f.); "*ḫamṭu*" : "*marû*" (Attinger 1993).

The *ḫamṭu* variant provides the base for a participle in -a (most probably not identical with the nominalizer [a], see 12.16): ^{d}Mes-lam-ta-è-a "(the god) who has come out of the Meslam (sanctuary)". It is, furthermore, used in the transitive conjugation pattern 2b (12.7.3) which most often corresponds to the Akkadian preterite *iprus*. It is also used in the intransitive conjugation pattern 1 (12.7.1).

The *marû* variant is used to form a participle in -e(d), -(ed): eme èd-dè-da-ni [ed-ed-ani] "while sticking out its tongue" Gudea Cyl. B xiv 7. It is, furthermore, used in the transitive conjugation pattern 2a (12.7.2) which most often corresponds to the Akkadian *iparras*.

Note: A verb is transitive if it displays the two conjugation patterns 2a and 2b.

A large group of verbs have only one conjugation pattern which may correspond to both Akkadian *iprus* and *iparras*. We traditionally call these verbs intransitive. For a restricted number of intransitive verbs, nevertheless, both a *ḫamṭu* and a *marû* base are found, and their distribution corresponds, once more, to Akkadian *iprus* and *iparras*: ba-ĝen "I went away", ì-du-un [i-du-(e)n] "I go".

12.3. Plural Verbs

Apart from the *ḫamṭu : marû* dichotomy, some verbs distinguish individual bases for whether the 'subject' (with intr. verbs) or 'object' (with trans. verbs) is in the sg. or pl. If one person is registered to "stay, live" somewhere, tìl is used; if there are two or more, the verb will be se_{12}.

12.4. Verbal base ḫamṭu/marû/sg./pl. grids

The Sumerian verbal base in *ḫamṭu/marû*/sg./pl. grids.

As noted above (12.1) it proves practical to enter the different attested base forms in a grid. We can offer eight variants. There may, however, be more because—most probably—the correct readings of some ambiguous cuneograms still escape us.

12.4.1.

	sg.	pl.
ḫ.	a	a
m.	a	a

šúm	šúm	gu$_7$	gu$_7$	sar	sar
šúm	šúm	gu$_7$	gu$_7$	sar	sar
"give"		"eat"		"write"	

This is the inalterable class. It has not yet been estimated how great a percentage the class represents in the total of (attested) Sumerian verbs.

12.4.2.

	sg.	pl.
ḫ.	a	a
m.	a'	a'

è	è	ti/te	ti/te
è(-d)	è(-d)	ti(-ĝ)/te(-ĝ)	ti(-ĝ)/te(-ĝ)
"come out"		"approach"	

Here, "vertically", a simple and an extended base are opposed. ti/te etc. mainly occurs in the compound verb šu ti "to bring the hand close (to something)" = "to receive" (see 12.15.1.2).

Note: In occasional Ur III administrative texts a reduplicated TI.TI stands for *marû* ti(-ĝ), e.g., šu ha-ba-an-ši-íb-TI.TI "he will certainly ([ha]) receive it ([b]) from him ([n-ši])"; see Krecher 1995, 161, 163–73, for similar cases of pseudo-reduplication of a verbal base to indicate the *marû*.

12.4.3.

	sg.	pl.
ḫ.	a	a
m.	a-a	a-a

and

	sg.	pl.
ḫ.	a	a
m.	a'-a'	a'-a'

ge$_4$	ge$_4$	zi(-g)	zi(-g)
ge$_4$-ge$_4$	ge$_4$-ge$_4$	zi-zi	zi-zi
"return"		"rise, raise"	

naĝ	naĝ	kur$_9$	kur$_9$	ĝar	ĝar
na$_8$-na$_8$	na$_8$-na$_8$	ku$_4$-ku$_4$	ku$_4$-ku$_4$	ĝá-ĝá	ĝá-ĝá
"drink"		"enter"		"set"	

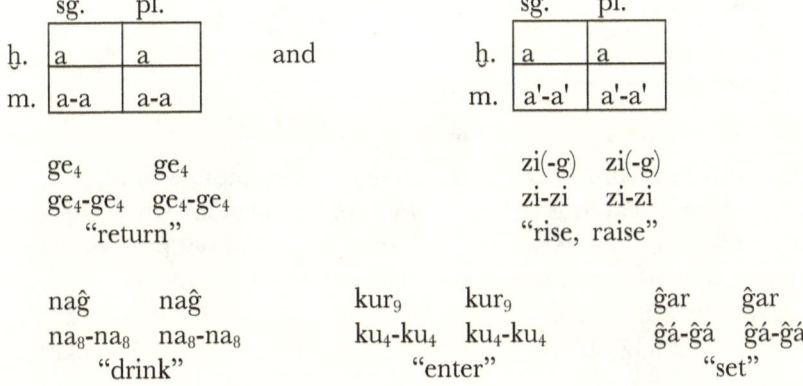

In this class, "vertically", the opposition is between a simple *ḫamṭu* and a reduplicated *marû* base. If the simple form ends in a consonant, this final consonant is omitted in reduplication; note, however, class 4. If the simple form ends in a vowel, it is reduplicated without alteration.

Unfortunately, different cuneograms are only used with ĝar/ĝá-ĝá. In the other cases the morphological evidence has to be inferred from the behaviour of the suffixed particles or from non-orthodox spellings.

12.4.4.

	sg.	pl.
ḫ.	a	a
m.	a'+a"	a'+a"

sùh	sùh	$tuku_4$	$tuku_4$
[sish]	[sish]	[tutk]	[tutk]
"confuse, trouble"		"tremble"	

For si-is-he [si(h)s(i)h-e] or tu-ut-ke [tu(k)t(u)k-e] see Falkenstein 1959 b, 99 f. This type of reduplication where $C_1VC_2(V)$-$C_1VC_2(V)$ turns into $C_1VC_1C_2$, recalls the nominal reduplication *deli-deli > dedli (see 5.3.4).

Type 4 is, strictly speaking, a variant of type 3. But we are unable to state why *zig-zig became zi-zi instead of *zizg.

Krecher 1995, 173–77.

12.4.5.

	sg.	pl.	non-fin.
ḫ.	a	b	
m.	b	b	c

dug_4	e	
e	e	di
"speak, do"		

This verb most probably forms a unique class and we have termed it "irregular". There is a heteronymic differentiation between *ḫamṭu* and *marû* in sg., but *marû* [e] also intruded in to *ḫamṭu* pl. Moreover, there is a third heteronymic base for non-finite *marû*.

Although dug_4/e is a transitive verb, the pl. base is used for plural 'subjects', not 'objects' (see below 12.4.7), this being another irregularity.

M. Civil and R. D. Biggs proposed that DUG_4 should occasionally be read as e_x (apud Steinkeller 1979, 61). But there is no proof for such an assumption.

Exhaustive information on dug_4/e/di is found in Attinger 1993 where also the astounding number of over 210 compound verbs is treated in detail.

12.4.6.

In types 1–4 there was a "horizontal" *ḫamṭu : marû* division of the grid. In types 6–9 the "vertical" sg.: pl. division becomes relevant. Unfortunately, some of the grids can only be partially filled out as yet.

	sg.	pl.
ḫ.	a	b
m.	a	b

gub	$šu_4$-(g)/su_8(-g)	úš	ug_7
gub	$šu_4$-(g)/su_8(-g)	–	–
"stand" (intr. only)		"die"	

tìl	se_{12}(sig_7)
–	–
"live, dwell"	

For gub, see Krecher 1967, 8–11; for tìl : se_{12}(SIG_7) see Steinkeller 1979, 55 with fn. 5 (with previous lit.). When someone died it was noted as ba-úš; in the case of two or more dead, OS ba-ug_7-ge(-š) is found.

Note: See Steinkeller 1979, 55 fn. 4, for the graphic difference between (OS)  ÚŠ and  BAD.

It is important to observe that the above verbs belong to class 6 only as long as they are intransitive. Transitive gub "to put, place" is turned into the non-changing class 1: cf. mu-gub-ba-$\hat{g}u_{10}$ ma-an-gub-bu-uš [ma-n-gub-eš] "they set before me my 'standing lines'" Schooldays 6. The same holds for ug_5 "to kill".

Note: A widespread (universal?) rule is that verbs which display morphological pecularities in their primary form become "regular" in derived forms. Cf. the uniform vocalization of (derived) D stem verbs in Akkadian and other Semitic languages; German sitzen → setzen, English sit → set, etc.

12.4.7.

	sg.	pl.
ḫ.	a	c
m.	b	c

	"sit"		"carry away"	
ḫ.	tuš	durun	de$_6$	lah$_5$(DU.DU) lah$_4$($^{DU}_{DU}$)
m.	dúr	durun	tùmu	lah$_5$(DU.DU) lah$_4$($^{DU}_{DU}$)

Here, the grid is divided both "horizontally" and "vertically". The sg. has different bases for *ḫamṭu* and *marû*, and there is a base for the plural of both *ḫamṭu* and *marû* (formally related to *m.* sg.?).

Steinkeller 1979, 55 f. fn. 6, noted that OS TUŠ.TUŠ stands for durun$_x$ (not *durun-durun, as was supposed by Yoshikawa 1981, 115). Note also Krecher 1995: TUŠ.TUŠ = durun$_x$. Cf. above 12.4.2 for Ur III TI.TI = *marû* [tiĝ-e].

ki-dam-A-NE-a-ti-ka ì-dú-ru-né-ša-àm [i-durun-eš-am] "they reside with A.'s wife" NG no. 214:41.

For lah$_5$ and lah$_4$ see Steinkeller 1979, 54–67, esp. 57–60.

Whereas tuš etc. is intransitive, de$_6$ etc. is transitive. With de$_6$, therefore, the absolutive to which the plurality refers is the 'object'. However, apart from being transitive, [lah] may occur as a passive: ba-lah$_5$ "were carried away" (Steinkeller 1979, 59 f.).

Note: Steinkeller 1979, 65 compared Caucasian (Georgian, Svan, etc.) and North American Indian languages (Athapascan, etc.) for pl. verbs implying a pl. object.

12.4.8.

	sg.	pl.
ḫ.	a	c
m.	b	d

	"go"	
ḫ.	ĝen	[ere]
m.	du	su$_8$(-b)

The verb "to go" presents pecularities and irregularities in so many languages that there is no need to quote examples. It is no surprise that "to go" holds the record in Sumerian for base variants and that, what is more, all four are heteronymic.

The decisive study of these variants is Krecher 1967, 1–11 "Die pluralischen Verben für 'gehen' und 'stehen' im Sumerischen".

Pl. *ḫamṭu* DU.DU and $\frac{\text{DU}}{\text{DU}}$ represent the same evolution of spelling as with the pl. of gub "to stand" (see 12.4.7).

[ere] is noted, in non-orthodox spelling, as e-re and e-re$_7$(DU) (or ^{e}ere).

ì-im-e-re-ša "who had come here" UET 3, 1633:11; see, for more forms, Wilcke 1988, 32.

As in classes 6 and 7, plurality refers to the absolutive case, the 'subject' of the intransitive verb.

12.5. Sorts of plurality (*ḫamṭu* reduplication)

Apart from the *ḫamṭu : marû* and sg. : pl. distribution patterns as shown in 12.4.1–8, the unaltered *ḫamṭu* base can also be reduplicated for a variety of reasons: to denote different sorts of plurality or totality of the 'subject' or 'object'; to stress its size, strength, or general importance; or to stress the durative or iterative character of the action (Edzard 1971, 226–32; Steinkeller 1979, 63 f.).

The difference between this type of reduplicated base and the *marû* reduplication is transparent in the spellings ĝá-ĝá (*marû*) and ĝar-ĝar.

This kind of "free reduplication" of the *ḫamṭu* base may occur both in the *ḫamṭu* and *marû* conjugation patterns:

igi hé-mu-e-ši-bar-bar-re "may Utu—again and again—look on you" Enm. 95

igi nam-bar-bar-re-en "you are not supposed to stare at everything" Scribe and Son 31.

siki-udu-⌜gan⌝-na-kam šu-a mi-ni(-n)-ĝar-ĝar "(instead of the whip) he put wool of ewes in the hand (of all the overseers)" Gudea Cyl. A xiii 2.

dam dumu-Ku-li, dumu-Ba-ba-ĝu$_{10}$-ke$_4$-ne(-r), ba-an-da-zàh-zàh-éš, dumu-Ba-ba-ĝu$_{10}$-ke$_4$-ne mu-un-dab$_5$-dab$_5$-bé-éš "the wife and children of Kuli had all fled from the children of Babaĝu, (but) the children of Babaĝu seized them all" NG no. 41:11'–13'.

iku-zi-dam éše ì(-n)-ĝar-ĝar "(Gudea) laid—along all sides—the measuring rope to (a square corresponding) exactly to an iku" Gudea Cyl. A xviii 26.

Note: Not "gána", as transliterated in ZA 61, 229.

12.6. Note on verbal reduplication

The form a verbal case takes when it is reduplicated cannot be established beforehand. It differs from one verb to the other. We may generally distinguish between two ways of information: (1) standard orthography: repetition of the sign used to render the simple form or, very rarely, of a variant form (e.g., ĝá-ĝá instead of ĝar-ĝar); (2) unorthodox spelling: the scribe tried, to the best of his ability, to render in syllabic script the actual pronunciation of the reduplicated form.

12.6.1

a) Full reduplication: gi_4-gi_4, bad-bad (Šulgi A 45 with var. ba-ad-ba-ad in Susa MDP 57 no. 200).

12.6.2

b) Loss of final consonant: ĝar → ĝá-ĝá; kur_9 → ku_4-ku_4; naĝ → na_8-na_8, and see above 12.4.2.

c) Loss of final consonant in first base: bi-bi-z(é) < *biz-biz (Gudea Cyl. A xxviii 11, 24; šu ba-ba-r(a-da) < BAR-BAR Gudea Cyl. B xv 7; la-la-ah < LAH_4-LAH_4, see ZA 53, 99 with fn. 16.

d) Assimilation of final consonant in first base to following initial consonant: bar_6-bar_6 → UD (babbar), ba(-ab)-ba-ar Proto-Ea 157 (MSL 14, 38).

e) Loss of consonant in second base: gen → (*gen-gen) ge-en-ge-te [genge(n)-(e)d-e] "make firm" Innin šag. 118 (var. to ge-en-ge-en), see Å. Sjöberg, ZA 65 (1975) 188.

f) VC-VC > VCCVC (loss of hiatus): ul_4 → ul-lu-ul "to hasten" ibid. (as e) 116 (var. ul_4-ul_4).

g) $C_1VC_2(V)$ → $C_1VC_1C_2(V)$ (loss of consonant in first, of vowel in second base): bir-bir CT 15, 22:8 // bi-ib-ri VS 2, 2 iv 20 (see Falkenstein 1959 b, 99 with fn. 17).

$tuku_4$ → tu-ut-ke see above 12.4.3.

h) $C_1VC_2VC_3$ → C_1V-$C_1VC_2VC_3$ (loss of second syllable in first base): ù-bi-GALAM-GALAM$^{\text{ga-ga-la-am}}$: *gana utlellī* "rise high (O Inanna)" TCL 6, 51:37 (Hruška 1969, 483 f.).

zu-lu-un → zu-zu-lu-un, sù-sù-lu-un = *ruṣṣunu* "roaring" see CAD R 183 *raṣānu* lex.

i) $C_1VC_2VC_3$ → C_1VC_2-$C_1VC_2VC_3$ (loss of the end of the second syllable in first base): zalag → za-al-zu-le-g(a) = *nuwwurum* "illuminate" (var. to ZALAG-ga) Innin šag. 160, see Å. Sjöberg, ZA 65 (1975) 194.

Note: za-al-za-le-bi ibid. 124 does not belong here according to Sjöberg, ibid. p. 235.

The change of vowel in [zalzuleg(a)] is noteworthy and it is probable a phenomenon occurring much more frequently than may be guessed from standard spelling.

Besides reduplication of the verbal base, triplication and even quadruplication may be observed, but only much less frequently. Cf. Attinger 1993, 190 (with previous lit.).

12.7. Conjugation

As the Sumerian verb is essentially person-oriented it is appropriate to speak of its "conjugation" (or of "verbal inflection").

There are three patterns, (1) one for intransitive (and passive) verbal forms, exhibiting absolutive person elements only; (2) two patterns for transitive verbs showing both ergative ("subject") and absolutive ("object") person elements.

Forms of pattern (1) are rendered in Akkadian by both *iprus* and *iparras*. For (2) there is one (2a) normally translated by *iprus* and one (2b) by *iparras*. This distribution has led former grammarians to speak about (1) the "intransitive standard form" ("Normalform") and (2a) "preterite" and (2b) "present-future" (see above, p. 73 f. n.).

The three patterns may be reconstructed with relative certainty during and after Ur III. In OS, and to some degree still in Ur III, spelling only partly represents the full form because of a marked tendency to neglect syllable-closing consonants in writing: Note the ubiquitous šu ba-ti for [šu banti] or the above-quoted OS ba-ug$_6$-ge(-š) [ba-ug-eš].

12.7.1. *Conjugation pattern 1: Intransitive (and passive)*

sg. 1st	ba-zah-en (Ur III -èn)	[ba-zah-en]	"I run away"
sg. 2nd	ba-zah-en	[ba-zah-en]	
sg. 3rd	ba-zah	[ba-zah]	
pl. 1st	ba-zah-en-dè-en	[ba-zah-enden]	
pl. 2nd	ba-zah-en-zé-en	[ba-zah-enzen]	
pl. 3rd	ba-zah-eš (Ur III -éš)	[ba-zah-eš]	

The pattern may be extended by adding -e(d) to the base: [ba-zah-ed-en] "I will flee" in the oath ba-ra-ba-zah-e-dè-en "I swear I will not run away (another time)" (said by a captured runaway slave) (negative affirmative particle [bara], see 12.11.4). [ed] here serves to express more precisely the temporal situation (future).

Note: The homophony—at least according to spelling—of 1st and 2nd person sg. is striking. Was there originally only an opposition of "I" or "you" : "he, she, it"?

Phonetic pecularities: The [e] of [en, enden, enzen, eš] may yield to the final vowel of the preceding base: ì-du-un [i-du(e)n] "I/you go".

Or this [e] may assimilate to a non-final vowel of the base: *ba-šúm-mu-uš [ba-šum-eš] "they were given" (example made up from corresponding active forms of pattern 2b).

Assimilation of the vowel is not yet predictable for us: cf., e.g., ga-ba-húl-le-en-dè-en [ga-ba-hul-enden] "let us rejoice over it", not *[-hul-unden].

Conjugation pattern 1 is neutral as for tense or aspect (except when the base is extended by [e(d)]). This is easily explained by the fact that it has only one participant (absolute) while patterns 2a and 2b, with their distinction of perfective (*ḫamṭu* based pattern) and imperfective (*marû* based pattern) are essentially characterized by the presence of two participants: absolutive and ergative.

12.7.1.1. The verb me

The verb [me] "to be" and the copula [me] have conjugations which differ only in the 3rd sg., where there is both a free and a bound form (copula).

sg. 1st	ì-me-en	-me-en	[men]	"I am"
sg. 2nd	ì-me-en	-me-en	[men]	
sg. 3rd	ì-me(-àm) (OS -am_6)	-àm (OS -am_6)	[am]	
pl. 1st	ì-me-en-dè-en	-me-en-dè-en	[menden]	
pl. 2nd	ì-me-en-zé-en	-me-en-zé-en	[menzen]	
pl. 3rd	ì-me-eš (Ur III -éš)	-me-eš (Ur III -éš)	[meš]	

In the majority of cases, the bound form occurs, e.g., lugal-me-en "I am king", "I, the king".

For the free form cf. ba-ra-me "he certainly will not be" NG no. 18:34; ì-me-àm "he was" NG no. 63:12, 70:9; ì-me-àm [i-me-a-am] "who is" NG no. 6:2, 26:2, 75:2; ì-me-ša-ke_4-éš [i-me-(e)š-a-(a)k-eš] "pertaining to the fact that they are" = "because they are (. . .)" Gudea Cyl. A xxvi 15.

Thomsen 1984, 273–78; Attinger 1993, 312 f.

The free form is mainly used when [me] is understood as a "preterite" or "future" and when the form is nominalized by the particle [a].

The [a] of [am] may be superseded by a preceding vowel: -bi-im [bi-(a)m]" "it is its (. . .)"; -zu-um [zu-(a)m] "it is your (. . .)". It is unlikely that there was an original distribution of two forms: [am] after C and [m] after V because we find, e.g., hé-àm.

[am] was written by AN in OS, transliterated as am_6. From the frequent combination of the nominalizing particle [a] + copula [am], -a-am_6 [a'am] the more recent (Ur III) spelling A.AN = àm arose, probably after the hiatus originally present in [a'am] had disappeared, resulting in [âm].

After the genitive particle [ak] and after [d] or [n], the CVC cuneograms kam, dam, and nam are normally used: za-a-kam [za(e)-(a)k-am] "it is yours", min-nam [min-am] "it is two".

For enclitic [am] derivation from *i-m(e) (or *a-m(e)), i.e., a reduced free form with prefixed particle [i] or [a] has been proposed: Poebel 1923, 72 ff., followed by Falkenstein 1949, 147. A heteronymous form is, however, more probable, because heteronymy in the copula conjugation is also found in other languages, e.g., Indo-European.

12.7.2. *Conjugation pattern 2a: Transitive*

Given its great similarity to pattern 1, we describe pattern 2a, *marû*, imperfective, before pattern 2b, *ḫamṭu*, perfective.

sg. 1st	ì-lá-en	[i-laH-en]	"I pay"
sg. 2nd	ì-lá-en	[i-laH-en]	
sg. 3rd	ì-lá-e	[i-laH-e]	
pl. 1st	ì-lá-en-dè-en	[i-laH-enden]	
pl. 2nd	ì-lá-en-zé-en	[i-laH-enzen]	
pl. 3rd (person class only)	ì-lá-e-ne	[i-laH-ene]	

The pattern offered here has been simplified because only one participant has been noted, the suffixed ergative markers; the second participant, the 'object' denoted by absolutive markers, has been disregarded here (see below p. 84 f.).

Pattern 2a is formally identical with pattern 1 in the 1st and 2nd persons; for the 3rd p. pattern 2a replaces absolutive (-Ø, -eš) by ergative (-e, -ene).

In verbs with differing *ḫamṭu : marû* bases pattern 2a is linked to the *marû* base(s) (cf. above 12.4).

It is probable that 3rd sg. [e] and 3rd pl. [ene] have the same origin as the nominal ergative particles sg. [e] and pl. [ene].

Phonetic details: As in pattern 1, the [e] of [en, e, enden, enzen, ene] may yield to the final vowel of the preceding base: ì-ĝá-ĝá-ne [i-ĝaĝa-(e)ne] "they set, place (something)"; or it may be assimilated to the non-final vowel of the base: -šúm-mu-un, -šúm-mu [šum-en], [šum-e] "I/you give, he gives", also pl. -šúm-mu-un-dè-en, -šúm-mu-ne [šum-enden], [šum-ene]; ba-tar-ra-aš [ba-tar-eš] "they were split" Lugale 72. But, as with pattern 1, assimilation cannot be predicted.

Discussion has arisen about whether the [e] of [en] etc. is part of an autonomous marker of the conjugation pattern, or should be considered a separate "*marû*" marker so that -en of ì-lá-en [i-laH-en] would have to be segmentized as -e-n. Such a "*marû*" [e] would, then, only occur in verbs with a non-alternating base (cf. 12.4.1).

Put another way round, we would have to ask whether in 3rd sg. -ge_4-ge_4 [gege], [gege] would represent *gege + e, with [e] superseded by the final vowel of the base; or whether [gege] would have been self-sufficient to indicate 3rd p. sg.

Note: Krecher 1995, 183 § 43, joined Yoshikawa 1974, 18, and Jacobsen 1988, 180, in asserting that [e] is not part of the person elements.

Since the great majority of—reduplicated or unreduplicated—*marû* bases end in a vowel, there is the danger of a circular argument. However, in case of è (*ḫamṭu*)/e(-d) (*marû*) "come/bring out", -è-dè [ed-e] can only represent the marû base + additional, autonomous, [e].

The same holds for the verb te/ti (*ḫ.*)/te(-ĝ) (*m.*) "to come/bring close (to something)", with -te-$ĝe_{26}$(GÁ) as *marû* base + [e]. Here, some authors have posited, ad hoc, the *marû* base to be [teĝa].

Verbal forms of conjugation pattern 2a normally express—or at least imply, if graphically unrealized—absolutive elements for the person or non-person class 'objects'. The system runs:

sg. 1st	-(e)n-B(ase)
sg. 2nd	-(e)n-B
sg. 3rd person	- n-B
sg. 3rd non-person	- b-B

pl. 1st	?
pl. 2nd	?
pl. 3rd person	-ne-B

^{d}En-líl-le im-ma-ši-in-gi$_4$-gi$_4$ [imma-ši-(e)n-gigi] "Enlil sends me back (against the rebel lands)" Römer 1969, 298:109 (see Attinger 1985, 166); more references for 1st sg. "me" in Attinger 1993, 163–67.

Ha-ba(-n)-zi-zi [ha-ba-(e)n-zizi] "May (the personal god) raise you here" (= PN) Limet 1968, 311 f.; more references for 2nd sg. "you" see Attinger 1985, 167–75.

Note: Until—and partly including—Ur III the consonants representing the absolutive elements are disregarded in spelling (because of their position at the end of a closed syllable), and their restitution depends entirely on our (subjective) understanding of the context.

ha-ra-ab-šúm-mu [ha-(e)ra-b-šum-e] "let him give it to you".

ha-mu-ra-ne-šúm-mu [ha-mu-(e)ra-ne-šum-e] "let him give them (pers.) to you". ITT 1,1100:16.

[For Table of absolutive-ergative combinations in conjugation pattern 2a see p. 86.]

In literary texts of OB date, -(e)n- before the base often alternates with -e- (Attinger 1985, 163 ff. passim).

The fact that the absolutive markers for the 1st, 2nd, and 3rd sg. person class, i.e., -(e)n-, -(e)n-, -n-, may have been homophonous (they are so at least in our Latin transliteration), can hardly have contributed much to clarity. The coexistence of homophonous morphemes has, however, never been an obstacle to practical understanding, as is shown by English multifunctional [s] in (1) wings, (2) sings, (3) king's, (4) kings', (5) it's, (6) he's (has).

The 1st and 2nd pl. forms of the absolutive marker are still unknown. If they existed they may have been replaced over time by periphrastic expressions by means of the free forms of the personal pronoun (see 9.1).

It is still open to research whether Sumerian, in the transitive verb, distinguished between determinate action implying an object (e.g. "he fights an enemy") and indeterminate action not implying an object (e.g., "he fights").

Final note to 12.7.2.: We have described conjugation pattern 2a in terms of ergativity although, since Michalowski 1980, the opinion has been voiced that Sumerian was a language with "split ergativity" (accepted by Attinger 1993, 150–52) where only conjugation

Table of absolutive-ergative combinations in conjugation pattern 2a

absolutive →

ergative ↓

	1st sg.	2nd sg.	3rd sg. p.	3rd sg. non-p.	1st pl.	2nd pl.	3rd pl. p.
1st sg.	X	-(e)n-B-en	-n-B-en	-b-B-en	X	?	-(e)n-B-en (?)
2nd sg.	-(e)n-B-en	X	-n-B-en	-b-B-en	?	X	-(e)n-B-en (?)
3rd sg. p.	-(e)n-B-e	-(e)n-B-e	-n-B-e	-b-B-e	?	?	-(e)n-B-e (?)
3rd sg. non-p.	-(e)n-B-e	-(e)n-B-e	-n-B-e	-b-B-e	?	?	-(e)n-B-e (?)
1st pl.	X	-(e)n-B-enden	-n-B-enden	-b-B-enden	X	?	?
2nd pl.	-(e)n-B-enzen	X	-n-B-enzen	-b-B-enzen	?	X	?
3rd pl. p.	-(e)n-B-ene	-(e)n-B-ene	-n-B-ene	-b-B-ene	?	?	-(e)n-B-ene (?)

Crossed-out boxes would imply reflexive forms (I-myself, etc.) which the Sumerian verbal system does not express.
Boxes with a question mark refer to forms where the absolutive element cannot be safely stated or reconstructed.

pattern 2b (*ḫamṭu*) would be termed ergative, while pattern 2a as well as the imperative and cohortative would have to be considered as functioning on a nominative-accusative level. The question will be discussed in more detail in 12.7.4.

12.7.3. *Conjugation pattern 2b: Transitive*

sg. 1st	-(V-)lá
sg. 2nd	-e-lá
sg. 3rd p.	-n-lá
sg. 3rd non-p.	-b-lá
pl. 1st	-lá-enden (see note)
pl. 2nd	-e-lá-enzen (see note)
pl. 3rd p.	-n-lá-eš

In pattern 2b the ergative markers for sg. and 3rd pl. immediately precede the verbal base (in its *ḫamṭu* variant if such exists). 3rd p. -n- and -b- appear identical with the absolutive markers of pattern 2a.

Note to 1st sg.: The ergative marker can hardly have been zero, but its original vocalic quality can no longer be ascertained. Some rare OB verbal forms have [e] before the base, thus suggesting identity with the 2nd sg. [e], but this may be a late analogy formed on the identity of the absolutive/ergative markers [en] of 1st and 2nd sg. Note Falkenstein 1949, 159 fn. 2: "Vielleicht ist das Personenzeichen der 1. ps. sg. mit dem der 2. ps. sg. -e- identisch".

Jacobsen 1988, 198, preferred "Poebel's first suggestion [1923, 175] of a mark zero".

Extensive discussion by Attinger 1993, 217 § 139a, without a definite result.

Note to 2nd sg.: Krecher 1985, 144, proposed identifying the ergative marker as [e(r)] because he analysed the dative and directive elements -e-ra- and -e-re- "to you" as [er-a/e] instead of [e-r-a/e]. He is followed by Attinger 1993, 217–20 and passim.

Before Krecher, -r- had been explained as a Hiatustilger (the [r] being borrowed from the dative case particle [ra]). Now since *[er] only occurs between vowels and would otherwise have to be reconstructed as *[e(r)], Krecher's argument clearly is circular. Moreover, in such cases as á mu-e-da-a-áĝ [mu-e+da-e-aĝ] "you (moved the arm with me =) ordered me" one would have expected [*r] to be indicated before the vowel of áĝ.

Note to 1st pl.: A form -*me-lá, postulated by Poebel 1923, 173 n. 176; Falkenstein 1949, 160 fn. 2; 1959, 40; Thomsen 1984, 148 (but with caution in fn. 43), has not yet been demonstrated. The form -lá-enden is rarely attested in OB; cf. Attinger 1993, 22. It looks like a 'late' suppletive form.

It is probably just by chance that very few texts record the speech of more than one person. Letters and depositions of witnesses always happen to be in the sg. There was no pluralis maiestatis ("we" for "I").

We hesitate to posit the ergative 1st pl. marker as (sg.) [(V)] + . . . -enden because cross-linguistically "we" is rarely expressed as "I" + pl. (cf. above 5.2). However, formation by analogy with 2nd pl., (sg.) [e] + . . . -enzen, cannot be excluded.

Note: For exceptions cf. Maghrebi (and Maltese) Arabic 1st pl. *niqtlu* (1st sg. = *niqtil*) or Chinese *wo-men* "we" = "I" + pl.

Note to 2nd pl.: A form -e-ene-B was offered by Thomsen 1984, 148, mechanically appending pl. [(e)ne] to sg. [e]. However, the Enlil-bāni (of Isin) 'key text' HSM 1384 has in line 11 nu-mu-⌜e⌝-š[úm-m]u-un-zé-en [nu-mu-e-šum-e-nzen] "you did not give (it)" (Edzard 1976, 160; 165).

The absolutive markers of conjugation pattern 2b are placed after the verbal base in suffix rank 2 (after [ed]):

sg. 1st	-B-en
sg. 2nd	-B-en
sg. 3rd p.	-B-Ø
sg. 3rd non-p.	-B-Ø
pl. 1st	-B-enden
pl. 2nd	-B-enzen
pl. 3rd p.	-B-eš(?)

These elements are identical with the absolutive markers of conjugation pattern 1. Since one 'slot' can only receive either an ergative or an absolutive marker, in cases where both might be wanted a selection had to be made, and in such cases it is ergative that prevails: in-túd-dè-en [i-n-tud-en] "he (erg.) beat me (abs.)" cannot be transformed into "they beat me", because a form *[i-n-tud-eš-en] would require to fill one 'slot' with both [eš] (erg. 3rd pl.) and [en] (abs. 1st sg.). Therefore, would such a phrase have to be expressed differently? The same applies to forms such as *"we beat you (pl.)", "they beat us", etc.

Table of absolutive-ergative combinations in conjugation pattern 2b

absolutive →

ergative ↓

	1st sg.	2nd sg.	3rd sg. p.	3rd sg. non-p.	1st pl.	2nd pl.	3rd pl. p.
1st sg.	X	-V-B-en	–	–	X	-V-B-enzen	?
2nd sg.	-e-B-en	X	–	–	-e-B-enden	X	?
3rd sg. p.	-n-B-en	-n-B-en	–	–	-n-B-enden	-n-B-enzen	?
3rd sg. non-p.	-b-B-en	-b-B-en	–	–	-b-B-enden	-b-B-enzen	?
1st pl.	X	–	–	–	X	–	–
2nd pl.	–	X	–	–	–	X	–
3rd pl. p.	–	–	–	–	–	–	–

Crossed-out boxes would imply reflexive forms (I-myself etc.) which the pattern does not serve.
Boxes with a dash refer to forms where one 'slot' would have to be filled by two elements at the same time, so that one must have been selected at the expense of the other.
Boxes with a question mark refer to forms where the absolutive marker cannot be securely reconstructed.

12.7.4. *Prefixless finite verbal forms*

Old Babylonian literary texts occasionally offer prefixless verbal forms which still have to be considered finite because their suffixes evidently represent ergative or absolutive elements of conjugation pattern 1, 2a and 2b. The motivation for these forms is still unknown nor do we know how far they were productive.

Examples known as of 1965 have been collected and commented on by Römer 1965, 220–23.

èn-šè nú-dè-en [nud-en] "how long (O Gilgameš . . .) will you (lie =) sleep?" Gilg. Huw. A 76, 80 (var.s ì-nú-dè, ì-nú-na).

u_4-da kur-šè àm-e_{11}-dè-en-na (var.s mu-un-e_{11}-[. . .], e_{11}-dè-en) "today I am about to descend to the (Foreign Country =) Netherworld" Inana's Descent 32.

har-ra-an lú-du-ù-bi nu-gi_4-gi_4-dè šà-zu a-gim túm-mu-un "how did your heart (bring =) move you to (take) the road whose traveller will not return?" Inana's Descent 84.

a-re-eš dug_4-ge-eš "they praised" Ur-Ninurta B 28.

12.7.5. *Was Sumerian a language with "split ergativity"?*

The question has been raised whether Sumerian was a fully-fledged ergative language (with both the nominal and the verbal inflections displaying definite ergative characteristics) or whether it belonged—at least from a given period onward—to the type of language defined by "split ergativity". In the latter case only part of the system is ergative (with ergative and absolutive cases and ergative behaviour of the verbal inflexion) whereas another part of the system has a nominative-accusative construction.

"Split ergativity" may affect both the nominal and the verbal syntax; or the noun may go on exhibiting ergative and absolutive case while only the verbal system suffers the "split".

On "split ergativity" cf. R. M. W. Dixon 1994, 70–110: "Types of split system". Michalowski 1980 passim, Thomsen 1984, 51, and Attinger 1993, 150–52, define Sumerian as a language with "split ergativity". The nominal system is definitely ergative, and only during the OB period some scribes lost the notion of when to apply a "subject case" in -e and when not—an evolution that happened in the final stage of the development of the Sumero-Akkadian linguistic area.

For the verb, conjugation pattern 2b (Black's "standard construction", see 12.3) is ergative. However, the imperative (see 12.13) and cohortative (see 12.11.3), both using the *ḫamṭu* base, are claimed to show non-ergative, nominative-accusative, construction.

A non-ergative, nominative-accusative, construction is equally claimed by the authors quoted for conjugation pattern 2a (transitive, *marû*).

In forms like in-na-an-du_{11} [i-na-n-dug] "he (erg.) said (it) to him" "it" has to be understood, the "slot" for absolutive [b] before the base, being already filled by ergative [n].

du_{11}-ga-na-ab [dug-a-na-b] "say it to him/her". Here the ergative of the person who is commanded to speak, is implied in the imperative itself; a "slot" has become open for absolutive [b] "it".

The same holds true for the cohortative ga-na-ab-dug_4 [ga-na-b-dug] "let me tell it to him/her". Here again, because the cohortative particle [ga] automatically implies a 1st person subject, a "slot" has become free for absolutive [b] "it".

This explanation may be viewed as more plausible than the overall proposal to "split" conjugation patterns 2a (*marû*) and 2b (*ḫamṭu*, plus imperative and cohortative) into individual patterns, one nominative-accusative and the other ergative-absolutive.

Do we have to see conjugation pattern 2a (*marû*) as evidence for "split ergativity" at all? Compare two examples:

(a) ses-gal-e dumu-é-dub-ba-a in-túd [i-n-tud] "the (big brother =) school overseer hit the pupil". Here, [n] indicates the ergative; there is no "slot" for the absolutive which would equally be [n], before the base [tud].

(b) ses-gal-e dumu-é-dub-ba-a in-túd-dè [i-n-tud-e] "the school overseer will hit the pupil". Here, both ergative [-e] and absolutive [n] are noted in their individual "slots". We do not have to re-name them "nominative" and "accusative" while the nominal subject of the phrase, ses-gal-e, is in the ergative case.

Either way, the question of "split ergativity" does not seem to be of any importance in Sumerian.

12.8. Dimensional indicators

The Sumerian verb is characterized by a series of up to six prefixed particles. Their main and original—but no longer exclusive—function is to indicate arrest and movement, direction, separation, company and related notions.

These indicators frequently correspond to case particles 4–9 (see 5.4.2.4–9) to suffixed nouns in the same phrase. The dimensional indicators are arranged in a string within which the individual elements have their fixed and inalterable rank.

Many dimensional indicators can be segmentized into a pronominal head and a case element, e.g., [na] "for, to him/her", consisting of 3rd sg. person-class [n] and the (dative-)locative element [a], or -(e)ne-da [(e)ne-da] "with them", where pl. [(e)ne] is combined with comitative [da].

Note to -da-: Due to the uncertainties of Sumerian spelling, esp. with regard to the frequent non-notation of syllable-closing consonants, we sometimes cannot know whether -da- was meant for [nda], [bda], [mda], or [da] alone, and similarly for -ši-, -ta-, etc.

See 12.8.3 for the question whether dimensional indicators could also occur without reference to a person.

For each dimensional indicator there exists a variant with prefixed [m(u)], e.g., -na- : (-)mu-na-; (-)ba- : (-)V-m-ma-. Following the grammatical terminology of Akkadian, Foxvog 1974 and 1975, 400 f. with fn. 17, proposed "Sumerian ventive" for the m-forms; see Attinger 1993, 270–80 with lit. p. 270.

If one wonders about the coincidence of both languages using an [m] element for ventive, it should be borne in mind that the Akkadian ventive marker is (historically) [aC] (before *-k*, *-n*, *-š*), and it is only [am] before *-m* or in word-final position. There is no need, in Akkadian, to construe ad hoc assimilation rules like "*am-kum*" > *akkum* etc. Rather, the ventive (as opposed to affirmative) function of Akkadian [aC/am] may have been a re-interpretation of this morpheme under Sumerian influence, at the beginning of the Sumero-Akkadian areal interaction. See Pedersén 1989, 434 for derivation of the Akkadian ventive from common-Semitic affirmative (energetic) [an].

Note: The [m] of the Akkadian dative pronouns *-kum*, *-šum*, *-nim*, etc., has, most probably, to be kept separate from the [m] of the ventive final form *-am*.

It seems practical to arrange the dimensional indicators in numbered grids and to refer to the numbers for reference. We will present a grid each for "non-ventive" and "ventive" indicators. The grids have a horizontal division by cases and a vertical division by person. Boxes left blank reflect forms that the system did not allow, but have been numbered for the sake of completeness.

Grid 1 (non-ventive) has no entries for the 1st (sg. or pl.), because 1st person would automatically require ventive.

Dimensional indicators non-ventive

	Dative-loc.	Comitative	Ablative	Terminative	Directive	Locative 2
2nd sg.	era (1)	eda (6)	(11)	(e)ši (16)	(e)ri (21)	–
3rd sg. person	na (2)	nda (7)	nta (12)	nši (17)	ni (22)	–
3rd sg. non-person	ba (3)	bda (8)	bta (13) ra	bši (18)	bi (23)	ni (26)
2nd pl.	(4)	(9)	(14)	(19)	(24)	–
3rd pl. person	(e)nea (5)	(e)neda (10)	(15)	(e)neši (20)	(e)ne (25)	–

Dimensional indicators: ventive

	Dative-loc.	Comitative	Ablative	Terminative	Directive	Locative 2
1st sg.	ma (27)	muda (34)	(41)	muši (48)	mu (55)	–
2nd sg.	mura (28)	mueda (35)	(42)	mueši (49)	muri (56)	–
3rd sg. person	muna (29)	munda (36)	(43)	munši (50)	muni (57)	–
3rd sg. non-person	mma (30)	mda (37)	mta (44) mmara	mši (51)	mmi (58) mmeri	mini (62) mmini
1st pl.	mea (31)	mueda (38)	(45)	(52)	me (59)	–
2nd pl.	(32)	(39)	(46)	(53)	*muri-. . .(60) -enzen	–
3rd pl. person	munea (33)	muneda (40)	(47)	muneši (54)	mune (61)	–

Note: Variants are not indicated; see the individual paragraphs (ns. 1–62) below. In many cases where [i] is shown, [e] may be preferable. In view of our general reluctance to propose a clear phonemic distinction between Sumerian [e] and [i], we have left NI as ni and RI as ri instead of né and re.

12.8.1. *Non-ventive indicators (1–26)*

12.8.1.1. [era, (V)ra]:

e-ra-an-du$_{11}$ "he told (it) to you" Inanna/Enki, StPohl 10, 32 II i 15.

Note: Spelling does not allow us to decide whether [era] was preceded by the indicator [e, i] (12.9), but non-ventive e-na-, ì-na- "to him/her" (12.8.1.2) rather favours a positive answer.

ga-ra-ab-šúm "let me give it to you".

ki a-ra-du$_{11}$-ga : *ašar aqbûkum* "where I told you" MSL 5, 196:12.

For mu-ra- and ma-ra- see (28)

Note: [era] has mostly been analysed as [e] + [a] with [r] as a Hiatustilger. See the discussion above, 12.7.3, note to 2nd sg.

12.8.1.2. [na]:

"to him/her" is the most easily predictable dimensional indicator when the phrase contains a noun in the dative (with case particle -ra).

e-na(-n)-šúm "he/she gave (it) to him/her".

na-e-a [na-b-e-a] "what you will say to him/her (is this)", OS letter opening formula, written na-ab-bé-a from Ur III on.

Note: It is interesting to note, diachronically, that the verbal-base ['e] turned into [e], the latter no longer causing a hiatus between absolutive [b] and the base.

ù-na-a-du$_{11}$ [u-na-e-dug] "(after you said to him/her =) please say to him/her" (polite imperative, see 12.11.2.2).

For mu-na- see (29).

12.8.1.3 [ba] : [ba] is treated here on the assumption that it is composed of [b] and [a], in accordance with the general pattern of non-ventive and ventive dimensional indicators.

Doubts have been raised about this interpretation, e.g., by M. Civil apud Postgate 1974, 20 fn. 11: "(while) the prefix ba- has no connection with a locative element /a/", and Thomsen 1984, 176 ff., treats ba- (as well as bí-) as "conjugation prefixes".

OS texts from Šuruppag (Fāra) and Abu Ṣalābīḫ as well as Sumerograms used in Ebla lexical and administrative texts use both BA (ba) and GÁ (ba$_4$) as verbal prefixes in a distribution still imperfectly understood. They do not seem to be mere graphic variants: šu ba$_4$-ti "he received" has no correspondence šu *ba-ti and ĝeš ba-tuku "he heard" is not paralleled by ĝeš *ba$_4$-tuku.

Note: See d'Agostino 1990, 77–82 (monolingual and bilingual lexical entries ba-B) and 83–87 (monol. and bil. lex. entries ba$_4$-B) with no overlap (with the seeming exception of ba-DU and ba$_4$-DU where we should possibly reckon on two different readings of DU). See also Krebernik 1998, 287.

At present, the diachronic evidence cannot be said to support a hypothesis that the two spellings go back to two different morphemes, [ba_x] and [ba_y].

For general discussion see Attinger 1993, 204 and 280–84.

ki-a-naĝ-e ha-ba-gub "let (the stela) stand at the libation place" Gudea Stat. B vii 55.

šu ba(-n)-ti "he (brought the hand to it =) received (it)".

Note: The compound verb šu ti offers a typical example of the frozen use of a directive indicator.

Apart from indicating locative proper, [ba] may also, with verbs of motion, denote moving away, e.g., picking up something here and taking it there. Note the contrast between ba(-n)-de_6 "he carried (it) away" and mu(-n)-túm "he brought (it) here", where non-ventive [ba] is in clear opposition with ventive [mu].

Note: In the second example, the ventive function of [mu] is general, not linked to a specific goal (person, non-person).

A special function of [ba], first attested in Ur III, is to denote passive voice. The origin of this usage is not entirely clear. Edzard 1976, 169 f., tried to derive it from ocurrences such as ba-an-šúm [ba-n-šum] "he (gave him to =) ordered him to (do something)" where without ergative [n] a neutral form ba-šúm "he was given to (. . .)" would have arisen.

Note the frequent variants in Ur III year formula: mu-un-hul "he destroyed" and ba-hul "(a city) was destroyed".

More research on the origin of passive [ba] is, however, very desirable.

Passive [ba], being disconnected from dimensional notation, has no counterpart in ventive [mma] (30).

Although, in principle, locative [ba] and dative [na] are found in complementary distribution, ba-na- is attested when [ba] denotes passive, e.g., ba-na-ge(-n) "(someone/something) was confirmed/awarded to him" NG III p. 114.

12.8.1.4: A dative "to you (pl.)" is not attested as a dimensional indicator.

12.8.1.5 [(e)nea]:
hé-ne-ab-šúm-mu [he-(e)ne-a-b-šum-e] "let him give it (= the rent for the hired boat) to them (= PN_1 and PN_2)" TCS 1 no. 135:7; cf. no. 365:6 (Ur III).

The dative "to them" is more frequently replaced by the directive [(e)ne] (25).

12.8.1.6 [eda]: ùĝ e-da-lu ùĝ e-da-daĝal "people will multiply, people will spread (with you =) during your reign" SKIZ 211:55.

ba-ra-ba-a-da-gi$_4$-gi$_4$-dè(-n) [bara-ba-eda-gigi-(e)d-en] "I will not, I swear it, come back (with =) against you (with a claim)" Genava NS 8 (1960) 306 no. 20.

For mu-e-da-, mu-ù-da- see (35).

12.8.1.7 [nda]: in-da-ĝál-àm "(PN's tablet) is (with =) at the disposition (of PN$_2$)" NG no. 208:14.

di in-da-tuku-àm "it is that he had a lawsuit with him" PBS 13, 32:3.

Note: Before [ni], [da] may be assimilated to -di(TI)-; see (26) for Ukg. 34:1.

For mu-un-da- see (36).

12.8.1.8 [bda]: bala-nam-lugal-la-ka-ni 3 še:gur-ta . . . kù-babbar 1:gín:e hé-eb-da-sa$_{10}$ [he-bda(-n)-sa] "when he ruled as a king, one shekel of silver bought, so I affirm, 3 kor of barley . . . each" Sin-kāšid 8:13–22 (and see 10:13–20, etc., see RIME 4, 454 ff.).

Note: bala- . . . -ka-ni is virtually in the comitative. D. Frayne, RIME 4, 545, translated "3 gur of barley . . . cost one shekel of silver". But 1:gín:e, i.e., *gín-diš-e, can only be the subject (ergative) of the sentence.

For -b-da- cf. -e-da- in 12.8.1.6.

12.8.1.9: I cannot offer an example for "with you" (pl.).

12.8.1.10 [(e)neda]: e-ne-da-tuš "he is residing with them" Nik. 309 r. 4.

It is impossible to decide whether or not [(e)neda] was preceded by the neutral, non-ventive, indicator [i/e].

Poebel 1931, 16–19, suggested that -PI- might have been an allograph for -be(da)- "with them" in OS Ĝirsu, with non-person class [b-e] serving in lieu of person class 3rd pl. [(e)ne]. Falkenstein, resuming the question in AfO 18 (1957/58) 94 (d) f., preferred [(e)ne-da], and so did Sollberger 1961, 39:233, though with a question mark. Cf. DP 621 iii 1 e-PI-ĝál "it is with them", and see Poebel 1931, 16 fnn. 1–4, for more examples.

12.8.1.11: No example available.

12.8.1.12 [nta]: Although ablative is generally incompatible with person class, an exception may be found in the Ur III PN In-ta-è-a "Having come out from her" (i.e., from the mother's womb, whether it refer to the real mother of the child or to the protective deity); see Limet 1968, 438 who, however, prefers to see -nta- as a variant of -bta- (p. 79 ad 237).

Note: J. N. Postgate suggests in-ta "from the stalk" (*išinnu*) (referring to the ancestors).

In the frequent OS PN E-ta-è (Struve 1984, 63–66) incomplete spelling conceals from us whether -ta-, -bta- or -mta- (44) is intended.

12.8.1.13 [bta], [ra]: íb-ta-ni(-n)-è "he let (the boundary ditch) go out from . . . to . . ." Ent. 28 ii 3.

iti-ta u_4-n-kam ba-ta-zal "the nth of the month had ended" is a frequent note at the end of Ur III administrative documents; it varies with simple ba-zal "had ended" and ba-ra-zal (for [ra] see below), and the—pleonastic?—form ba-ta-ra-zal; cf. Falkenstein 1949, 215 fn. 5.

Note: -(b)ta- or -ra- have been inserted into the frozen ba-zal. Falkenstein's proposal to explain ba-ta- as [bta] has not been maintained since Postgate 1974, 17 f.

[ta] has a variant [ra] which looks out of place in a beautifully regular system. Attinger 1993, 256–58, showed that the two morphemes are in contemporary distribution: [ta] follows a consonant and [ra] a vowel, [ra], therefore, being incompatible with a consonantal pronominal element ([n], [b]). This observation does not, however, explain the phonetic situation; for [t] and [r] (at least in our Latin transliteration) do not form a pair.

á-sàg . . . é-ta ha-ba-ra-è "the asakku (demon) definitely left the house".

ní-te-ne-ne ba-ra-an-sa_{10}-aš [ba-ra-n-sa-(e)š] "They sold themselves" TMH NF 1/2, 53: 8' (cf. Falkenstein, NG I 84 f.).

Falkenstein 1939, 180–94; id., NG III 152 f; Steinkeller 1989, 153–62, "Excursus: the verb sa_{10} and the noun (níg-)sám".

12.8.1.14: No example available.

12.8.1.15: No non-ventive example available; see (47).

12.8.1.16 [(e)ši]: šu ba-a-ši-íb-TI [šu ba-eši-b-teĝ-e] "he will receive it from you" Gudea Cyl. A vii 3.

12.8.1.17 [nši]: in-ši(-n)-sa_{10} "(purchaser) bought (object) from (seller)" Falkenstein, NG III 153 b. The action of buying is made "in the direction" of the seller.

12.8.1.18 [bši]: igi-zi ba-ši-bar [ba-bši-n-bar] "he looked friendlily at it".

igi na-ši-bar-re [na-bši-bar-e] "let him not look at it" Gudea Stat. B ix 18.

12.8.1.19: No example available to me.

12.8.1.20 [(e)neši]: in-ne-ši-sa_{10} [i-(e)neši-n-sa] "(purchaser) bought (object) from (sellers)" UET 3, 27:6; cf. 41:6.

Note: in- of in-ne- has been taken over mechanically from the much more frequent sg. in-ši- (see 17).

12.8.1.21–26.

The complex of directive and locative 2, closest to the absolutive/ergative elements or directly before the base, is the most difficult in the system of directional indicators. It has been exhaustively dealt with by Wilcke 1988, 1–49, Attinger 1993, 234–47 and, most recently, by Zólyomi 1999 (as well as B. Jagersma apud Zólyomi), 215–53. We owe to Wilcke the decisive breakthrough.

Both person and non-person class 3rd sg. [ni] (22) and [bi] (23) as well as locative 2 [ni] (26) have variants [n] and [b] which might easily be confused with the absolutive or ergative elements [n] and [b]. These variants occur only in a position immediately before the base:

bi	-	X	-	base	-ni	-	X	-	base
Vb	-	Ø	-	base	-Vn	-	Ø	-	base

Moreover, comparable to [ba] (3) with its secondary function of a passive indicator, 3rd sg. person class [ni] (22) and non-person class [bi] (23) also developed a secondary function: they may denote a causative where [ni] or [bi] are turned—at least in our view—into a secondary 'subject'. Here, the parallel with [Š] in the causative formation of the Akkadian verb leaps to the eye: *ušākilšu* "he (subj. 1) saw to it that he (subj. 2) ate (it)" = "he made him eat (it)". If we acknowledge the existence of a Sumero-Akkadian linguistic area (see 17) we cannot help seeing a correlation between Sumerian [ni], [bi] and the Akkadian causative markers [šu], [ša], [š].

Note: The bilingual grammatical lists abound in 'equations' between a Sumerian verbal form with -ni- or bi- and an Akkadian Š-form. See, e.g., MSL 4, 79 ff., OBGT VI 19 ĝar-ma-ab: *šuknam* "set (it) to me", ĝar-ma-ni-ib: *šuškinam* "have (it) set to me", and passim; see, generally, Black 1991, 27–35. Black, however, admits, p. 34, that "All in all, the Sumerian of the causative sections . . . is complicated and awkward. We can only say that the Babylonian grammarians seem to have tried to force Sumerian into a straight jacket by devising un-idiomatic forms which would correspond to those of the complex and productive causative system possessed by their own language".

It is uncertain whether the directional indicator for locative 2, [ni] (26), is secondary in the system and a deviant of the directive set (21–25), or whether it is original to the system and there was perhaps homography (not necessarily homophony) between [ni_a] (22) and [ni_b] (26). See the discussion below.

12.8.1.21 [(e)ri]: dUtu-eri(URU)-è "the Sungod has risen next to you" (PN).

Note: In OS, URU = eri occurs as one of the extremely rare bisyllabic syllabograms; see also Sollberger 1952, 78.

nam ge_4-rí-íb-tar[ar] nam-dùg gú-mu-rí-íb-tar[ar] "let me make a firm promise for you, let me make a benevolent firm promise on your behalf" Šulgi D 384 f. (Klein 1981, 88).

Note: The contrast of non-ventive [eri] and ventive [muri] implies growing intensity.

ĝá-e ga-ri-ib-zu-zu "let me make it all known to you" TMH NF 3, 25:13 f. (Akkadian gloss *lu-uq*[!]*-bi-ki*); see C. Wilcke, AfO 23 (1974) 84–87.

Note: [eri] may be analyzed as e+r-i/e with -r- as a Hiatustilger. Cf. above [era] (1), and ibid. for Krecher's interpretation of [er] as an indissoluble unit.

12.8.1.22 [ni]: (PN_1-e PN_2-ra object) al ì-ni(-n)-du[g_4] "(PN_1) demanded (object) [to =] from PN_2" NRVN 1, 247:3.

túg ì-ni-in-dul "he draped a garment over her" ZA 55 (1962) 70, 1:10.

I cannot offer non-ventive examples for person class [ni] in causative function; for ventive mu-ni- see (57).

12.8.1.23 [bi]: [bi] is, next to [mu] and [ba], the most frequent opener of Sumerian verbal forms.

In Pre-Sargonic Girsu, there was an orthographic distribution of bé- [BI] and bí- [NE] which Kramer 1936, following Poebel 1931, explained by way of regressive "vowel harmony": V_1 occurs if the following syllable contains V_a; and V_2 if there is V_b. bé-, according to Poebel, stood before a syllable with a vowel close to the opening grade of [a], and bí- before a syllable with a vowel close to the opening grade of [i]: e.g., bé-ra, bí-ri. It goes without saying that we often risk a circular argument based on our Latin transliteration. Still, there is some chance that the distributional pattern worked, more or less, along the lines described by Poebel and Kramer. See also below, 12.9.

Be that it as it may, although "vowel harmony" is ubiquitous in languages of the agglutinative type, it would completely upset our ideas about Sumerian phonetics, if we applied such a phenomenon not to the language as a whole, but only to a very restricted sector. OS Ĝirsu spelling usage should, therefore, probably be seen as an isolated phenomenon which realized in writing peculiarities that were perhaps more widely present in the spoken language.

An-né Ki-en-gi-ra nam bí-in-tar^{ar} "An made a firm promise to Sumer" Šulgi F 30 (see Zólyomi 1999, 249:74).

Note: Here again, as in (21), nam tar governs the directive.

šà-kù-ge bí(-n)-pà "(the lord Ningirsu called =) chose (Gudea) unto his pure mind" Gudea Cyl. A. xxiii 22 f.

Note: The directive expresses motion close to, but not into, something.

šu-a bí(-n)-ge$_4$ "he (returned into the hand =) delivered (objects)" AWL 81 v 3 f.

Cf. šu-na ì-ni(-n)-ge$_4$ "he delivered (object) (into her hand =) to her" AWL 178 v 4–5 (see Zólyomi 1999, 231:26 f.).

Eridu^{ki}-gin$_7$ ki-sikil-la bí(-n)-r̂ú "(Gudea) built (the temple) on a place as pure as Eridu" (or: "pure as if (in) Eridu) Gudea Stat. B iv 8–9.

eri-ni Niĝin^{ki}-šè ka-Niĝin^{ki}-ke$_4$ má bí(-n)-ús "(Gudea, on his way) to her city N. (let the boat come close =) moored the boat at the harbour of N." Gudea Cyl. A iv 4.

Note: This example is especially instructive because it shows that ergative (Gudea) and directive (harbour) may co-occur as two cases marked by [e]. See 5.4.29.

For the shortened form [b] preceded by [i] or [a] note: kišib-PN$_2$ . . . -a(k) íb-ra [i-b(i)-ra] "(instead of PN's seal) PN$_2$'s seal has been (struck =) rolled (on the document)" ITT 2/1, 3470 r. 1–2.

Note: The directive is used to denote immediate contact of the seal with the surface of the tablet.

ì-íb-ĝál "there is (. . . on the field)" CT 7, 18 r. 2 (Zólyomi 1999, 227:15).

Cf. ì-in-ĝál "there is (in the basket)" UET 3, 153:4 (Zólyomi, ibid. 16; with locative 2).

Note: Wilcke 1988, 35, suggested that ì-íb-ĝál means "is found on (the surface of) something" and ì-in-ĝál "is found in it", thus explaining the contrastive use of directive [b(i)] and locative 2 [n(i)].

ab-ús-sa [a-b(i)-us-a] "(house) which is bordering on (. . .)" Ukg. 4/5 xi 3.

ab-r̂ú-a "(pedestals) which had been erected (at . . .)" Ent. 28/29 ii 41.

Parallel to person class [ni], non-person class [bi] may assume the function of expressing causative:

ud$_5$-dè níĝ-àr-ra bí-íb-gu$_7$-en "I will (make eat =) feed the goats with groats" Nanna's Journey 271.

níĝ-àr-ra "groats" is in the absolutive ('object'); the ergative subject of the one who feeds is implied in the verbal form. The second 'subject', the one being fed, cannot stand in a second absolutive case (in Akkadian: double accusative); it is in the directive.

Edzard 1976b, 72 f., attempted an explanation of the Sumerian causative construction: The Akkadian sentence *šarrum šakkanakkam ālam ušēpiš* "the king had the general build a city" cannot be rendered in Sumerian with two absolutive ("accusative") cases. The person caused to act (*šakkanakkum*) has to stand in a dimensional case, preferably in the dative if it is a person: lugal-e (ergative) šagin-ra (dative) eri (absolutive). The dative šagin-ra cannot, however, be resumed by the infixed particle of the dative, -na-, because a sentence *lugal-e šagin-ra eri mu-na-an-r̂ú would mean "the king built a city for the general"; instead of -na-, directive -ni- is used.

Zólyomi 1999, 219 with fn. 9, quotes, but rejects Edzard's explanation, but the author would still maintain his position.

Note: Zólyomi's example (1999, 318:6) É-an-na-túm-ra lú ti mu-ni(-n)-ra "someone (struck =) sent an arrow against E." has no causative implication at all and cannot serve as an argument.

12.8.1.23a: The imperative šúm-me-eb "give it to us" has most probably to be interpreted as a ventive form; see (59).

12.8.1.24: No examples available to the author for "to you (pl.)".

12.8.1.25 [(e)ne]: gú-ne-ne-a e-ne(-n)-ĝar [i-ene-e-n-ĝar] "he (put (it) on their neck =) charged (it) to their account".

Note: More frequent in the sg. gú-na e-na(-n)-ĝar where dative -na- (2) is used. While the sg. offers a clear locative : dative correspondence, in the pl. it is locative : directive. For reasons still unknown to us *[i-ene-a-n-ĝar] has been replaced by [i-ene-e-n-ĝar].

12.8.1.26 [ni]: Falkenstein 1949, 206 f. (also 1959[a], 48), had defined [ni], reduced [n], as a positional variant of [bi] in ba-ni- or mu-ni-, each time allegedly caused by dissimilation of the second of two labials (*ba-bi-, *mu-bi-). However, Sumerian has no general aversion against bab(V)-, mub(V)-; cf. only mu-bi "this year" or gub-ba-bi, šub-ba-bi "its being placed, having fallen".

Falkenstein was criticized by Gragg 1973, 69–90, and Postgate 1974, 21 f. Gragg 1973, 73 ff., has extensive material for locative [ni], and Postgate showed that [ni] in mi-ni- (< *bi-ni-) and im-mi-ni- (not = im-ma-ni-!) cannot be identical with the directive element. Also, mi-ni- and mu-ni- have to be kept strictly apart; see for more discussion (62).

An autonomous locative element [ni] had already been noted by Jacobsen, MSL 4 (1956) 39* ("allocative"), Sollberger 1952, 90–96 ("locatif"), again Jacobsen 1965, 95 ("neuter allative-illative"), and see most definitively Wilcke 1988, 40 f.

We prefer to write "locative 2" in order not to have to rename the locative dimensional indicators [ba] (3) and [(m)ma] (30).

At any rate, the directive dimensional indicator and locative 2 may follow each other and do not fall into the same "slot", so that they definitely have to be kept apart.

tu^{mušen}-min-nam igi-ba šembi ba-ni(-n)-ĝar "he put kohl on the eyes of two pigeons" Ean. 1 xviii 2–3.

e-bi íd-nun-ta gú-eden-na-šè íb-ta-ni(-n)-è "(Enmetena) made his ditch-and-dyke come up from the 'High Canal' to the 'Border-of-the-Steppe'" Ent. 28–29 ii 1–3.

e(-n)-da(-n)-dug$_4$-ga-a [e-n-da-n-dug-a-a] šu nu-dì-ni(-b)-bala-e [nu (-b)-da-ni-b-bala-e] "he (Erikagina) will not (turn the hand over (-a) =) change what Ningirsu had (spoken with =) agreed upon with (Erikagina)" Ukg. 34:1.

Note: Comitative [da] (8) has become dì(TI) by regressive assimilation to [ni].

ì-in-ĝál "it is contained therein" Wilcke 1988, 24 f.

ba-an-ku$_4$ "it has been brought in there" Wilcke 1988, 27 n. 97 bottom.

Note: [ban], reduced from [bani], forms a closed syllable. In this case, in OS spelling, the syllable-closing consonant is most often omitted in writing. Therefore, OS ba- may stand for (1) ba-Ø-, e.g., ba-úš "he died"; (2) ba-n- (-n- being the absolutive or ergative element) and (3) ba-niØ-, reduced to ba-n(i)Ø/-. This polyvalence of spelling does not facilitate the modern interpreter's task.

12.8.2. *Ventive indicators (27–62)*

In the following series of ventive dimensional indicators the translations do their best to render the nuance given to the verbal forms by these indicators.

12.8.2.27 [ma]: Dimensional indicators for the 1st p. sg. (and pl.) are to the best of our knowledge exclusively ventive. For whereas in the 2nd or 3rd person there may always have been a choice between "to you/him here" and "to you/him there", the 1st person "to me/us", "with me/us", etc., always implies motion towards the person (or object).

ma-a-dug$_4$ [ma-e-dug] "you told me".

^{d}En-líl-le-ma-an-ba "Enlil attributed to me (the child)" (PN, cf. Akkadian *Enlil-iqīšam*).

Note: The verb ba, in spite of Akkadian *qâšu* "to give as a present", is primarily "to allocate (something to someone)", and the idea of a gift is secondary.

ma-an-ĝál "he let (it) be there for me".

12.8.2.28 [muera]: ĝá-e mu-zu-šè ĝi$_6$ an-bar$_7$-ba ^{giš}gag-ti mu-e-ra-TAR.TAR "(as for) me: (for your name =) on your behalf, day and night, (the ribs are being cut for you =) I get upset because of you" Father and Son 121.

nam-ti ha-mu-ra-sù(-d) "may life be long for you".

šu-zi ma-ra-a-ĝar "I (put a faithful hand to you =) did faithfully obey you" Gudea Cyl. B ii 20.

Note: mu-ra- and ma-ra-, both for [muera], may have been synchronic options. The regressive vowel assimilation in ma-ra- was most probably conditioned by 1st person [ma] "to me".

12.8.2.29 [muna]: mu-na- is one of the most frequent sequences among linked dimensional indicators. This is mainly due to its ubiquitous occurrence in building inscriptions: mu-na(-n)-r̂ú "he built for (DN)", in dedications: a mu-na(-šè)(-n)-ru "he dedicated (object) to (DN) (for the life of PN)", or in dialogues: gù mu-na-dé-e "he says to him".

ha-mu-na-ab-šúm-mu [ha-mu-na-b-šum-e] "let him give it to him" Ur III, see Sollberger 1966 glossary p. 169 f.: 640 s.v. sumu.

Since its publication, OS RTC 19 has been used to demonstrate the contrast of (non-ventive) e- and (ventive) mu-:

šu mu-na(-n)-taka "(visiting lady) conveyed (gifts) to her (= person visited)" iii 2.

mu(-n)-da-ĝen-na "(PN) who had come with her (on her way to person visited)" iii 6 (seen from the side of the visiting person).

mu-na(-n)-šúm "(visiting lady) gave (gifts) to her (= person visited)" iv 3.

And contrast šu e-na(-n)-taka "(receiver of gifts) conveyed (gifts in return) to her (= visiting person)" r. ii 3.

e(-n)-da-ĝen "(PN) had come with her (on her way to person visited)" r. ii 5 (seen from the side of the person visited).

e-na(-n)-šúm "(receiver of gifts) gave (gifts in return) to her (= visiting person)" r. iii 5.

Note: The document was drawn up at the residence of Bara-namtara, wife of ensi Lugal-anda of Lagaš. All actions and motions in her direction are noted as ventives; all actions and motions referring to the visiting person, Nin-ĝiškimti, wife of the ensi of Adab, are noted as neutral non-ventives.

12.8.2.30 [mma]: An zà-gal-la mu-na(-n)-tuš, An-ra ^{d}En-líl im-ma-ni(-n)-ús [-mma-ni-n-us], ^{d}En-líl-ra, ^{d}Nin-mah mu-ni(-n)-ús "(Gudea) seated An for him (= Ningirsu) at the (big side =) seat of honour, he made Enlil sit there next to An, (and) he seated Ninmah at Enlil('s side)" Gudea Cyl. B xix 18–21.

Note: The seating at the banquet was Ningirsu-An-Enlil-Ninmah. The change from [muna] to [immani] to [muni] was probably made for reasons of style, avoiding repetition, rather than for morpho-syntactic subtlety.

dumu-ù ama-ni-ra KA-ȓú-a nu-ma-na-dug$_4$ [nu-mma-na-n-dug] "no child would (say a 'stuck-in' word on something to =) disobey its mother" Gudea Cyl. A xiii 4–5.

For more Gudea examples see Falkenstein 1949, 202.

Umma^{ki} e-ma-zi(-g) [e-mma-zig] "Umma rose against it" Ukg. 6 iv 10'–11'.

Íl-e nam-énsi Umma^{ki}-a šu e-ma(-n)-ti [e-mma-n-ti] "Il seized for himself the ensi-ship at Umma" Ent. 28/29 iii 37.

12.8.2.31 [mea]: Alongside the frequent Ur III PN (in Umma) ^{d}Šára-mu(-n)-túm "Šara brought (the child)" (e.g., Limet 1968, 528), there are variants of the name: ^{d}Šára-me-a-túm "Šara brought us (the child)" Johnes/Snyder 1961, 270:53, and DN-me-túm (see 59).

Note: The pronominal element of the indicator, [me], is also found as the 1st pl. of the possessive particle (cf. 5.2).

Is [me] self-sufficient, or is it the result of haplological ellipsis: *[mume] > [me]? See (38) for [mueda], probably resulting from hypothetical *[mumeda].

12.8.2.32: No example available.

12.8.2.33 [munea]: No example available; see (61).

12.8.2.34 [muda]: ha-mu-da-gub "let (Nanše) stand by me" Gudea Cyl. A i 25.

12.8.2.35 [mueda]: á-šè mu-e-da-a-áĝ [mu-eda-V-áĝ] "I (passed (it) to the arm with you =) ordered you"

šà-bi nu-mu-ù-da-zu [nu-mu-e-da-V-zu] "I did not learn (with =) from you (about) (its heart =) the matter" Gudea Cyl. A viii 22.

Note: [e] of [eda] assimilated to preceding [u].

12.8.2.36 [munda]: á mu(-n)-da(-n)-áĝ "he (passed the arm with =) ordered him" Gudea Cyl. A xv 11.

eri-ni ki-Lagas[ki]-e si_{11}-lí-a u_4 mu(-n)-dì-ni-íb-zal-e [mu-nda-ni-b-zal-e] "his city (and) the land of Lagas spend the day here with him in rejoicing"

Note: [a] of [da] assimilated to following [i] of [ni]; cf. above (26) Ukg. 34:1.

ad mu-un-di_1-ni-íb-ge_4-ge_4 "(the king) takes council with her" Three Men of Adab 17, see Alster 1991–93, 32.

12.8.2.37 [mda]: ad im-dab_5-ge_4-ge_4 [i-mda-b-gege] "(Nisaba) was consulting with (the tablet) for herself (ventive)" Gudea Cyl. A v 1.

[d]Utu im-da-húl "the Sungod rejoiced over (the brick)" Gudea Cyl. A xix 19.

Note: In hé-em-ši-húl "let him rejoice over it" the object of joy is noted in the terminative (51).

12.8.2.38 [mueda](?): a nu-mu-e-da-ĝál "there was no water (with =) for us" Three Men of Adab 6, see Alster 1991–93, 31.

Note: Is [mueda] a dissimilated form of *[mumeda]? Or is it literally "with you (sg.)" as a rhetorical form used by the story-teller?

me-e-de-en-ha-ze "he will seize him (= Dumuzi) from us (= the demons)" VS 2, 2 ii 44, 46.

12.8.2.39: No example available.

12.8.2.40 [muneda]: No example available.

12.8.2.41–43: No examples available.

Note: Ablative is generally incompatible with 1st and 2nd persons as well as with 3rd person person-class; see, however, discussion on possible [nta] in 12.8.1.12.

12.8.2.44 [mta], [mmara]:

a) [mta]: lú E-ninnû-ta im-ta-ab-è-è-a "he who would remove (the statues) here from the Eninnû" Gudea Stat. B viii 7.

Note: The parallel version of Stat. C iv 6 has the non-ventive form íb-ta-ab-è-è-a. This is hardly a free variant, but has to do with the fact that in Statue C the temple is Inana's Eana and not Nin̂girsu's own Eninnû. So, imta- refers to her own, ibta- to another, environment.

b) im-ma-ra-an-dú-ud [i-mmara-n-dud] "she gave birth from (her) own (vulva)" Enki-Ninh. 253, etc.

Note: We follow Attinger's translation proposal (b), see ZA 74 (1984) 46; his alternative (a) was "(X) est né(e) pour toi" where -ra- would be taken as the directive indicator [era] (1).

šà-bi-ta nu-ù-ma-ra(-n)-è-a [nu-mmara-n-e-a] "(he swore) he had not removed (anything) from (the storehouse)" NG no. 205:53.

Note: An alternative interpretation would be [mma + ra], i.e., locative + ablative.

12.8.2.45–46: No examples available (see note on 12.8.2.41–43).

12.8.2.47: No example available.

NG no. 51:15 mu-ne-ra-è "(two witnesses) came forth (against two other persons)" only seemingly contains [(e)nera] "from (among) them". [(e)ne] is in fact virtually a dative, replaced by the directive (cf. 12.8.2.5, 25, and 61). This becomes clear from NG no. 127:16 mu-na-ra-ni-è-eš "they came forth (as witnesses) against him (-na-)"; see also no. 129:13. In cases without dative (or directive) of the person, è(-d) "to come forth" is construed with im-ta- or íb-ta- (see NG III 105) s.v. è(-d) 3. The ablative is used here either to refer to the group of persons from which the witnesses rose or it has become "frozen" to denote the special meaning of è(-d), "to come forth". See Falkenstein, NG I 68 f. fn. 4.

Note: [ra] probably never has a preceding pronominal element. See below 12.8.3 for the question whether other dimensional indicators could occur only with general reference to the verb's semantic meaning and with no (even suppressed) pronominal element.

12.8.2.48 [muši]: mu-ši-in-še "he favoured me".

12.8.2.49 [mueši]: ^{d}En-líl-le igi-zi mu-e-ši-in-bar [mu-eši-n-bar] "Enlil looked at you full of joy" Iddin-Dagan Hymn: SKIZ 209:5.

Ki-en-ge-re$_{6}$ kur-kur igi-bi ha-mu-ši-ĝál "all the countries, let their eyes be directed to (you, O) Sumer" Gudea Cyl. B xxii 20.

Note: [Ki-engere] is taken here as a vocative. If it were an ergative and if 2nd sg. were not intended, one would expect rather *hé-em-ši-ĝál (51).

12.8.2.50 [munši]: ki mu-un-ši-KIĜ.KIĜ "he looks for (someone)" Lugalbanda I 270 f.

12.8.2.51 [mši]: hé-em-ši-húl "let him rejoice over it".

12.8.2.52: No example available.

12.8.2.53: No example available.

12.8.2.54 *[mu-ne-ši]: No example available.

12.8.2.55 [mu]: mu-šè mu-še$_{21}$(SA$_{4}$) [mu-V-n-še] "he gave me as a name ('. . .')" Gudea Cyl. A x 5, 14.

12.8.2.56 [muri]: nam ge$_{4}$-rí-íb-tar^{ar} nam-dùg gú-mu-rí-íb-tar^{ar} Šulgi D 384 f., see above (12.8.1.21).

12.8.2.57 [muni]: mu-šè mu-ni-še$_{21}$ "he gave him as a name ('. . .')"

Note: mu-šè mu-na(-n)-še$_{21}$ means "he gave (the statue) as a name ('. . .') for his/her (= the deity's) sake" Gudea Stat. A iv 3; D v 7; etc. Here, -na- refers to the deity to whom the statue is dedicated, not to the person or object named.

na-ám-zé-eb du$_{10}$-mu-ni-ib-tar^{ar} "let me make a firm promise for him" (Emesal) TLB 2, 2:36, 38, 41 (Šulgi).

Note: Only a short excerpt of the vast and complicated morphological evidence for the verb nam tar could be offered; see also 12.8.1.23, 2:56.

mu-ni-ús see above (12.8.2.30).

12.8.2.58 [mmi], [mmeri]:

a) [mmi]: e-ba na-ȓú-a e-me-sar-sar [e-mmi-n-sarsar] "at the dyke here (on this side) he inscribed stelae" Ent. 28/29 ii 4–5.

tu^{mušen}-min-nam saĝ-ba eren ì-mi-du$_{8}$ [i-mmi-n-du] "he stuck 'cedar' (twigs) at the heads of two pigeons (of his)" Ean. 1 obv. xviii 4, xxi 16, etc.

é . . . an-né im-ús "the House . . . borders on Heaven" Gudea Cyl. B i 6.

Note: [mmi] here is reduced to [m(mi)] immediately before the base. For more Gudea examples see Falkenstein 1949, 207 f.

lú GN-ta ì-im-e-re-ša [i-m(mi)-ere-(e)š-a] "(persons) who had come here from GN" UET 3, 1633:11, and see Wilcke 1988, 32.

Note: Many more examples for i-im-B in Wilcke 1988, 15; 19–32.

b) [immeri]: hur-saĝ-umun$_7$-e im-me-ri-BAL.BAL [i-mmeri-BALBAL] "he crossed seven mountain ranges" Enm. 171, and cf. Lugalbanda I 252.

Note: The form is difficult to explain. Jacobsen 1965 (= 1970), 265 analysed it as containing "(b)ri 'beyond it', 'over it'" (= "Neuter Superlative").

[immeri] is hardly imaginable without the model of [immara] (see 12.8.2.44.b), for which an alternative interpretation as [mma+ra], locative + ablative, was suggested (see 12.8.2.44 end). Was, therefore, [immeri] just a "rhyming" form of [immara]?

Note: In OB Sumerian, apparently, no fixed form is used when "crossing, passing over (something)" is to be expressed. Traditionally, one would expect [bta] (13) or [mta] (44), e.g., ĝeš-gán-na ib-ta(-n)-bala "he made (someone) step over the wooden rod" (cf. Edzard 1970, 8–53).

When the hero crosses mountain-ranges, OB texts offer a variety of forms: in-ti-bala/bal-lam Gilg. Hu. A 61 ff.; bé-ri-bala, in-TE-bala (ibid.); see Edzard 1991, 187 f.

12.8.2.59 [me]: ^{d}Nanna-me(-n)-túm "the Moongod brought us (the child)" Limet 1968, 75.

Note: [me] is probably a (free?) variant of [mea], for which see above (12.8.2.31).

šúm-me-eb [šum-me-b] "give it to us" Inana's Descent 278.

Note: See above (12.8.2.31) note on whether [me] is self-sufficient or the result of haplological ellipsis.

12.8.2.60: No example available.

12.8.2.61 [mune]: diĝir-gal-gal-Lagas^{ki}-ke$_4$-ne(-r) é-a-ne-ne mu-ne-r̂ú [mu-(e)ne-e-n-r̂u] "he built here their houses for the great gods of Lagas" Gudea Stat. I iii 6; P iii 7.

15.8.2.62 [mini], [mmini]:

a) [mini]: é-e hur-saĝ-gin$_7$ . . . saĝ an-šè mi-ni-íb-íl "the House (raised the head =) proudly looked up to Heaven . . . like a mountain range" Gudea Cyl. A xxi 23.

b) [mmini]: (é . . .) DUGUD-gin$_7$ an-šà-ge im-mi-ni-íb-DIRI.DIRI-ne "they let (the House) soar into the midst of Heaven as if it were a cloud" Gudea Cyl. A xxi 20.

12.8.3. *Dimensional indicators without reference to a person?*

The question must be asked whether in principle a dimensional indicator could occur with general reference to the verb's semantic meaning, but with no (even suppressed) pronominal element. Were there -da- "with", -ta- "from", or -ši- "toward" indicating that the verb implied the general idea of having something with it, stemming from, moving towards a goal? The question is extremely hard to answer because of our well-known difficulties interpreting Sumerian syllabic spelling where, until the beginning of the 2nd millennium B.C., syllable-closing consonants could be neglected in writing: did, e.g., -da- always stand for [nda], [bda], [mda] or could [da] alone be intended?

So far the only possible exception seems to be ablative [ra] (see 12.8.1.13, 12.8.2.44) which is never found with a person element, e.g., *[bra] or *[mra]. But [ra] is an extraneous element anyhow in the system of the dimensional indicators.

12.9. Prefixed indicator [e, i]

Prefixed [e] or [i], spelled e- or ì-, is difficult to define. It has challenged Sumerologists for more than a century. If a basic function once existed it may well have vanished over the long period during Sumerian was spoken and written.

Note: Our transliteration NI = i is confirmed by allograph i- from Ur III onward. Vanstiphout 1985, 1–2, resumed the Forschungsgeschichte; see, thereafter, Wilcke 1988, 2–4.

It is advisable to start from forms where [e]/[i] precedes the verbal base as the only element and where no suffixes occur, i.e., 3rd sg. forms of the intransitive conjugation pattern 1 (see 12.7.1): e-ĝen "he went", e-ĝál "it is/was present", ì-til "he lived, stayed".

The function of [e]/[i] may be defined here as an element moving the verbal base out of its neutral (lexical) mode into a finite verbal mode, i.e., indication—or implication—of a pronominal participant.

[e]/[i], seen this way, is left without an oppositional mark. It could not be defined as, e.g., "non-ventive" in a general way because it may

occur at least with a ventive directional indicator of the 3rd person non-person class, cf. above [mma] 12.8.2.30, [mda] 12.8.2.37, etc.

The idea of two allegedly opposed elements [mu] and [e, i], termed "Konjugationspräfixe" by B. Landsberger apud R. Scholtz 1934, 2, which was essential to Falkenstein 1950, 158–181; 1959, 45 f., 58 f.; Römer 1982, 65–69; Yoshikawa 1979, 185–206 and others, lost its relevance since the discovery of the Sumerian "ventive" (above 12.8, p. 92) of which [mu] is but part.

Falkenstein supposed ì- to constitute a nasalized vowel (still maintained in Thomsen 1984, 162 f. and passim) because he analysed im-ma- as *ĩ-ba-. This theory, involving a circular argument, has been disproved by Gragg 1973, and Postgate 1974.

Poebel 1931 demonstrated that in the pre-Sargonic texts from Girsu (Lagas) e- and ì- show complementary distribution, each form determined by the quality of the vowel in the following syllable; 12.8.1.23 cf. e.g., e-sar, e-da-, e-ta-, e-šè- versus ì-gu_7("kú"), ì-rí-, ì-mi- etc.

In a number of cases, Poebel begged the question. Because of e-ur_4 (instead of *i-ur_4) "he sheared", Poebel postulated e-or_4; see also his e-sor, e-ne-sor for -sur.

See above, 12.8.1.23, on alleged "vowel harmony".

Krecher 1985 proposed to reduce—or even partially eliminate—the existence of a Sumerian verbal prefix [e]/[i]. He claimed that the vowel was mainly part of the pronominal element constituting or opening a verbal prefix (series). So, he proposed to define pronominal elements (-)n-, (-)b- as original in-, ib-, thus including an alleged prefix [e]/[i] as part of the pronominal prefix. Krecher's view was refuted by Wilcke 1988 who brought ample evidence of pre-OB spellings ì-íb-, ì-in-, ì-im- (as well as a-ab-, see below 12.10) constituting a prefix series which could not possibly have been rendering merely a non-functional [i].

Even if we cannot recover the original function of [e]/[i], we may repeat that the prefix served, before a simple base, to indicate "finalization" or "pronominalization" of the base. By extension, it may then also have been used when absolutive, ergative and dimensional indicators preceded the base: in-sar [i-n-sar] "he wrote", in-da-ĝál [i-nda-ĝal] "it is/was present with him", etc.

There is a distribution rule limiting the use of [e]/[i]: (1) It occurs with all non-ventive indicators except with [ba] (3); there is no *[iba].

(2) It does not occur with ventive indicators except with the 3rd sg. non-person class series [mma] (30), [mda] (37), [mta], [mmara] (44), [mši] (51), [mmi], [mmeri] (58), and [mmini] (62). There is no *[ima], *[imuda] etc.

For peculiarities of [ba] (3) which are still in need of further elucidation see above 12.8.1.3.

12.10. Prefixed indicator [a(l)]

a- and al- both indicate the notion of state (not necessarily passive) or habitualness, as against the notion of action, mobility, or becoming.

enim-bi al-til "the respective matter is in the state of having being settled" (ubiquitous in pre-Ur III and Ur III court documents).

x y-šè ab-ši-ĝar "(x is set in relation to y =) x equals y", e.g., NRVN I 202:3.

al- was until recently seen as unique among Sumerian verbal prefixes because of its alleged inability to combine with any other morpheme—apart from prospective [u]: *ù-al- > ù-ul-.

Attinger 1993, 267–69 (a-) and 269 f. (al-), both with extensive literature, clearly states (p. 269) that "[al] semble être le pendant de [a] dans le cas où la base n'est pas précédé d'un préf. III (i.e., the group next to the base: absolutive, ergative, dimensional indicator) ou d'un préfixe II (i.e., the group next-but-one to the base, [i], ventive indicators)"; he stresses that a- before the base must always go back to a-x-B and that "la seule fonction de -l-" (i.e., in [al]) "est d'indiquer que [a] est directement suivi de la base, que donc al-B représente morphématiquement [a+B]".

Thus Attinger implicitly stated that a- and al- are found in complementary morphemic distribution.

Since an element [l] encountered exclusively in [al] would be hard to explain, it seems preferable to posit with Attinger just the one morpheme [a(l)], with the allomorphs [a] and [al] depending on Sumerian syllable structure: *[alb] > [ab], *[alnda] > [anda], etc.

Note: As a matter of fact, a circular argument is involved: The Sumerian system of syllable writing which we can only see through "Akkadian glasses", had no room for such notations as [alb], [bla], [albra]. We, therefore, discount the possible occurrence of such consonantal clusters in Sumerian syllable structure. Therefore this line of reasoning only really holds good for a Semitic language such as Akkadian where such clusters do not occur.

a- *[a(l)-n(i)]: é me-lim$_5$-bi kur-kur-ra a-dul$_5$ "the awe of the House is spread over all the countries" Ent. 8 vi 2.

For the formula u$_4$ an-r̂ú enim an-ĝál see Edzard 2003a, 89.

ab- *[a(l)-b(i)]: bára-r̂ú-a-diĝir-ré-ne nam-nun-da-ki-ĝar-ra ab-r̂ú-a "the pedestals of the gods, which had been erected there in Namnunda-kiĝara" Ent. 28–29 ii 39–41.

ab-da- [*a(l)-b-da]: (silver) máš-bi-šè dam-[a-ni] . . . ab-da-gub "for its interest PN, [his] wife, (stands =) guarantees" TMH NF 1–2, 32:1–4.

àm- *[a(l)-m(mi)]: en-na àm-ĝen igi-ĝu$_{10}$-šè enim-bi a-bala-e na-ba-an-r̂ú "until he came here to report before me, he (= the addressee) should not be (stuck in =) kept" TCS 1 no. 125:8–9.

an- *[a(l)-n]: a-na-gin$_7$ an-AG "(the one who had one son, . . .) how does he fare?" Gilgameš, Enkidu and the Netherworld 255 and passim.

an-da- *[a(l)-n-da]: an-da-tuku "(creditor, erg.) has (a credit) with him (= debtor)" SR 99 iv 12–15.

ú-[ni al]-bar a-ni al-bar ú-gíd al-gu$_7$-e a-gíd al-na$_8$-na$_8$ eri-bar-ra-a al-tuš "[his] (grass =) food is separate, his (water =) drink is separate, he is supposed to eat (long =) faraway food, he is supposed to drink faraway water, he sits at the suburb" Gilgameš, Enkidu and the Netherworld. (UET 6/1, 58:6).

Note: For more evidence, see Edzard 2003a, 87–98.

12.11–12. Modal and connecting indicators

It seems advisable to treat these two kinds of indicators together because their functions partly interlink. The following chart is divided into a positive left and a negative right part.

Ind.	Ø- Ø-	(1st–3rd p.) 12.13.1	12.11.1 INGA	Neg Ind.	NU- NU-	(1st–3rd p.) 12.13.2	12.11.2 NGA
Coh.	GA- GA-	(1st p.) 12.13.3	12.11.3	Neg Coh.	BARA-	(1st p.)	12.11.4
Prec.	HÉ- HÉ-	(2nd, 3rd p.) 12.13.4	12.11.5 NGA	Vet.	BARA-	(2nd, 3rd p.)	12.11.6
Aff. 1	HÉ-	(1st, 3rd p.)	12.117	Neg.Aff.	BARA-	(1st, 3rd p.)	12.11.8
Aff. 2	NA$_{II}$- NA$_{II}$-	(1st, 3rd p.) 12.13.5	12.11.10 NGA	Prohib.	NA$_{I}$-	(2nd, 3rd p.)	12.11.9

Table (*cont.*)

Aff. 3	ŠI- ŠI-	(1st, 3rd p.) 12.13.6	12.11.11 NGA	
Frustr.	NUŠ- NUŠ	12.11.12 12.13.6	 INGA	
Prosp.	Ù	12.12.1		

Note to the chart: NA_I and NA_{II} are, very probably, of the same origin, but have diverged, NA_I referring to future, NA_{II} to past events. NA_{II} as an affirmative may go back to a negative rhetorical question (see 12.11.9). For allomorphs see below.

The table "Construction of Finite Forms" in Thomsen 1984, 139 is an over-simplified presentation of the "Modal prefixes".

12.11. Modal indicators

12.11.1. *Indicative*

Simple statements, in the "indicative mood", are not specially marked.

12.11.2. *Negative indicative*

Its mark is [nu] (for allomorphs see below). [nu] is used independent of conjugation pattern, and it may also be prefixed to non-finite verbal forms such as participles or infinitives.

šà-bi nu-zu "I did not understand its (heart =) meaning" Gudea Cyl. A i 28.

šà-ga-ni nu-mu-zu "I did not understand what he meant with respect to me" Gudea Cyl. A iv 21.

From NS onward, [nu] has the allomorph [la] before the dimensional indicator [ba] (3): á! (DA)-bad-ĝu$_{10}$ la-ba-ta-è "nobody escaped my outstretched arm" Gudea Cyl. A iv 26.

'Archaizing' nu-ba- instead of *la-ba- is found in alan-e . . . kiĝ-ĝá nu-ba-ĝá-ĝá "for this statue . . . nobody was supposed to use (silver . . .) as a working material" Gudea Stat. B vii 53. nu-ba- may have been conditioned by the fourfold occurrence of suffixed -nu in preceding lines 50–52.

In OB, the allomorph [la] before [ba] was extended to [li] before [bi]: za-e šu-ĝar-lugal-zu li-bí-in-gi$_4$ "you(!) have not avenged your king" Ali Letters B 5:7, as compared to earlier ér nu-bí(-n)-dug$_4$ "she uttered no laments thereon" Gudea Stat. B v 4.

It is an open question whether allomorph [la] has been influenced by the existence of Akkadian *lā* "not". There is a parallel, equally unexplained, in the relation between Sumerian nu-banda "foreman" and the Akkadian loanword *laputtûm* < *la-pant-.

[nu] may be spelled nu-ù-, probably when followed by [i]: nu-ù-me-en "I am not" NG no. 32:3.

[nu] is not used if a modal form is to be negated, as with vetitive (12.11.6) or prohibitive (12.11.9).

Note: Similarly Babylonian Akkadian would not use *ul* except for a negated indicative in a main clause; *lā* is used in a dependent clause or in prohibitive, *ay*, *ē* in vetitive.

[nu] is used, however, in negative infinitive constructions even where they may have a modal connotation, e.g., final "in order not to . . .", nu-B-(e)de/-(e)da (see 12.14.3).

12.11.2.1. Suffixed -nu

[nu] occurs suffixed to a noun as the negation of the copula [am] (see 12.7.1.2):

dam-ĝu$_{10}$-nu dumu-ĝu$_{10}$-nu é-ĝu$_{10}$-nu im-me "he exclaims 'my wife/my child/my house is no more'" LamSumUr 95–97.

Note: Michalowski 1989, 43 understood the passage as "he says not, Oh, my wife!", assuming a verbal form nu-im-me.

Nin-nu-nam-šita$_x$ "(There) being no Lady, (would there be) a prayer?" (PN) DP 113 iv 4; 114 iv 3; HSS 3, 17 iii 10; 23 ix 26.

munus-bi a-ba me-a-nu a-ba me-a-ni "that woman: who being (was she) not, who being (was) she?" = "that woman, whoever was she?" Gudea Cyl. A iv 23.

Note: me-a-ni is an example of the "pronominal conjugation" (see 12.14.4).

ù kù-nu za-gìn nu-ga-àm ù erida-nu nagga-nu sipar-nu "it is not silver nor is it lapislazuli, and it is neither copper nor tin nor bronze" Gudea Stat. B vii 50–52.

Note: nu-ga-àm [nu-(i)nga-am] contains the connecting indicator [inga] for which see 12.12.1.

OB grammatical and lexical texts show suffixed -nu with pronouns, e.g., me-en-dè-nu [menden-nu] : *ul nīnu* "it is not us" MSL 4, 51:419 (OBGT); a-ne-da-nu [ane-da-nu] : *baluššu* "it is (not with =) without him" MSL 13, 86: E 31 (Proto-Kagal).

In practice, suffixed -nu has often become a substitute for the syntagma X-da nu-me-a "(not being with =) without X" (see 5.4.2.6).

12.11.2.2. [nu] as a separate verbal base

dub-sar šu nu-a nar míli (KA × LI) nu-a "a scribe having no hand (is like) a cantor having no voice" SP II 43.

ud_5 máš nu-a "a goat having no kid" TrDr. 26:9.

u_8 $sila_4$ nú-a "a ewe having no lamb" TCL 2, 5621:1.

Note: The lexical passage u_8 $sila_4$ nú-a: *ša puḫādsa nī*[*lu*] "a ewe whose lamb is resting" (see CAD L 42 *laḫru* lex.) most probably has to be kept separate from the Ur III reference (TrDr. 26:9) where -nu-a would not be an abbreviated spelling for *-nú-a.

in-nu [i-nu] has become the expression for "No!" by OB.

nu may also be considered a base of its own in the phrase a-ba-àm lugal a-ba-àm nu lugal "who is it (that was) king, who is it (that was) not king?" = "whoever was king?" Sum. Kinglist vii 1.

For nu in OS Ean. 1 r. x 2 see 12.11.11.

12.11.3. *Cohortative*

The cohortative mood occurs only in the 1st sg. and pl. It is denoted by prefixed ga-, with allomorphs (Ur III) ge_4-(rí-) and gú-(mu-). The cohortative is found in complementary distribution with the precative, which supplies the 2nd and 3rd persons, see 12.11.5.

ga- is essentially linked to verbal forms with the *ḫamṭu* base and, therefore, is not marked with a suffix (denoting person) after the base:

ga-tìl$^{(il)}$ "(let me live =) ex-voto object".

nam $gé_4$-rí-íb-tar^{ar} etc. Šulgi D 384 f. (*NS), see above 12.8.1.21.

Although combined with conjugation pattern 1 in the case of an intransitive verb, there is no ending -en after the base. Apparently, ga- alone was sufficient to mark the 1st sg. In the pl., however, -enden is suffixed: ga-ba-húl-húl-le-en-dè-en [ga-ba-hulhul-enden] "let us mightily rejoice over it" ZA 45 (1939) 119.

The (irregular) verb dug_4/e "to speak, do" behaves in a special way in OB: silim-ma ga-na-ab-bé-en [ga-na-b-e-(e)n] "let me say 'hail' to her" Iddin-Dagān B 1–3, 6, etc. where we do not find the expected ga-na-ab-dug_4 [ga-na-b-dug] as in Gudea Cyl. A iii 22 f.

e-ne-sù-ud ga$^!$-da-e [ga-eda-e-(e)n] "(let me play with you =) let us have sex together" TMH NF 3, 25:20.

Note: Here the pl. base [e] may have been chosen because the intended act implied two (active) participants.

See Attinger 1993, 222 f.; 476.

12.11.4. *Negated cohortative*

Negative exhortation, "let me not . . .", "I will certainly not . . .", is expressed with the bi-syllabic prefix [bara], a multi-functional morpheme which is also found in the vetitive (12.11.6) and in the negative affirmative (12.11.8).

The negative cohortative is restricted by definition to the 1st person and found with the *marû* verbal base and personal suffixes if the form is transitive.

ki-sur-ra-dNin-ĝír-su-ka-ke$_4$ ba-ra-mu-bala-e(n) "I swear I will not transgress, as regards me, Ninĝirsu's boundary" Ean. 1 xx 19.

di ba-ra-a-da-ab-bé-en$_6$ [bara-eda-b-e-(e)n] "I promise I will not go to court (with =) against you" NG no. 28:8.

12.11.5. *Precative*

The precative mood is used with 2nd and 3rd person, "you may . . .", "he may . . .", "let him/her . . .", etc. It is found in complementary distribution with the cohortative (12.11.3).

Precative is marked by the prefix HÉ-, graphically realized as hé- or ha-, as well as (OB) hu- before mu-.

Precative forms are found with the *marû* form if the verb is transitive.

The distribution of [he] and [ha] is not entirely clear, but, according to Attinger 1993, 292 f. § 191, hé- is "sans hésitation possible la forme de base", being found in a wider range of phonetic contexts than is [ha].

In Ur III letter-orders hé-na-ab-šúm-mu and ha-na-ab-šúm-mu "let him/her give it to him/her" (Sollberger 1966, 169 f. s.v. sumu) the relative frequency of the two forms is 125:15. As both hé-na- and ha-na- occur at Ĝirsu, local variation should be discounted. Moreover, there are 'mixed' spellings HÉ-ab-, HÉ-an- (see below), but none of a type *HA-eb-, *HA-en-.

Note: For another allograph, hi- (Ur III, Šulgi hymns), see Attinger 1993, 293 with fn. 838, where also reference is made to Ebla, d'Agostino 1990, 128–34.

ĝìri-bi ha-ma-ĝá-ĝá "may (Nanše) show me the way there" Gudea Cyl. A ii 19.

ĝiškim-ĝu$_{10}$ hé-sa$_6$ "let my sign be favourable" Gudea Cyl. A iii 18.

E$_4$-nun-na bar-ĝu$_{10}$-a šùd hé-mi(-b)-sa$_4$(-n)-za(-n) [he-mmi-b-sa-(e)nzen] "O Enūna (pl.), may you say a blessing thereat on my behalf" Gudea Cyl. B ii 6.

kalam-e hé-ĝál-la šu HÉ.A-da-peš-e [he-eda-b-peš-e] "let the Land (stretch out the hand =) gain in abundance (with you =) under your rule" Gudea Cyl. A xi 9.

mu-ni . . . dub-ta hé-em-ta-ĝar "may his name . . . be (set =) taken off the tablet" Gudea Stat. B ix 16.

hé-àm "let it be" became in effect an expression for "yes", in contrast to in-nu "no" (cf. 12.11.2.2).

Note: See also Edzard 1971, 213 f. (note that in TCS 1 no. 82:4 there is 3rd, not 2nd person).

hé is used as an independent verbal base in the expression A hé-a B hé-a (= *lū* A *lū* B), ("A WISH-ing, B WISH-ing =) be it A, be it B", e.g., in blessing or curse formulae, en hé-a lugal hé-a "whether he be a lord or a king".

12.11.6. *The vetitive (negative precative)*

It is used with the 2nd and 3rd person, "you/he should not", "please do not", etc. It is found in complementary distribution with the negative cohortative (1st person, see 12.11.4).

Like the negative cohortative, vetitive is marked by the prefixed particle [bara]. It is found with the *marû* verbal base if the verbal form is transitive.

mí-ús-sá-zu mí-ús-sá-ĝu$_{10}$ ba-ra-me "the son-in-law you (had in mind) should certainly not be(come) my son-in-law" NG no. 18:24 (oath).

Note: Since the copula is intransitive and has no opposed *ḫamṭu* : *marû* forms, it is difficult to decide whether this is a vetitive or a negative affirmative "will certainly not . . ."; cf. 12.11.8.

12.11.7. *Affirmative 1*

Like the precative (see 12.11.5) it is marked by the prefixed particle [he] and its allomorphs. As against precative (occurring with 2nd and 3rd persons), affirmative 1 occurs in the 1st and 3rd persons. It refers to something in the past and, therefore, is found with conjugation pattern 2b (see 12.7.3) and the *ḫamṭu* verbal base if the verbal form is transitive.

Edzard 1971, 213–25.

"Affirmative 1" is a catch-all term. The main function of this mood is to remove doubt, on the side of the listener, about what is being said.

Note: Cf. "honest!" in colloquial English, which serves to remove doubt.

Affirmative 1 is extremely popular in royal statements about what the ruler did, achieved, performed. It might then be rendered by a pluralis maiestatis, "we . . .", instead of "I verily . . .".

Note: In the royal hymn Šulgi A nearly all statements of the king's activities made in the 1st sg., are preceded by hé-, with the exception of subordinate clauses and of lines where the copula -me-en "I am" is used.

Affirmative 1 does not occur with the 2nd person.

12.11.8. *Negative affirmative*

The negative affirmative is marked by the prefixed particle [bara] which also serves the negative cohortative (12.11.4) and the vetitive (12.11.6). It occurs in the 1st and 3rd person. As it refers to something in the past, it is found with the *ḫamṭu* verbal base and with conjugation pattern 2b (see 12.7.3) if the verbal form is transitive.

Edzard 1971, 218 f.

As with positive affirmative 1 (12.11.7), the main function of negative affirmative is to rule out doubt, on the side of the listener, about what is being said.

nu-mu-un-su lú-á-tuku-ra ba-ra-na-an-ĝar "he did not—do not doubt it—(set =) pledge (as a security) a widow to a wealthy person" Ur-Namma Code 115.

ní ba-ra-ba-da-te su ba-ra-ba-da-zi "Yeah! I (the king) was not afraid of it, did not let (my) hair stand on end because of it" Šulgi A 70.

12.11.9. *Prohibitive*

The prohibitive mood is prefixed by the particle [na] graphically (and phonetically?) identical to the affirmative 2 particle [na]. Directed at a 2nd person it expresses prohibition, and as such it is the negation of the imperative. With a 3rd person form it equally implies strict interdiction. As against the negative cohortative [bara] (see 12.11.4) it does not occur with the 1st person (nor does the vetitive, 12.11.6).

túg-tán-tán-na na-an-mu_4-mu_4-un [na-ni-mumu-(e)n] "do not wear a clean garment there" Gilg., Enkidu and the Nether World 185.

ì-du_{10}-ga bur-ra na-an-$še_{22}$-$še_{22}$-en "do not anoint (yourself) there with sweet oil from a jar" ibid. 187.

Edzard 1971, 219 f.

We summarize the negative moods:

(1) negative cohortative [bara] (1st person, 12.11.4): strict instruction not to act or to repeat an action.

(2) vetitive [bara] (2nd, 3rd persons, 12.11.6): interdiction, or recommendation not to act.

(3) negative affirmative [bara] (1st, 3rd persons, 12.11.8): assertion that something has not occurred, or that someone has not done something.

(4) prohibitive [na] (2nd, 3rd persons, 12.11.9): negative imperative; interdiction (theoretically).

See also table on p. 112 f.

12.11.10. *Affirmative 2*

Affirmative 2, prefixed by particle [na], has been amply treated by Falkenstein 1942, 181–223. It serves to draw attention to the importance of something that was there or happened, but is still meaningful for what is to come. For that reason, it is usually found with the *ḫamṭu* base and conjugation pattern 2b (see 12.7.3), if the verbal form is transitive. It is often found at the beginning of tales:

ĝéštu-ga-ni na-an-gub [na-n-gub] "You should know that (Inana) (set her ear =) decided to move (from the great Heaven to the great Earth)". Inana's Descent 1.

é ur$_5$-gin$_7$ dím-ma énsi-deli-e ^{d}Nin-ĝír-su-ra nu-na(-n)-r̂ú na-mu(-n)-r̂ú "a house built that way no single ensi had (ever) built for Ninĝirsu; (now, however) he (= Gudea) did build it" Gudea Stat. B vii 4.

Edzard 1971, 220–21.

Affirmative na- can rarely be confused with prohibitive na- (12.11.9) because the latter uses the *marû* base and conjugation pattern 1 (see 12.7.2) in the case of transitive verbal forms.

For affirmative 2 na- and prohibitive na-—instead of chance homophony—a common origin is plausible. Affirmative 2 na- may go back to a rhetorical negative question: "has it not . . . by all means?" turning into "it definitely has . . .".

Note: Phonetic assonance or even identity of elements denoting negation, question (and affirmation) are found in diverse languages: Latin *ne* and enclitic question marker *-ne*; Turkish *-m*V- (negation) and *-m*V (question), e.g., bil-mi-yorum "I do not know", evin-mi "your house?"; Semitic *lā* "not" and affirmative and/or optative elements containing *la* (see D. Testen, JSS 38 [1993] 1–13); cf. also in colloquial English the negative tag question ". . . isn't it?" meaning "it is really . . .".

hé-àm "it is really so" (= "yes", see 12.11.5 end and 15.8) has a counterpart in na-nam "it definitely was, and still is, so". It is a pleonastic formation of *na-àm [na-am] turned into [na-na-(a)m] and could be extended still further to (ur$_5$) hé-na-nam-ma(-àm).

Note: Pleonastic extensions frequently occur in languages; cf., e.g., French le lendemain "the next day", starting out from *main (< mane), then extended as demain "tomorrow", en-demain, l'endemain.

For the UD.GAL.NUN correspondence ŠA = NA see below, 12.11.11.

12.11.11. *Affirmative 3*

Affirmative 3 ša-, ši-, with allomorph (OB) šu- before mu-, is found only in literary contexts, and it is unknown whether it also occurred in colloquial Sumerian.

Beside the extensive treatment of the morpheme by Falkenstein 1944, 73–118, cf. the note of M. Civil apud Heimpel 1974, 44 and 48 fn. 25; Edzard 1971, 222; Attinger 1993, 294 f. (with more lit.).

The main function of [ša] is to reconfirm something that already had been stated or had occurred (Civil 1974: "Main event precedes"), as against affirmative 2 [na] which stresses the importance of something in the past, still meaningful for the future.

na-rû-a mu-bi lú-a nu(-àm) mu-bi ši-e "the name of the statue—it is not a person's (name)—its name (says =) reads (as we already know): '. . .'" Ean. 1 r. x 1–3.

di-ku$_5$ ka-aš bar-re-da [z]a-a-da ša-mu-e-da-ĝál "Pronouncing decisions rests (as it always has) with you (= Nergal)" SRT 12.:20, see Römer 1965, 91.

Note: A. Ganter (Zgoll) contrasted [ša] and [na]: "ša- weist mit Nachdruck—affirmativ—auf etwas schon Vorliegendes, Vorauszusetzendes zurück; im Gegensatz zu na-, das primär auf etwas Kommendes, zu Erwartendes verweist" (Sumerian Grammar Discussion Group, Oxford 1993; see Zgoll 2003).

12.11.12. *Frustrative*

The prefixed particle nu-uš- (var. nu-úš- and nu-šV-) expresses a hypothetical wish: something should be or have been, occur or have occurred. The term "frustrative" was proposed by Jacobsen 1965, 74 (= 1970, 249). [nuš] was thoroughly analysed by Römer 1976, 371–78. See Attinger 1993, 297 with more lit.

[nuš] is so far only found in literary and lexical contexts. Ebla NU.UŠ = *lu-wu-um, (l)a-wu-um* represents, in its Akkadian column, precative [luw] and hypothetical [law] in substantivized form. Cf. Krebernik 1983, 23 f. n. 78; 45:1439, as well as apud Edzard 1984, 115 n. 1.

sipa-ĝu$_{10}$ hi-li-a-ni nu-uš-ma$^{!}$(-da)-an-ku$_{4}$-ku$_{4}$ [nuš-ma/mada-n(i)-kuku] ĝá-e ba-ra-ku$_{4}$-ku$_{4}$-dè-en "Would that my shepherd (= the dead Ur-Namma) (could still) bring in unto me (var. with me) his beautiful features; as for me (= lamenting Inana), I will certainly not enter (there again)" Ur-Namma's Death 213.

u$_{4}$-ba ^{geš}ellag-ĝu$_{10}$ é-naĝar-ra-ka nu-uš-ma-da-ĝál-la-àm = *ūma pukku ina bīt naggāri lū ezib* "If only on that day my hoop(?) had stayed with me in the carpenter's house" = "had the hoop(?) but stayed on that day in the carpenter's house" Gilgameš, Enkidu and the Netherworld 172 (= EG XII 1).

[nuš] may perhaps be segmentized into negative [nu] + [Š], but the nature of the second element would remain quite uncertain. Civil 1983, 51, proposed *nu-šè-; but *nu-ši-, i.e., a—rhetoric?—negation of affirmative 3, cannot be ruled out, nor can some other unknown origin.

For rare spelling variants nu-úš-, né-eš-, and ni-iš- see Attinger 1993, 297.

12.12. Connecting indicators

12.12.1. Prospective

Prospective [U] has two main functions: (1) it serves to indicate that the verbal idea expressed by form A precedes (in time or argument) the verbal idea expressed by a subsequent form B, e.g., "after I had done A, I did B". A syntagma [U]- . . . -A, . . . -B sometimes comes close to a conditional clause, "if A, then B".

(2) [U] expresses a polite imperative: "after you did A (I would be grateful)" = "would you please do A".

Note: Cf. English "if you would (kindly) close the window" which equals "close the window, please".

[U] is written ù- (also u- in post-OB or in Emesal); a- before ba- (a-ba-), and ì- before bí- (ì-bí-).

The prospective cannot, most probably, be negated: *"after I did not see him, I went home"; at least, no examples are known.

Attinger 1993, 295 f. with lit., esp. Heimpel 1974, 229–233 with over 70 strings of prefixed particles starting with [U].

12.12.1. *A precedes B*

kalam-e zi-šà-ĝál ù-ma-šúm [u-mma-n-šum], lú-deli lú-min-da kiĝ mu-da-ak-ke_4 "after he (= the Northwind) has given life to our Land, one single person will (do work with a second person =) work as much as two" Gudea Cyl. A xi 24–25.

2 še gur a-šà ù-gíd, máš-a-šà-ga a-ba-ra-zi, úgu-ba máš ì-íb-ĝá-ĝá "(when =) if he (= the tenant) (only) tilled (the amount of) 2 kor of barley; when the interest of the field will have been raised he (= the lessor) will set his rent/interest thereon" TCL 5, 6170:13–15 (NG no. 144, and see Wilcke 1988, 10 with fn. 39).

12.12.2. *Polite imperative*

There is a universal tendency to moderate the harsh form of a direct imperative: "pass me the salt"—"would you please pass me the salt".

In OS, the author of a letter addresses the scribe by dug_4-ga-na (-b) "tell it to him" in order to convey the message to the addressee, e.g., Michalowski 1995, 11 no. 1:6 [dug_4]-ga-⌜na⌝ (= CIRPL Enz. 1). Later on this quite direct formula was generally replaced by a verbal form using the prospective: ù-na-dug_4 [u-na-e-dug] "after you said to him/her" = "would you please tell him/her". The formula must often have been pronounced [unêdug] in order to account for the Akkadian loanword form *unetukku* (see above 3.1.2).

A typical example of polite imperatives are Ninĝirsu's instructions given to Gudea to tell him how he should construct his (= Ninĝirsu's) chariot and accessories:

kìšib ù-mi-kúr [u-mbi-e-kur] ĝeš ù-ma-ta-ĝar [u-mba-(b)ta-e-ĝar] . . . ^{ĝeš}gigir ù-mu-silim [u-mu-e-silim] ANSE.DUN.ÙR ù-ši-lá [u-bši-e-laH] . . . šu ù-ma-ni-tag [u-mba-ni-e-tag] "would you please break the seal (on your storehouse), lay out the wood from there, . . . fit together a chariot, harness to it a donkey stallion . . ., decorate (that chariot)" Gudea Cyl. A vi 15–19.

An Ur III (or earlier) collection of medical prescriptions nearly twenty times offers prospective verbal forms which should be considered as suggestions, i.e., polite imperatives: Civil 1960, 61:54

ù-dé [u-e-de] "would you pour", ibid. 58 ù-gaz "would you crush", and see 66, 80, and passim.

A frozen form ù-/u-me-ni-B "would you please . . ." is found in post-OB incantations, in prescriptions to perform a ritual, e.g., e_4 . . . ù-me-ni-dé, [ĝeš]šinig . . . ù-me-ni-šub "would you pour water (in a jug), throw a (twig of) tamarisk into it" Falkenstein 1931, 90:28 f.

12.12.2. *Connecting indicator [inga]*

The preposed particle [inga] occurs in its full form, inga-, in verb initial position (see 12.12.2.1) as well as after [nuš] (see 12.12.2.7); it is -Vn-ga- [nga] after a preceding vowel (see 12.12.2.2–6).

The question arises whether [inga] might be segmentized into [i] + [nga]. In such a case we would have to define [i] (see 12.9) as the modal indicator for the indicative (cf. table on p. 112 f.), instead of giving it the value [ø].

Thomsen 1984, 169–72, only notes an element [ga] instead of [inga]. In her theory, [i], preceding [ga], is nasalized, so that [inga] would represent *[ĩ-ga]. See above, 12.9, for arguments militating against the existence of a nasalized element *[ĩ].

As a connecting indicator, [inga] stands out by its ability to combine with at least five positive modal particles (GA-, HÉ-, NA_{II}-, ŠA-. NUŠ-) as well as with negative NU-.

The functions of [inga] have been summed up by Attinger 1993, 297 f., as indicating "et alors", "et par conséquence", "(et) aussi . . . que", "et de plus", "(et) de nouveau", "non seulement . . . mais encore". See 12.12.2.1 ff. [inga], as a rule, only occurs with a second (or third . . .) verbal form in a series, and it is only found in first position when it is followed by a second verbal form with [inga].

[inga] was given much attention in the grammatical lists, both OBGT and NBGT. Cf., e.g., in-ga-me-en-dè-en, in-ga-me-en-da-nam—*nīnuma* "it is we; we too" OBGT I 410 f. (MSL 4, 51), also lines 412–418 where, each time, [inga] is rendered by suffixed *-ma* in Akkadian.

The NBGT 205–208 (MSL 4, 137) list un-ga, an-ga, in-ga, en-ga (in the well-known u-a-i(-e) sequence) = *ù* "and", preceded by lines 202–204 ù, bi, bi-da = *ù* "and". un-ga etc. were treated separately from such strings as nu-un-ga-; na-na-ga-, ga-an-ga-; in-ga-, ši-in-ga-; hé-en-ga-—an example of the efforts of cuneiform scribes to define grammatical elements whose structure cannot be rendered with syllabic signs.

See also MSL 4, 199:21; 145:395–398; 150:37–40; 163:12–15 (new: MSL 5, 198).

12.12.2.1. in-ga-

Lagaš^{ki} gaba-bi šu e-ma-ús . . . gaba-bi šu e-ga-ma-ús [inga-mma-n-us] "(Umma) (came close to the breast of =) defied Lagaš, . . . it (also =) once more defied it" Ean. 1 ii 27–iii 22.

gal mu-zu gal ì-ga-túm-mu "(Gudea) is wise (and) (also brings forth great (things) =) able, too, to realize things" Gudea Cyl. A vii 10.

eri^{ki} in-ga-àm eri^{ki} in-ga-àm šà-bi a-ba mu-zu "it is (such) a city, it is (such) a city, (who knows its heart =) that no one can know its heart" Keš Hymn 59.

lugal-ĝu$_{10}$ za-gin$_7$ a-ba an-ga-kal a-ba an-ga-a-da-sá "my lord, who is as powerful as you are, who would also (= [anga]) be able to compete with you?" Šulgi D (MBI 3 i 23–25).

This passage may be interpreted in two ways: (1) a-ba an-ga- is a contraction of a-ba (i)n-ga-. (2) (i)nga is preceded by indicator [a(l)] (see 12.10).

a-a-ĝu$_{10}$ a-a-zu-gin$_7$ in-ga-dím "my father is (made =) as good as your father" Sefati 1998, 195:11.

12.12.2.2. [nu-nga]

a-na gur-si-sá-ta, àm-áĝ[-ĝá], ù ĝá-[e], (1) gur ki-su$_7$-ta, nu-ga-áĝ [nu-nga-V-aĝ] "what(ever) may have been measured out from the regular kor, as for me, I did not measure out (one) kor from the threshing floor" BIN 8, 156:7–11 (letter, unclear context).

. . . me-zu mah-àm . . ., ^{d}Nanše me-zu me-na-me nu-un-ga-an-da-sá "your ordinances are the greatest . . ., and, O Nanše, any other ordinances could certainly not rival with you(rs)" Nanše Hymn 251.

For Gudea Stat. B vii 50 nu-ga-àm "nor is it" see 12.11.2.1.

[. . .] mu-tar, Ur-^{d}Nin-ĝír-su, ù nam-érim, nu-ga-ma-tar "[. . .] has sworn, as for U., he did not swear an (assertive) oath in my favour" ITT II 5758 r. 1'–4'.

12.12.2.3. [ga-nga]

gan ga-ni-re$_7$-en-dè-en gan ga-an-ga-àm-gi(!)-dè-en [ga-nga-mm(i)-gigi(!)-(n)den] "come, let's go there, come, let's also return here" The Three Ox Drivers 13.

12.12.2.4. [he-nga]

é ki-hur-sa$_6$-ga-ù$\hat{g}$-sa$\hat{g}$-$\hat{g}$i$_6$-ga ì-me-en-na-ke$_4$-eš, ì-ze-è$\hat{g}$-bi-ta íb-ba su-mu-ug-ga hé-en-ga-mu-e-da-TAB.TAB-e-eš "although, O House, you used to be the place of joy for the Black-headed ones, instead of its festivals (emesal for ezem) they (doubled with you =) gave in return to you both wrath and disaster" Lament of Ur 116–117.

12.12.2.5. [na-nga]

en-e ní$\hat{g}$-du$_7$-e pa na-an-ga-àm-mi-in-è (var. naM-ga-), . . ., an ki-ta baD-$\hat{r}$e$_6$-dè sa$\hat{g}$ na-an-ga(-àm)-ma-an-šúm "the Lord, you should know (na-), made appear here what is due, in bright fashion, . . . and, moreover, he in fact gave heed to separate heaven from earth" Creation of the Pickaxe 1 . . . 5.

Note: The actions described in lines 1 and 5 are connected by (i)nga . . . (i)nga, lit. "both . . . and . . .". na- in line 1 is the affirmative na$_{II}$- frequently found at the beginning of tales (see 12.11.10), and it is repeated in line 5, most probably because of rhyme.

en-na W. ù N. na-an-ga-ti-la-aš igi-ni-ne-šè ì-gub-bu(-d) as long as either W. or N. will actually be alive, he (= the adopted person) will (stand before them =) be at their service" ARN 7:8–11.

É-an-na-túm-me gal na-ga-mu-zu "Eanatum in fact also knows this: . . ." Ean. 1 xxi 12–13, r. i 31–32, etc. (the phrase each time introduces the magic ritual performed with pigeons).

ki šà-$\hat{g}$u$_{10}$ na-an-ga-ma-ab-bé-a "(I will loosen my sandals) at whichever place my heart tells me" Lugalbanda I 178 (this is the climax after a series of cohortative verbal forms introduced by ga-).

Mu-ni-na-ga-me "Whichever be his/her (= the divinity's) name" Old Sum. PN, DP 95:4, etc.; see Struve 1984, 124.

na-an-gaba(!)-ti-[l]a-da [na-nga-ba-til-ed-a] "as long as he lives" NRVN 1, 236:4.

[nanga] occurs in a frozen form in u$_4$ na-an-ga-ma [na-nga(-i)-me-a?] "whichever day it actually was" in the sense of "formerly" (see Wilcke 1969, 159 ad line 74).

Note: For the 'inverted' sequence inga-na- see below, 12.12.2.8.

12.12.2.6. [ši-nga]

u$_4$-ba $\hat{g}$éštu-diri . . . ki-tuš-a-ni-ta šà-di$\hat{g}$ir-re-e-ke$_4$ ši-in-ga-zu-a . . . á im-ma-an-á$\hat{g}$ "then the very wise one . . . who even from his residence finds out about the (heart =) intentions of the gods . . . gave instruction" Inanna and Enki SLTNi. 32:9–10 (Farber-Flügge 1973, 18).

nin_9-$\hat{g}u_{10}$ ama-$\hat{g}u_{10}$ ši-ga-mi-in-na "my sister who, as we know (ši-), are also my mother" VS 2, 27 v 7.

. . . me-e ši-in-ga-m[èn-na], . . . me-e ši-in-ga-mèn-[na] "I who, as one knows, am . . ., and who, as one knows, also am . . ." SBH 56:18 f. and 22 f. (see Falkenstein 1944, 92).

Kèš[ki]-gin_7 rib-ba lú ši-in-ga(-an)-túm-mu, . . . ama ši-in-ga-an-ù-dú "will someone bring forth somebody who would be as overwhelming as Keš, or will a mother bear somebody (who would be as overwhelming as Ašgi, the warrior (of Keš))?" Keš Hymn 18–19 (as well as at the end of each 'House' section).

12.12.2.7. [nuš-inga]

lugal-$\hat{g}u_{10}$ ní-huš-rib-ba-za, nu-uš-in-ga-zu-àm, . . . ní-mah-a-za, nu-uš-in-ga-⸢zu-àm⸣ "My lord, would that your overwhelming fierce awe were known, . . . that your unsurpassed awe were known" Ninurta G 174–177 (and see 179, 181, 183), M. E. Cohen 1975, 29.

Note: The fivefold repetition of [inga] might be rendered by "firstly", "secondly", etc.

nu-uš-in-ga- is spelled with 'hiatus' above, but note Ur Lamentation 101 nu-ši-in-ga- with var. nu-uš-in-ga- in UET 6/2, 136:96.

12.12.2.8. 'Irregular' [inga-na]

Attinger 1993, 297: "Que [(i)nga] n'est ni un préf. I ["préformatif"] ni un préf. II ["préfixe de conjugaison"], mais une sorte de "prédicat conjonctif" (§ 90.e [p. 149]), ressort clairement du fait qu'il peut être aussi bien précédé que suivi du préf. I assertif (na) (comp. in-ga-na(m)-mu-na-be_2(-en) et na-an/nam-ga-)".

According to Attinger who rather associates [inga] with -bi, -bi-da, ù "and" (p. 149 f.), [inga] should not find its fixed position in table on p. 112 f. In fact, [inga] might be isolated as "also" in GilgHuw. I 91 mìn-kam-ma-šè in-ga(-)nam-mu-na-ab-bé "a second time, still, he definitely addresses him". But in most of the other occurrences, [(i)nga] appears inseparably embedded in the prefix string of the verb.

Note: Only a living informant would be able to say whether or not [inga-na-mu-na-b-e] and *[na-nga-mu-na-b-e] were freely exchangeable.

At any rate, Attinger's position will have to be submitted to further research, in a comprehensive study of the particle [inga].

For bibl., see Attinger 1993, 297.

12.12.2.9. Summary of [inga].
After Attinger's definition (1993, 297; see above 12.12.2), the main functions of [inga] may be tentatively summed up as follows:

1. Simple [inga] denotes "also", "too", with an antecedent not provided by [inga]; [inga] in consecutive verbal forms means "both . . . and . . .".
2. X Y-gin$_7$ [inga] means "X equals Y (nominal antecedent)".
3. [nu-nga] "not even".
4. [he-nga] "also really/verily", "instead of".
5. [na-nga] "also in fact".
6. [ši-nga] "also, indeed, as we already know".
7. [nuš-inga] "let/may also . . ." (rhetorical question).

12.12a. [IRI]

A verb-connected element [iri], spelled i-ri, i-rí, iri, is so far attested only before [(i)nga]. We have not entered it in table on p. 112 f., because we are at a loss to define its function. See, for discussion and bibl., Attinger 1993, 296 f. ("Ni la fonction ni même la catégorie grammaticale de {iri} ne peuvent être déterminées".)

12.13. Imperative

The Sumerian imperative is regularly formed with the verbal *ḫamṭu* (alternatively the reduplicated *ḫamṭu*) base without any prefixed particles. There are basically two types: 1) the unextended imperative consisting of the base and an additional vowel whose quality is unpredictable to us, i.e., B-V; 2) the extended imperative; here, one or more (up to four) particles, otherwise prefixed to the base, follow either the base itself or the base+V.

The element V following the base has, since Poebel 1923, 278 f. §§ 676–678, been interpreted as a reflex of the prefixed indicator [e, i] (see 12.9); cf. Attinger 1993, 298. This explanation does not, however, account for the vocalic diversity. Therefore, we prefer to see V as a mark of imperative as such.

We are unable so far to predict the imperative of a given Sumerian verb—as against many languages (Indo-European, Semitic, and others).

The plural of the Sumerian imperative is formed by the addition of [nzen] after V or [zen] after C; correlation with 2nd pl. [(e)nzen] is obvious.

In the extended imperative, as in the cohortative (see 12.11.3), the absolutive 'object' of the 3rd sg. is noted by [n] (extremely rarely) or [b]. This fact has been claimed as an argument for Sumerian being a language with "split ergativity"; but see our alternative explanation above in 12.7.4.

So far, no context examples are available for the 1st (sg. or pl.) absolutive 'object', i.e., e.g., *"push me", *"push us". The 2nd (sg. and pl.) may be safely excluded, because forms like *"put yourself (in my position)" would be reflexive and require ní-zu(-ne-ne) "yourself", "yourselves".

The OBGT in their ĝar = *šakānum* paradigm, offer two examples for an imperative + "me": ĝar-mu-un = *šuknanni* "set me (here)" MSL 4, 80 OBGT VI 46; [ĝar]-mu-ub = *šuškinanni* "cause me to be set (here)" ibid. VI 51. The first of the two forms may be segmentized into [ĝar-mu-(e)n] with [(e)n] as the absolutive "me" of the transitive conjugation pattern 2b (see 12.7.3). As for the second example, we are at a loss to explain the relation existing between the Sumerian and Akkadian forms.

Note: "Help me" which in our language would imply a 1st person absolutive 'object', occurs as dah-ma-ab, lit. "add it to me" in GilgHuw. A 110 za-e ĝá-e dah-ma-ab "(as for) you, help me". The construction is with the dative.

12.13.1. *Unextended imperative (base + V)*

gi$_4$-a "go back", "return" Gilg. Huw. A 117, 118.

ér šéš-a "shed tears" Inana's Descent 42, 51, 59.

^{ĝeš}šudun gú-ba ĝar-ì "set the yoke on their neck" Ur-Ninurta B r. 6; šu-ni-šè ĝar-ì "put into her hands" Message of Ludiĝira 7; but note ĝar-ra [ĝar-a] šukun "set" OBGT VI 1 (MSL 4, 79).

é ĝál-ù (var. ĝál-lu) "open the house" Inana's Descent 75 f.; Nanna's Journey 260–264, etc.

Note: The verb "to open" is ĝál taka; either [ĝal-u] is an irregular imperative, or the imperative still preserves a verbal form that was otherwise extended to ĝál taka.

ki-gub-za nú-ì "lie (down) at your resting place" Copper and Silver 33 (SRT 4:33).

ní-za ĝéštu AG-ì "heed yourself" Grain and Sheep" 162 (ASJ 9, 26).

ĝen-na "go" Inana's Descent 70.

ĝá-nu (or $ĝe_{26}$-nu?) "come on" Lugalbanda I 135.

Note: The two imperatives of ĝen (*ḫamṭu*)/du (*marû*) "to go" have been generally discussed by Wilcke 1969, 172 f., who also dissociated the exclamation [gana] (see 15.7).

The plural of the unextended imperative is relatively rare; cf. e.g.,

ĝen-na-an-zé-en [ĝen-a-(e)nzen] "go" Inana's Descent 227.

gu_4-ud-an-zé-en [gud-a-(e)n-zen] "jump, dance" SRT 5:42, 44.

12.13.2. *Extended imperative*

The extended imperative may contain such additional information as ventive, dimensional indicators, or absolutive. As a rule, one to three of these elements occur (the plural marker not counted), exceptionally as many as four (see 12.13.2.4).

12.13.2.1. One element

ĝìri kur-šè nú-ba-an-zé-en [nu-ba-nzen] "(lay down the feet =) slide down (on your behinds) toward the Nether World" Inana's Descent 227.

12.14.2.2. Two elements

má-a dab_5-dab_5-ba-ab [dabdab-ba-b] "take (all the cattle) on the boat" SR 87:5.

dah-ma-ab [dah-ma-b] "add it to me" Gilg. Huw. A 110.

tuku-ba-an [tuku-ba-n] "marry her" NG no. 6:8.

Note: ba- is here a frozen indicator, referring to implied nam-dam-šè "for marriage".

a naĝ-mu-ub-zé-en [naĝ-mu-b-zen] "give me water to drink" Schooldays 13.

zi-mu-ub-zé-en [zi-mu-b-zen] "wake me" Schooldays 16.

Note: [b] is difficult to explain here. Does it 'rhyme' with [b] in the preceding imperatives?

ní te-ba-ab téš tuku-ba-ab "be devoted, be reverent (in face of my words)" Father and Son 101.

du_{11}-ga-na(-b) [dug-a-na-b] "say it to him (there)" CIRPL N 12 iii 1.

šúm-me-eb "give it to us" Inanna's Descent 245, 266, 269.

12.13.2.3. Three elements

ur$_4$-ur$_4$-u$_4$-mu-na-ab [ururu-mu-na-b] "collect it for him" SRT 12:60.

é-diĝir-re-e-ne nigin-na-ma-ni-ib [nigin-a-ma-ni-b] "go around the houses of the gods for my sake" Inana's Descent 36.

ĝiškim-a-ni [e-ne-ra] du$_{11}$-mu-na-ab [dug-mu-na-b] "give [him] a sign (or: an identification) of his" ELA 496.

12.13.2.4. Four elements

⌜sá du$_{11}$⌝-ga-àm-mu-⌜na-ni-íb⌝ [dug-a-mu-na-ni-b] = ⌜*šutakši*⌝*daššum* "cause him$_1$ to be brought in close contact with him$_2$" OBGT IX 52 (MSL 4, 106).

[sá du$_{11}$]-⌜ga-ba-na⌝-ni-íb [dug-a-ba-na-ni-b] = *šutak*⌜*šidsum*⌝ "cause him$_1$ to be brought close to him$_2$" OBGT IX 40 (MSL 4, 105).

Note: Neither AHw. nor CAD K s.vv. *kašādu* (*šutakšudu*) has offered a convincing translation of these Akkadian imperatives. Both the Sumerian and the Akkadian forms look like learned scribal efforts—as do some other forms in the sá-du$_{11}$(-g) = *kašādu* section of OBGT.

Attinger 1993, 298 f. with lit.

As in many languages, there is no negated imperative in Sumerian. Instead, vetitive [bara] (12.11.8) or prohibitive [na$_I$] (12.11.9) are used.

12.14. Non-finite verbal forms

Non-finite verbal forms lack any of those prefixes or suffixes by which state or action can be linked to a 'subject' of 1st, 2nd, or 3rd person, sing. or pl. Cf. 12.7.1, 12.7.2, and 12.7.3 for the conjugation patterns of the Sumerian verb.

There are three types (see 1–3) of non-finite verbal forms. Moreover, there is a 'hybrid' type (see 4) where particles of possession (see 5.2) occur.

In all except (1), the distribution of the *ḫamṭu* or *marû* bases is relevant.

(1) B-[Ø], B-B-[Ø].
(2) B-[a] and B-[e(d)], without or with copula.
(3) B-[ede], B-[eda], B-[ada].
(4) 'Conjugated' participle or 'pronominal conjugation'.

It seems practical to call (2) participles, (3) infinitives, and (4) a conjugated participle.

12.14.1. *B-[Ø], B-B-[Ø]: unextended bases*

The unextended verbal base (single or reduplicated) occurs by itself as an abstract lexical unit and as such it is the form regularly used for entries in the lexical lists.

Note: In Innin šagura, the section [d]Inana za-a-kam "it is yours, O Inana" (Sjöberg 1975, 188 ff. lines 115 ff.) contains verbs cited both as B(-e)-dè and as unextended forms, e.g., šár-šár (= *šutābulum*) "to interchange" (p. 192: 140 f.). The unextended bases are cited here in the manner of entries in a lexical list.

The unextended base may be joined to a preceding substantive (in the absolutive case). In our translation, the substantive may be seen as an object dependent on the verb.

dub-sar "tablet write" = "(who writes tablets =) scribe".

kù-dím "silver form" = "(who forms silver =) silver-smith".

The loanwords in Akkadian, *tupšarru* or *kuttimmu*, show that the verb actually stands as the base by itself, without any further affix.

kù nu-zu(-ù)-ne "(people) not knowing silver".

kur gul-gul "destroying the (foreign) countries".

níĝ-kur-du$_{11}$-du$_{11}$ = ni$_5$-in-kur-du-tu "constantly saying hostile things", "deriding" (= *epēš namûtim* "derision") Inin šagura 159.

ùĝ-ge-en-ge-en "establishing the people".

Note: Reduplicated B-B (base-base) has to be understood as the 'free' (non-*marû*) reduplication of the base (cf. 12.5) which occurs in the *ḫamṭu* variant (if there is any). The clearest example is supplied by du$_{11}$-du$_{11}$ from the *ḫamṭu* base of the verb du$_{11}$(-g)/e/di.

For more examples see Edzard 1972, 5 f.:12 "(Der mah-di-Typus und) der dub-sar-Typus"; 6.8 "Der kur-gul-gul-Typus (freie Reduplikation)".

In some compounds of the type noun—B, the noun cannot be interpreted as an object depending on B:

ki-bala "place transgressing" = "rebellious land".

Note: bala has neither the suffix -a nor -e(d). This becomes clear from the spelling ki-bala-e sá-di "conquering the rebellious land" Gungunum 1:7. See Edzard 1972, 9 fn. 108.

sá-du$_{11}$(-g) = *sattukku* "arrival" = "(regular) delivery" (cf. Krecher 1978, 388), with a pre-verbal element sá "be equal, comparable" (cf. Attinger 1993, 642 f.).

ĝeš-hur = *gišḫurru* "wood carve" = "engraving, design, ground plan". This is not the dub-sar type, because ĝeš is not 'governed' by the verb hur.

ki-gub "place stand" = "position", ki-tuš "place sit" = "dwelling place", ki-nú "place lie down" = "bed".

All these compounds appear to be 'archaic' formations which had already ceased to be productive in Old Sumerian.

Edzard 1972, 8 f. "Der sá-du$_{11}$(-g)-Typus".

12.14.2. *B-[a], B-[ed], without or with copula*

In view of the function which they assume in Sumerian syntax, B-[a] and B-[ed] may be called participles. B in B-[a] is regularly represented by the *ḫamṭu* base of the verb, B in B-[ed] by the *marû* base. Both formations remained productive throughout.

Note: The "mah-di-Typus", proposed by Edzard 1972, 2–5, and contrasted there with the "dub-sar-Typus" (see above 12.14.1), is not a formation of its own, but simply corresponds to B-[ed].

Whereas [a] undergoes no variation, [ed] has four allomorphs: (1) [ed] after a consonant (including H, cf. 3.1.2 p. 19f.) and before a vowel, e.g., nam tar-re-dè [tar-ed-e] "to make a binding promise"; (2) [(e)d] after a vowel and before a vowel, e.g., r̂ú-dè [r̂u-(e)d-e] "to build"; (3) [e(d)] after a consonant in final position, e.g., šúm-mu(-d) [šum-e(d)] "someone who will give"; (4) [(e)(d)] ge$_4$-ge$_4$ [gege(e)(d)] "someone who will return". Moreover, the [e] of [ed] may be assimilated to a preceding (first) vowel in the same way as the [e] of the verbal particles [en], [enden], [enzen], [eš], and the first [e] of [ene]. See above šúm-mu [šum-e(d)].

[ed] marking the *marû* participle is most probably identical with the [ed] occurring in the extended conjugation patterns 1 and 2a (see 12.7.1 and 12.7.2), e.g., ba-ra-ba-zah-e-dè-en [bara-ba-zah-ed-en] "I swear I will not run away (again)".

12.14.2.1. B-[a]; mes-Ane-pada construction

12.14.2.1.1. B-[a]

^{d}Mes-lam-ta-è-a [e-a] "the one having come out of Meslam (sanctuary)" (name of a god). Compare eme è-è(-d) [ed-e(d)] "(snake) darting (its) tongue in and out" Gudea Cyl. A xxvi 25.

kaš naĝ-ĝá [naĝ-a] "who has drunk beer" Lugalbanda B 24.

An-gin$_7$ dím-ma [dim-a] "made like An" (first line and title of Return of Ninurta to Nibru).

kù lá-a-bi-im [laH-a-bi-(a)m] "(NN) was the one weighed the silver" Forde Nebraska 63:13.

As shown above, the verb in the B-[a] participle may in principle be either transitive or intransitive. However, seen statistically, examples of intransitive participles by far outweigh transitive ones.

Edzard 1972, 10–12; Thomsen 1984, 255 ff. passim.

12.14.2.1.2. The mes-Ane-pada construction

A special use of B-[a] is found in the syntagma labelled "mes-Ane-pada" construction by Falkenstein 1949, 135, and 1950, 35 f. with fn. 2. Mes-An-né-pà-da [mes an-e pad-a], name of an Early Dynastic ruler of Ur, literally means "young male chosen by (the agency of) An (ergative)". It is a nominalized form of the phrase *An-e (erg.) mes (absol.) . . . -n-pà(-d) "An chose the young male".

Note: The closeness (and original identity?) of ergative and directive seems to become clear from the syntactical ambiguity of the construction which we may translate either "whom An chose" or "chosen (next to =) by An". It should be stressed, however, that the directive case in no other instance can be shown to express the 'ablative of agent' ("done by someone").

é-ninnû An-né ki ĝar-ra "the Eninnû founded by An" Gudea Cyl. A ix 11.

ninta-zi ^{d}Utu-ù [Utu-e] níĝ-si-sá saĝ-e-eš rig_7-ga "the trustworthy man whom the Sun god presented with righteousness" Šulgi D 5.

dumu Eridu^{ki}-ge dú-da "child born by Eridu" Gudea Cyl. A ii 16.

The full mes-Ane-pada construction may be reduced by the suppression of one or two of its components:

1) Suppression of the absolutive: hur-saĝ-e dú-da "born by the Mountain" Gudea frag. 8+3+5+4 iv' 3' (RIME 3/1, 103).

2) Suppression of the ergative: Lú-pà-da "person chosen (by . . .)" Ur III PN, see Limet 1968, 486; see also pre-Sargonic Lú-pà (for Lú-pad-a) in Struve 1984, 117.

3) Suppression of absolutive and ergative: ĝéštu šúm-ma in ĝéštu-šúm-ma-^{d}En-ki-ka-ke_4 "the one gifted with (ear =) wisdom of Enki" = "the one whom Enki gifted with wisdom" Ean. 2 ii 6–7. The originator of the gift, Enki, is expressed in the genitive, and the whole complex is in the ergative. The participial verbal element of the construction, šúm-ma, is extended by the addition of an 'object' (ĝéštu) in the absolutive case. ĝéštu-šúm-ma, therefore, is not "given wisdom", but someone gifted with wisdom although, formally, [ĝeštu šum-a] is identical with dumu-ki-áĝ-ĝá [dumu kiaĝ-a] "beloved child".

Edzard 1972, 12–14, where transformational rules are given.

12.14.2.2. B-[ed]; B-[ed+copula]

12.14.2.2.1. B-[ed]

Nam-tar-re(-d) "(the god) is making a firm promise", abbreviated PN, SR 65 iii 4.

The same person occurs in the ergative in the same document: Nam-tar-re-dè [namtar-ed-e] ibid. ii 3.

Note: In Yang Zhi 1989 no. A 661:3 an ergative Nam-tar-DU-e is noted (courtesy W. Sallaberger). It is uncertain whether a secondary ergative formation of Namtare is implied: Nam-tar-ré-e, or whether we have to do with a different name.

maškim-di(-d) "functioning as a inspector" Ukg. 4–5 vi 35.

gà-la nu-dag-ge(-d) "not dilatory" Išmē-Dagān A 33.

12.14.2.2.2. B-[ed+copula]

dEn-líl húl-le(-d)-me-en "you are one who pleases Enlil" Šulgi D 31.

níĝ-nu-kúr-ru-dam "it is something that will not be altered" Ninurta C iii 9.

kù máš ĝá-ĝá-dam [ĝaĝa-(e)d-am] "it is silver yielding interest" NG no. 135:2.

B-[edam] not unfrequently has a modal connotation: "has to . . .", "is to . . .", but it sometimes is a matter of subjective interpretation how a given form should be classified.

èn-bi tar-re-dam "to be (asked =) re-examined", final note in Ur III accounts when the calculation made by the scribe still has to be checked.

su-su-dam "to be replaced" UET 3, 37:6.

dah-he-dam "to be added" YOS 4, 18:10.

dam-A. ù M. ge-né-dam "A.'s wife and M. will (have to) prove it" NG no. 214:42.

Note: [gen-ed-am] is in the sing. in spite of the pl. subject. There probably was no form *ge-né(-d)-me-éš *[gen-ed-me-(e)š]. Maybe usage of the conjunction ù "and" caused the form to be understood in a distributive way: "A.'s wife and M. will each (have to) prove it". Or there is an anakoluthon: "A.'s wife and M.—(by them) it is to be established" (suggestion of J. N. Postgate). Edzard 1967, 36–40.

12.14.3. *B-[ede], B-[eda], B-[ada]*

The Sumerian verb has no infinitive form which serves for citation, corresponding to the Akkadian pattern *parāsum*. In lexical lists, verbs are quoted with their base, simple or reduplicated (cf. above 12.14.1).

There are, however, at least in NS and OB, bases with suffixed [ede], [eda], and [ada] which are rendered by Akkadian infinitive constructions in (OB) bilingual texts, e.g.,

bàd-Zimbir^{ki} r̂ú-ù-da saĝ-bi íl-i-da = *dūr Z. epēšam rēšīšu ullâm* "(he definitely ordered me) to build the wall of Sippar (and) to raise its head" RIME 4, 335 Hammu-rāpi 2:22–23 // 23–25.

The three Sumerian forms, B-[ede], B-[eda], and B-[ada] are treated together here because of their similar syntactic behaviour, although the proposed morphological analysis would not favour a parallel arangement of the respective forms.

12.14.3.1. B-[ede]

B is always represented by the *marû* base of the verb. A morphological analysis B-ed-e is obvious. This would, formally, constitute a *marû* participle B-[ed] with the addition of the directive particle [e]. sa_{10}-sa_{10}-dè [sasa-(e)d-e] "in order to buy" would, then, literally mean "at being buying", "at being a buyer".

The reading of -NE as -dè is substantiated by spellings -te (e.g., Sjöberg 1975, 190:120) or $-de_1$ (e.g., NATN 1, 702:2).

lú-Umma^{ki}-a . . . $^{a\text{-}šà}$aša$_5$ tùmu-dè an-ta bala-e-da . . . ^{d}En-líl-le hé-ha-lam-me "may Enlil destroy (any) person of Umma . . . who would cross over here from up there in order to (carry away =) seize fields" Ent. 28–29 A vi 9–20.

1 ma-na kù-luh-ha igi-nu-du$_8$-a sa$_{10}$-sa$_{10}$-dè U. dam-gàr- . . . -ke$_4$ ba-de$_6$ "U., the . . . merchant, took with him one mina of refined silver in order to buy (blind men =) garden workers" Nik. 293 i 1–5.

10 ì-nun : sìla ^{ĝeš}gigir-e AG-dè "10 pounds of butter to (make =) use for (lubricating) (at) the chariot (PN received)" BIN 8, 320:7–9.

^{d}E$_4$-nun-na ù di-dè im-ma-šu$_4$-šu$_4$-ge-éš "the Enūna stopped here to gaze in awe" Gudea Cyl. A xx 23; see Cyl. B i 11 (var. u$_6$).

u$_4$ šu-bala AG-dè ĝeš-hur ha-lam-e-dè . . . An ^{d}En-líl ^{d}En-ki ^{d}Nin-mah-bi nam-bi ha-ba-an-tar-re-eš "An, Enlil, Enki, and Ninmah have definitely decreed . . . that they would overturn the (appointed) time, forsake the (preordained) plans" Lament Sumer and Ur 1–55.

Note: There are in this passage 51 more B-[ede] forms which depend on nam-bi ha-ba-an-tar-re-eš, and there is no B-[eda] variant.

In all these examples and others, the subject implied in B-[ede] and the subject of the finite verb following B-[ede] are identical. Moreover, the subjects implied are all in the ergative. Identity of subject of

B-[ede] and following verb does not—as a rule—occur with B-[eda] for which see 12.14.3.2.

Edzard 1967, 43; but see the reservations made by Attinger 1993, 307.

12.14.3.2. B-[eda]

As with B-[ede], B is always represented by the *marû* base of the verb. In analogy to B-[ede], therefore, a morphological analysis B-ed-a is obvious. B-[eda] would, formally, constitute a *marû* participle B-[ed] with the addition of the locative particle [a].

é-a-ni r̂ú-da ma-an-du$_{11}$ "(Ningirsu) told me (to build =) I should build his house" Gudea Cyl. A iv 20.

ĝidri-u$_4$-sù-r̂á šu ĝá-ĝá-da . . . ^{d}Ig-alim . . . en ^{d}Nin-ĝír-su-ra me-ni-da mu-na-da-dib-e "(Gudea) brings Ig-alim along with himself (and introduces him) to the lord Ningirsu . . ., that he (Ig-alim) hand over a sceptre for long days" Gudea Cyl. B vi 16–23.

Note: Many parallel examples for B-[eda] in Gudea Cyl. B vi 11–x 17. They were listed in Edzard 1972, 25–27; see Edzard 1997, 92–94, for a recent translation. In all the examples (numbering 25) the subject implied in B-[eda] and the subject of the following verb are different, so that B-[eda] is clearly set off against B-[ede] (see 12.14.3.1).

Edzard 1967, 43; Thomsen 1984, 266. However, as with B-[ede], note Attinger's reservations (1993, 307).

In OB Sumerian literary texts, different manuscripts are occasionally inconsistent in their use of B-[ede], B-[eda], or even B-[edam], so that the awareness of the distinction of the respective forms may have been lost.

12.14.3.3. B-[ada]

Although B-[ada] occurs in contexts where it is clearly syntactically paralleled with B-[eda] [B-ed-a], it cannot be analysed as *B-ad-a because we know of no morpheme *[ad].

B in B-[ada] is always represented by the *ḫamṭu* base of the verb. B-[ada] forms are always intransitive or passive and never have an ergative subject.

Since we explain B-[ede] and B-[eda] as *marû* participle constructions, it would only be logical to define B-[ada] as the *ḫamṭu* participle with the addition of a case particle. Here, then, comitative [da] offers itself. Krecher 1978, 401 f. fn. 21, opened the way to this explanation.

Note: The analysis of B-[ada] as B-a-da may challenge our analysis of B-[eda] as [B-ed-a] (12.14.3.2), with locative [a], and lead to propose *[B-ed-da] instead of [B-ed-a]. While we cannot exclude such an analysis, the close contact between B-[ede] and B-[eda] rather favours the interpretation given above.

gú-eden-na eden-du$_{10}$-ge na-de$_6$ šúm-ma-da "that the Edge-of-the-Steppe, the best part of it, be subject to inspection" Gudea Cyl. B xii 8–9.

Contrast (a) eri-ni . . . na-de$_6$ šúm-mu-da [šum-ed-a] "that he might inspect his city . . ." Gudea Cyl. B vi 14 with (b) eri r̂ú-a-da ki-tuš ĝar-ra-da "that cities be built, settlements be founded" Gudea Cyl. B xii 19.

Here, in (a) šúm-mu-da there is a (hidden) ergative subject whereas (b) r̂ú-a-da and ĝar-ra-da have none.

Edzard 1972, 25–29, with many more examples for B-[ada], but still lacking a convincing morphological analysis; Wilcke 1990, 496 with fn. 84.

12.14.4. *Conjugated participle or "pronominal conjugation"*

Falkenstein 1949, 149, introduced the term "pronominale Konjugation" for participles which are 'conjugated' by the addition of particles expressing possession. The term has found wide acceptance in spite of the argument of Jacobsen 1988, 130 f., who took the term to be a misnomer, because "conjugation" should be restricted to the finite verb.

Note: F. Thureau-Dangin, RA 32 (1935) 108 f., to whom Falkenstein refers treats none of the examples quoted below.

The forms in question consist of (1) a *ḫamṭu* or *marû* participle, B-[a] or B-[ed], plus (2) an additional [a] after the *marû* participle plus (3) a particle of possession (cf. 5.2), and (4) in the 1st and 2nd persons, of an element -NE of unknown origin or function, with var. spelling -ni (see 12.14.2 ff. and esp. 12.14.4.13) suggesting -ne rather than -dè as had been assumed by most authors until recently.

The paradigm reads:

ḫamṭu

1st sg.	ku$_4$-ra-ĝu$_{10}$-ne	[kur-a-ĝu-ne] "when I entered"
2nd sg.	ku$_4$-ra-zu-ne	[kur-a-zu-ne]
3rd sg. p.	ku$_4$-ra-ni	[kur-a-(a)ni]
3rd sg. non-p.	ku$_4$-ra-bi	[kur-a-bi]
1st pl.	not attested	
2nd pl.	not attested	
3rd pl.	ku$_4$-ra-ne-ne	[kur-a-(a)nene]

marû

1st sg.	ku_4-ku_4-da-ĝu_{10}-ne	[kuku-(e)d-a-ĝu-ne]
2nd sg.	ku_4-ku_4-da-zu-ne	[kuku-(e)d-a-zu-ne]
3rd sg. p.	ku_4-ku_4-da-ni	[kuku-(e)d-a-(a)ni]
3rd sg. non-p.	ku_4-ku_4-da-bi	[kuku-(e)d-a-bi]
1st pl.	not attested	
2nd pl.	not attested	
3rd pl. p.	not attested, but see 12.14.4.10 for du-ne-ne	

In general, the forms with *ḫamṭu* participle express the idea of something having happened, occurred, and with *marû* participle of something about to happen, occur, or in course of happening, occurring—each time in anticipation of a following finite verbal form or a noun with copula.

A much-quoted contrastive example is ku_4-ra-ni "when she had entered (her bedroom)" Gudea Cyl. B v 12 versus ku_4-ku_4-da-ni "when (the warrior) was about to enter (or: was entering) (his house)" ibid. v 4.

12.14.4.1. 1st sg. *ḫamṭu*: nígin-na-ĝu_{10}-ne "when I had turned around (heaven, turned around the earth)" Inana/Ebeḫ 25 (see 26 f.).

u_4-da kur-šè ĝen-na-ĝu_{10}-ne "when today I will have gone away to the Nether World" Inana's Descent 33.

piriĝ-gin$_7$ KI-LUGAL.GUB-ta ní íl-la-ĝu_{10}-ne "having presented myself, clad in awe, (from =) on the royal dais" Šulgi A 56.

12.14.4.2. 2nd sg. *ḫamṭu*:

nú-a-zu-ne ùĝ ši-mu-e-da-nú-dè
zi-zi-da-zu-ne ùĝ ši-mu-e-da-zi-zi
"when you (O Sungod) have (lain down =) gone to sleep,
the people will also go to sleep with you,
(and) when you will rise again, the people will also rise
with you" Lugalbanda I 235 f.

za-e ĝál-la-zu-ne "now that you have been (back) again" Lugalbanda I 227.

mí du$_{11}$-ga-zu-ni "when you praised" Cohen CLAM II 503:33.

Note: The late version has mè[!?]-a du$_{11}$-ga-zu-ne = [*ṭ*]*āḫaza ina lapātika* "when you (touch =) engage in the battle" (Akk.); cf. Attinger 1993, 604.

12.14.4.3. 3rd sg. person-class *ḫamṭu*: an-gin$_7$ ri-ba-ni ki-gin$_7$ ri-ba-ni [rib-a-(a)ni] "(someone who) was enormous as the skies, enormous as the earth" Gudea Cyl. A iv 15–16.

enkara . . . zà-ga-na lá-a-ni "having tied the e.-weapon to (the king's) side" Martu A 49.

a-ba me-a-nu a-ba me-a-ni "(who not being, who his/her being =) who was it at all?" Gudea Cyl. A iv 23.

ku$_4$-ra-ni "when she entered" (see above p. 138).

The verb "to come, go" in Ur III administrative (messenger) texts merits special attention because of its irregular behaviour; see below 12.14.4.11.

12.14.4.4. 3rd sg. non-person class *ḫamṭu*: sig$_4$ é-šè saĝ íl-la-bi "as (more and more) bricks raised (their) heads =) were piled up for the house" Gudea Cyl. A xix 17.

[gú ^{id}Bu]ranuna-kù-ga-ka ȓú-a-bi [^{id}Bu]ranuna a na$_8$-na$_8$-da-bi "when (the tree) had been planted at [the bank] of the sparkling Euphrates, when it was drinking water (in =) from the Euphrates" Gilg., Enkidu and the Netherworld 28–29.

12.14.4.5. 3rd pl. person class *ḫamṭu*: gen-na-ne-ne "when they had gone (to take away . . .)" TUT 213 r. 7; see RTC 330:7; 335:8.

12.14.4.6. 1st sg. *marû*: u$_4$ zal-la-ĝu$_{10}$-ne e-ne di-da-ĝu$_{10}$-ne "when I spent the day, when I was playing around" = "when I spent the day playing around" TMH NF 3, 25:1 (cf. C. Wilcke, AfO 23 [1970] 84 ff.).

Note: For discussion of the element -ne see 12.14.4.13.

zi-zi-da-ĝu$_{10}$-ne "when I get up" Schooldays 18.

te-ĝe$_{26}$-e-da-ĝu$_{10}$-ne "when I was approaching" Letter Coll. A 1:12.

kur-šà-ga du$_7$-du$_7$-da-ĝu$_{10}$-ne "when I am goring at the innermost part of the foreign country" Inana/Ebeḫ 28.

12.14.4.7. 2nd sg. *marû*: ku$_4$-ku$_4$-da-zu-ni "when you are about to enter" CT 42 no. 3 ii 17, see D. Charpin, Le clergé d'Ur (1986) 282 f.: 7 (= Rīm-Sin D).

Note: For the element -ni (var. of -ne) see 12.14.4.13.

me-lim$_5$-nam-lugal-la mu$_4$-mu$_4$-da-zu-ne "when you robe yourself with the splendour of kingship" Samsu-iluna 50.

e-sír-ra dib-bé-da-zu-ne "when you walk along the street" Father and Son 31.

a-šà ur_4-ru-da-zu-ne "when you are working the field with the seeder-plough" Farmer's Instructions 48.

12.14.4.8. 3rd sg. person class *marû*: um-mi-a . . . èn tar-re-da-ni "when the headmaster . . . was asking" Schooldays 28.

ku_4-ku_4-da-ni "when he was about to enter" (see above p. 138).

For *marû* du-ni (instead of *du-da-ni) see below 12.14.4.11.

12.14.4.9. 3rd sg. non-person class *marû*: e-bi bala-e-da-bi "when (Umma) is about to cross this dyke-and-canal" Ean. 1 r. v 38.

Note: This example, which would be the oldest available, is not unambiguous because OS spelling prevents us from knowing whether a further (unwritten) syllable/particle followed bala-e-da-bi.

na_8-na_8-da-bi see above 12.14.4.4.

dal-le-e-da-bi [dal-ed-a-bi] "when (my sling-stones) are flying" Šulgi B 37.

12.14.4.10. 3rd pl. person class *marû*: hur-saĝ-$umun_7$-kam-ma bala-e-da-n[$e^!$-ne . . .] "when they were crossing the seventh mountain range" Gilg. Huwawa A 62.

Note: This is the var. of ex. NiAA (see Edzard 1991, 188:62). The other ex.s have bala-e-da-bi, bala-e-d[a-n]i, bala-da-ni, bi-ri-bala.

12.14.4.11. Irregular behaviour of the verb ĝen/du

The verb ĝen (*ḫamṭu*)/du (*marû*) "to come, to go" has a partially irregular behaviour with the conjugated participle. Whereas ĝen-na-$ĝu_{10}$-ne (12.14.4.1) or ĝen-na-ne-ne (12.14.4.5) are regular *ḫamṭu* formations, we find du-ni instead of *du-(e)da-ni and du-ne-ne instead of *du-(e)da-ne-ne.

Ki-maš^{ki}-ta du-ni "when he was arriving from Kimaš" HSS 4, 58:9 (see 12, r. 3 and 6).

Šušana^{ki}-šè du-ni "when he was leaving for Susa" HSS 4, 58:3 (see 6, r. 9 and 12).

du presents here an unextended *marû* participle du, i.e., without the addition of [ed]. Clear evidence for such a *marû* participle is offered by Enmerkar 157: lú-kin-gi_4-a kur-šè du-úr [du-r(a)] "to the messenger travelling to the foreign country".

du-ne-ne "when they were leaving (for Šimašgi)" HSS 4, 56 r. 10.

Note: There are spelling variants du-ni-ni ITT 3, 6332 r. 4; HLC 2, 58 85 r. 8; du-ni-ne RA 19, 43 XCII 7; in the latter form, the scribe probably added—mechanically—pl. -(e)ne to sg. du-ni.

For plenty more Ur III examples (as of 1955) see T. Fish, MCS 5, 13–26; also Edzard 1972, 17–19.

12.14.4.12. deli-ĝu$_{10}$-ne etc.

The formations B-a-ĝu$_{10}$-ne etc. have an unexpected parallel in a nominal compound where number "one" occurs in the position of a verbal base:

deli-ni "he/she alone", e.g., Angin dima 197.

deli-ĝu$_{10}$-ne "I all alone" Lugalbanda II 328.

deli-zu-ne "you all alone" Lugalbanda II 356.

Most interestingly, the variant spelling -ne/-ni is shared by B-(d)a-ĝu$_{10}$-ne/-ni and deli-ĝu$_{10}$-ne/-ni. For discussion see 12.14.4.13.

deli-zu-ne mah-me-en "(Suen, . . .) (of/in) your sole self, you are the greatest" ZA 63 (1973) 32 no. 5:20.

deli-zu-ni mah-me-en "(Nuska, . . .) (of/in) your sole self you are the greatest" ZA 63, 17 no. 3a:11.

Note: Å. Sjöberg, not yet realizing the parallel between -ne and -ni, read dili-zu ì-mah-me-en.

deli^{li}-zu$^{!}$-ni mah-me = *e-di-še-ka ṣí-ra-ta* VS 2, 89 obv.(?) 7' // 9'.

Note: I owe these—and more—examples to the late H. Behrens.

12.14.4.13. Conjugated participles: unresolved questions

Taken by themselves, 3rd sg. and pl. person class B-[a]-(a)ni, B-[a]-(a)nene as well as B-[ed]-ani, B-[ed]-anene would most easily be analysed as the *ḫamṭu* or *marû* participles + possessive particles [ani] or [anene].

Such an analysis is not compatible, however, with 1st and 2nd sg. *marû* B-[ed]-a-ĝu$_{10}$/-zu-ne or with 3rd sg. non-person class *marû* B-[ed]-a-bi. Here, before the possessive particle an element [a] is inserted which would remind us, at first glance, of the supposed locative particle in B-[ed]-a (see 12.14.3.2). But addition of a possessive particle after a (dimensional) case particle would disagree with the supposed hierarchy of suffixed nominal morphemes in Sumerian which is: possession—number—case, e.g., ses-ĝu$_{10}$-(e)ne-da "with my brothers" (see above, 8). Therefore, the element [a] in question might as well be of a different origin, with a different function. Or are B-[ed]-a-ĝu$_{10}$-ne, B-[ed]-ani, B-[ed]-a-bi, of different origin, converging to form a common paradigm, disregarding rules of suffix hierarchy?

The second problem is the suffix -ne (var. -ni) added after possessive particles -ĝu$_{10}$, -zu. The former reading -dè instead of -ne has been disproved by the variant spelling -ni, attested both synchronically with -ne and diachronically as a later variant.

Note: C. J. Gadd, Iraq 22 (1960) 161 f., note to line 7, ("-ni must arise from reading NE (regular here) as ne instead of dè"). The variant was also noted by Aro 1961, 327 fn. 1 ("Auffälligerweise ni statt NE (dè) geschrieben"). It was discussed by Attinger 1993, 107 and 311, but without definite conclusion.

To sum up, the function of this [ne, ni] is still unknown, and we cannot explain why it occurs only in forms of the 1st and 2nd person.

A completely analogous distribution of presence or absence of [ne/ni] is found in deli-ĝu$_{10}$/zu-ne "on my/your own", but deli-ni "on his/her own" (see 12.14.4.12).

12.15. Compound verbs

By "compound verbs" Sumerian grammars traditionally understand frozen combinations of a noun (mostly a substantive, rarely an adjective) and a verbal base. The meaning of the compound is not a simple addition of the meanings of the individual elements, but a new one: A+B = C or A+B ≠ A+B. This very often becomes clear from the Akkadian translation, e.g., ki áĝ, equated with *râmu* "to love", cannot be explained by combining the meanings "earth, ground" (ki) and "to measure out" (áĝ).

Note: A. Falkenstein, orally, suggested a gesture of reverence, making a generous move of the hand/arm towards the ground, as the origin of ki áĝ.

Postgate 1974, 35, proposed as "the most specific criterion for distinguishing a compound verb from a 'simple' one" the position of the nominal element immediately before the verbal complex. The nominal element may be extended by an adjective—or, occasionally, by a dependent genitive—but no independent word may enter between the nominal element and the verbal complex. Thus, ki mu-ra-áĝ-en "I love you" would not allow insertion of za-ra as in *ki za-ra mu-ra-áĝ-en "It is you I love".

Civil 1976, 148 f., and Attinger 1993, 179, have been sceptical about the criterion A+B ≠ A+B, "difficilement utilisable dans le cas d'une langue morte aux catégories de pensée étrangère aux nôtres". In fact, ĝéštu(-ga-ni) gub may be taken either literally as "to set (one's) (ear =) mind" or, on a more developed meaning, "to intend/plan to do".

Attinger 1993, 179, showed that there are two types of compound verbs: 1) Both the nominal and the verbal element have an originally independent status; 2) the verbal element serves as a verbalizer; the latter function is essentially restricted to du_{11}(-g)/e/di "to say, do" and AG "to do, make". While (1) may be said to be a closed class, limited by practical usage, (2) may be called an open class. So, e.g., the type nam-naĝar AG "to (do carpentry =) act as a carpenter" could theoretically be extended to as many nam-x formations as there are.

Note: In Akkadian corresponds . . . *-ūta(m) epēšu(m)* for which CAD E 201–225 offers over 50 examples.

Attinger 1993 listed as many as 213 examples for the verbalizer x(-y) du_{11}(-g)/e/di.

Karahashi 2000, 2–10, has reviewed former discussions of the topic, between 1908 and 1993; add Postgate 1974, 35–40.

See, moreover, Thomsen 1984, 269–72; Attinger 1993, 178–82; Krecher 1993, 107–18.

12.15.1. *Compound verbs: free formations*

Karahashi 2000 treated the subject with body-part terms as nominal elements, excluding formations with du_{11}(-g)/e/di and AG (see 12.15.2). On pp. 72–108 she listed over 130 compound verbs.

The main problem with the syntactical interpretation is the function of the nominal element: is it in the absolutive or may it also stand in a different case? Among Karahashi's examples, there are 91 (out of 130, i.e., 70%) with a nominal element which (in our Latin transliteration) ends in a vowel: á "arm, side", gaba "breast, chest", ĝìri "foot", gú "neck", gù "voice", igi "eye, front", ki "place", ní "self", su "body, flesh", šu "hand", zi "breath", zú "tooth". All these may, theoretically, be in the absolutive, or in the directive (with the [e] assimilated). So, šu ti/te(-ĝ) "to receive, to take" could be interpreted either as "to make (an object) (absolutive) come close to the hand (directive)" or as "to make the hand (absolutive) come close (to an object)". See below, p. 145f., for šu ti/te(-ĝ).

On the other hand, a nominal element ending in a consonant, e.g., dùg "knee", ĝéštu(-g) "ear", háš "thigh", saĝ "head", šà(-g) "heart, middle part", is clearly recognizable as an absolutive if it stands by itself. šà(-g) huĝ "to soothe the heart" can only have [šaĝ-Ø] as the nominal element, to the exclusion of *[šage] or *[šaga].

But a more important criterion for determing the syntactical character of the nominal element is the form taken by an "object" depending on a compound verb, whether as an independent part of speech or as an infixed particle.

If the nominal element is in the absolutive, there cannot be a second absolutive as a second "object" (or "subject" where the meaning of the verb is intransitive). It will have to stand in a dimensional case. Put the other way round, this means that if a second "object" (or "subject") is in fact in a dimensional case, it may be taken as proof that the nominal element of the compound verb is in the absolutive. This argument applies equally to dimensional indicators in the verbal chain (see 12.8).

tukumbi šu mu-ri-bar-re(-n) "if I set you free" Prov. Coll. 5.55:3 (E. I. Gordon, JCS 12 [1958] 46).

Here, the "object" of šu bar "to set free" is in the directive [(e)ri], and šu stands in the absolutive.

Note: For šu bar (< bar̂) see Krecher 1993, 113.

ninda [ninda-e] ĝeš ha-ba-ni-tag "I (Šulgi) indeed offered (bread =) food" Šulgi A 55.

Whatever the original meaning of ĝeš tag (touching wood in a ceremony?), ĝeš is in the absolutive.

nam ge$_4$-rí-íb-tar nam-du$_{10}$(-g) gú-mu-rí-íb-tar "let me make a firm promise for you, let me make a benevolent firm promise for you" Šulgi D 384 f.

nam is in the absolutive, the "object" in the directive [(e)ri].

é-e ĝál ba-an-taka "he (loosened the . . . at the house =) he opened the house".

ĝál (meaning unknown) is in the absolutive, the "object" in the directive.

Note: The nominal element ĝál is—graphically—the same as ig "door". It was also used for the abstract notion ĝál "to be, to exist".

urdu-dè lugal-ni [lugal-(a)ni-e] zà(-g) mu-da-DU-àm [mu-n-da-n-DU-am] "the slave (had it with him that he set the side next to his master =) was allowed to go side by side with his master" Gudea Stat. B vii 32–33.

zà(-g) "side" is in the absolutive and lugal-ni in the directive.

si-a ^{d}Inana me-kur-ra-ke$_4$ šu al-du$_7$-du$_7$ "be silent, Inana, the ordinances of the Netherworld are absolutely perfect" Inana's Descent 132, etc.

The original meaning of šu du_7 is probably "to move the hand directly (towards a goal)" (with du_7 "to make a direct movement (towards a goal)"). The "object" me-kur-ra(-k) is in the directive.

Gù-dé-a gal mu-zu gal ì-ga-túm-mu "Gudea knows much, and he (also brings great =) is able, too, to accomplish great things" Gudea Cyl. A vii 9–10.

Here, the nominal element is an adjective. It is probably to be understood in the absolutive case, but an unmarked adverb cannot be excluded.

12.15.1.1. Extended nominal element

The nominal element of a compound verb is occasionally extended by an adjective; it is uncertain, however, whether such an extension was a productive feature of the system or whether it was restricted in use by phraseology.

Beside igi bar "to look (at)" there is igi-zi bar:

^{d}En-líl-e en ^{d}Nin-ĝír-su-šè igi-zi mu-ši-bar [mu-n-ši-n-bar] "Enlil had directed his (true =) meaningful gaze toward the lord Ningirsu" Gudea Cyl. A i 3.

Only an informant would still be able to tell whether igi-zi bar was tantamount to zi-dè-eš igi bar "to look in a true, reliable, meaningful way". Be that as it may, the addition of zi after igi adds a shade of meaning to the verbal expression and may, therefore, well be called adverbial.

me-gal-gal ezem-An-na-$ĝu_{10}$ [ezem-An-a(k)-ĝu-e] šu-gal ma-du_7-du_7 "all the great performances, my 'festival of An', are performed for me in ritual perfection" Gudea Cyl. A x 18.

12.15.1.2. šu ti/te(-ĝ) and other compound verbs and the special behaviour of their "objects"

šu ti/te(-ĝ) "to receive, to take" is by far the most frequently attested compound verb, due to its ubiquitous usage in legal and administrative documents.

The subtle difference between OB Akkadian *maḫāru* "to receive" (without any ensuing consequence) and *leqû* "to receive" (with ensuing consequences, e.g., the obligation to repay a loan) has no counterpart in Sumerian where šu ti/te(-ĝ) is used in both senses.

For examples from literary texts, see Karahashi 2000, 168–71.

As a rule, the "object" of šu ti/te(-ĝ) is in the directive or locative, and the person from whom something is received is originally in the terminative:

lugal-a-ni (erg.) siskur ara_x(DU)-zu-ni [arazu-(a)ni-e] Gù-dé-a-áš en ^{d}Nin-ĝír-su-ke_4 (erg.) šu ba-ši(-n)-ti "his master (accepted) from Gudea, the lord Ningirsu accepted from him prayer and rite" Gudea Cyl. A ii 21–22; cf. iv 1–2; Cyl. B iii 3–4.

Occasionally, mostly in texts of OB tradition, the "object" of šu ti/te(-ĝ) is in the absolutive as if—contrarily to what one would expect—there actually were a second absolutive:

... ^{d}Nuska á-áĝ-ĝá-^{d}En-líl-lá šu ba-an-ti-a-ta "after ... Nuska had received Enlil's instructions" Enlil and Ninlil 2:44.

The "object" is [a'aĝa-Enlil-a(k)] instead of *[a'aĝa-Enlil-ak-e].

Falkenstein 1950, 134 n. 1 judged this as "der klarste Fall für die Beeinflussung der Konstruktion eines sumerischen Verbums durch die seines akkadischen Gegenstücks".

A comparable—secondary—construction is also found with si sá "to direct, adjust, etc.":

^{giš}ù-šub-kù(-g) [s]i íb-sá "a (clean =) brand-new brick-mould was adjusted" Gudea Cyl. A A v 6.

The "subject", in the passive construction, would be expected to be *[ušub-kuge].

For an exhaustive treatment of the compound verb si sá see C. Wilcke 2003.

In the above cases, the nominal element and the verbal base have practically coalesced so as to behave like a simple transitive verb. For this phenomenon two reasons may be adduced: (1) It was the result of an independent, internal evolution of Sumerian morphosyntax. (2) Or—more probably in view of the Sumero-Akkadian linguistic area—it was due to the influence of the syntax of the underlying Akkadian verb, e.g., *leqû* in the case of šu ti/te(-ĝ), or *ešēru, šūšuru* in the case of si sá (Falkenstein's position).

Note: In the case of šu ti/te(-ĝ), by Ur III also the notation of the person from whom something was received had undergone a change—at least in juridical and administrative contexts: Instead of PN-šè (see above, Gudea Cyl. A ii 21–22), ki-PN(-a(k))-ta "from (the place of) PN" or only ki-PN, became more customary. Here, the influence of *itti* PN *leqû* is obvious.

This change of syntax has a clear parallel in the verb "to buy", sa_{10}/sa_{10}-sa_{10}, where the seller was originally noted with the terminative, PN-šè, but by Ur III times with ki-PN(-a(k))-ta, or simply ki-PN; see J. Krecher, RlA 5 (1976–80) 496 r., and C. Wilcke, ibid. 505 r.

12.15.1.3. Complete incorporation of the nominal element

In a final—Old Bab.—stage of the evolution of the morpho-syntactic behaviour of compound verbs, the nominal element could be transferred to stand immediately before the verbal base, in finite and non-finite forms. Sometimes, in such cases, the nominal element was simultaneously kept in place, redundantly, before the string of prefixed verbal particles, e.g., si . . . -si-sá (see below).

é-ĝi$_6$-pàr-en-na . . . mu-un-ki-ĝar "I(!) founded . . . the abode of the en (priestess)" RIME 4, 472 f. no. 2:16–19 (Anam of Uruk).

A form *ki mu-un-ĝar "he laid the ground" has been transformed, but the reason remains unknown.

ga-bi nu-mu-ra-šu-gíd-e "(the sheep) no (longer) offer their milk to you" LamUr I 362.

So ms. C = STVC 17 v 2'; ms. N = MBI 6 ii 48' has ga nu-mu-ra-AG-e.

The underlying verb is šu gíd "to stretch out the hand (in either direction)" = "to offer, to receive" (cf. Karahashi 2000, 161 f.).

A post-OB example is hé-nir-ĝál "may he be authoritative" (PN) A. Moortgat, Rollsiegel ^{3}(1988) 554.

dumu-An-na An-x-la-ta téš mu-u$_8$-da-mah-di "daughter of An (= Bau), . . ., you alone are able to be as outstanding as An(?)" CT 36, 40 (r.) 7 (Bau B).

Note: Does Ur III PN Íb-ta-ab-PA-è RA 8 (1911) 184 no. 1:10' already represent a case of incorporated pa è "to come forth radiantly"? In view of Íb-ta-ab-è and Íb-ta(-b)-è (see Limet 1968, 431), Íb-ta-ab-PA-è has perhaps to be seen as a graphic variant.

The nominal element is sometimes found twice with the verb si sá:

šà-bi(-a) ur-saĝ-ur-saĝ-e-ne si mu-si-sá-e-ne "all the warriors go straightway into the interior (of the sanctuary)" Keš Hymn 60 (OB).

kù$^?$ a níĝ-izi-te-na si mi-ni-in-si-sá
ĝarza me-mah šu mi-ni-ib-šu-du$_7$

". . . water which quenches fire has been directed there, the rites and sublime ordinances have been performed there in the most perfect way (for us) Flood i 44–45.

Cf. Krecher 1987, 69; Karahashi 2000, 4; in general Wilcke 2003.

12.15.2. *Compound verbs with a verbalizer*

Attinger 1993, 179, noted that there is a group of compound verbs with the bases du_{11}(-g)/e/di or AG essentially serving the function of turning a noun into a verb, i.e., serving as verbalizers.

Note: Verbalization is a wide-spread phenomenon. It is realised, morphologically, either (a) by a special ending attached to the noun or (b) by a special verb. For (a) note, in Indo-European, -ize (English), -(is)ieren (German), -iser (French), etc., and for (b) etmek "to do" (Turkish), kardan "to do" (Persian). Semitic languages have not developed a productive way to verbalize nouns: here examples such as Akkadian *ruggubu* "to provide with a roof/an upper storey (*rugbu*)" or Arabic *talfana* "to telephone" (extremely unpopular) are rather exceptions to the rule. Sumerian would belong to category (b).

Attinger 1993 collected 213 examples for x du_{11}(-g)/e/di. A count for x AG has not yet been made. While verbalization applies to the majority of verbal compounds of the types x AG or x du_{11}(-g)/e/di, there certainly is a number of verbs which should rather be classified under 12.15.1, "free formations"; however, our modern interpretation is often arbitrary.

We will only quote a few examples each for (a) evident verbalization and (b) uncertain cases. In general, Attinger 1993 should be consulted for du_{11}(-g)/e/di.

12.15.2.1. Clear cases of verbalization

áš du_{11}(-g)/e/di "to say a curse" = "to curse"; di du_{11}(-g) "to say, make legal case" = "to judge"; A-nir du_{11}(-g) "to say a lamentation" = "to lament"; gù du_{11}(-g) to say, make a voice" = "to shout, yell, roar"; ĝiš du_{11}(-g) "to do the penis" = "to have intercourse with a woman"; maškim du_{11}(-g) "to do the bailiff" = "to act as a bailiff"; tu_6 du_{11}(-g) "to say an incantation" = "to conjure", etc.

Note: No references are offered because all the evidence is amply available in Attinger 1993, 414–765 (alphabetical catalogue).

[e_4] pa_5-bi šu-bala ba-ra-ak-ke_4(-n) "I will not—I swear—change (the course) of (Girsu's) canals and dykes" Ean. 1 r. i 20–21.

šu bala "to make the hand go across something" is a compound in itself; it has been verbalized—or re-verbalized—by the addition of AG "to make"; "to effect a change".

PN_{1-5} enim PN_6-ra in-na-an-eš-a [i-na-n-e-(e)š-a] šu-bala bí-in-AG-éš "PN_1 . . . PN_5 (changed =) contradicted what they had said to PN_6" NG no. 113:17–24.

sa-gaz lú mu-na [mu-n-a(k)] "someone committed a robbery here" NG no. 121:3.

Note: There is no need to restore mu-na<-AG>, as Falkenstein did in his edition.

12.15.2.2. Verbalization no longer recognizable to us

al du_{11}(-g)/e/di "to wish, to strive for" has a nominal element al with unknown etymology: see Attinger 1993, 443 with fn. 1179.

sá du_{11}(-g)/e/di "to reach, arrive" is derived from sá "être égal à" by Attinger 1993, 641; in fact, "to say 'equal'" = "to measure up to something", may be the appropriate etymology; but it is not certain.

a-ne/e-ne du_{11}(-g)/e/di "to enjoy, play" has a nominal element which Landsberger (see Attinger 1993, 472 fn. 1294) equated with the personal pronoun "he, she"; Landsberger saw the origin in counting-out rhymes: "it is him, her"; but this is uncertain.

12.15.3. *Difficult cases: artificial splits?*

saĝ(-[eš]) [rig] "to give as a present" has been claimed as a pre-Old Akkadian loan from Akkadian *šarākum* "to present" in its stative form *šarik*, with an artificial split of the Semitic root ŠRK into [sa(ĝ)] and [rig].

Cf. Karahashi 2000, 140 with fn. 93, and see already I. J. Gelb, MAD 3 (1957) 284.

Note: While the spelling of the first, 'nominal', element, [sa(ĝ)], is consistently SAG, [rig] offers several—diachronical—spelling variants, each one of the diri(g) type: PA.KAB = rig_8 (see below, Ean. 2 vii 6); KAB.[SA]G.DU = rig_9 (see below, Steible 1982 b 201); PA.KAB.DU = rig_7 in Ur III and OB. These spellings still remain unexplained.

^{d}Nin-ĝír-su-ra Lum-ma-gin_7-du_{10} saĝ-éš mu-ni-rig_8 "(Eannatum) gave (the canal) L. as a present to Ninĝirsu" Ean. 2 vii 3–6.

Note: Like with nam tar, saĝ(-[eš]) [rig] uses the directive for the (god or) person in whose favour the action is made.

[sa]ĝ r[i]g_9(KAB.[SA]G.DU Steible 1982 b 201: AnAgr. 4 ii 2' (OS, in broken context).

^{ĝeš}gu-za ^{d}En-ki-k[e_4] saĝ ha-ba-ra-PA.KA[B.DU]-ga-a suhuš-bi ha-ra-ab-ge-ge-in "I (= Ninlil) will certainly consolidate for you the throne which Enki has already given you as a present" Šulgi R 87.

Note: saĝ rig_7 here governs the dative (verbal infix [(e)ra]) instead of the directive—perhaps in parallel with the following [ha-(e)ra-b-gege-n].

^{d}En-ki-ke_4 Mar-tu máš-anše saĝ-e-eš mu-ni-rig_7 "Enki gave the cattle as a gift to the Amurru (nomad)" EWO 249.

Summing up, saĝ [rig] as a split of **šarik* would be quite an unusual type of borrowing. At least two arguments may be raised against a—direct—Akkadian origin of the verb in question: (1) Why was [saĝ] chosen to represent the first syllable of alleged *šarik*, instead of, e.g., sá? (2) Why was [saĝ rig] most often construed with the addition of the adverbiative ending [eš(e)] (cf. above 4.2.(5))?

For (2) one could refer to the parallel—post-OB—níĝ-ba-aš ba = *ana qīšti šarāku* "to give as a present" (see CAD Q 156 *qâšu* lex.). But given the late attestation of [niĝba-š ba], one would rather suggest that this idiom was formed by analogy with [saĝ-eš rig].

The question has to be left to further research.

A noun rig_7 "enclosed room(?)" was discussed by Krecher 1966, 153 f. It is not clear whether the spelling of the verbal element of [saĝ(-eš) rig] was derived from the respective noun or vice versa.

Some phonetic similarity has been noted between the noun ĝéštu (-g) (GIŠ.TÚG.PI and similar spellings) "ear" and the verb ĝeš tuku "to hear". Karahashi 2000, 84 f.: "in giš-tuku, giš is probably chosen not because of its literal meaning but because of its phonological proximity to geštú 'ear'"; see her excursus on "giš-tuku" ibid. p. 86 f.

There is hardly good reason to propose a "split" ĝéštu(-g) → ĝeš [tuG], and such was not Karahashi's intention either. For ĝéštu(-g) "ear" is regularly prolonged by -gV (e.g., ĝéštu-ga-ni [ĝeštug-ani] whereas tuku in ĝeš tuku is, without exception, prolonged by -a, -àm (see Karahashi 2000, 86 f.).

Whatever the etymology of ĝeš tuku, it cannot be directly related to [ĝeštug] "ear".

12.16. Nominalization of finite verbal forms

Sumerian finite verbal forms may be turned into nouns by the addition of a morpheme [a], the nominalizer. Once such a change from verb to noun took place, the newly attained nominal complex behaves like a noun: it may be inflected for case; possessive particles may be added. A nominalized complex cannot, however, be put in the plural.

Nominalization is important in Sumerian syntax because inflected complexes often stand for what we would interpret as subordinate clauses. Sumerian nominalization most probably influenced Akkadian which stands out, among other Semitic languages, by its great variety of infinitive constructions.

J. Aro, Die akkadischen Infinitivkonstruktionen (= StudOr. 26, 1961), esp. pp. 323–32, "Die sumerischen Entsprechungen und Vorbilder der akkadischen Infinitivkonstruktionen"; Thomsen 1984, 241–50; Attinger 1993, 305.

The origin of nominalizer [a] is unknown. It may be added to both *ḫamṭu* and *marû* bases along with the respective conjugation patterns. For this reason, identity of particle [a] with the ending of the *ḫamṭu* participle (r̂ú-a, see 12.14.2) is quite improbable.

lú . . . di-ku$_5$-a-na šu ì-íb-bala-e-a "he who . . . will (let the hand pass over =) disregard his (= Gudea's) judgment" Gudea Stat. B viii 42–43 (*marû*).

lú É-ninnû . . . in-r̂ú-a "who (had) built the Eninnû" Gudea Stat. A caption 4–6 and passim in the Gudea Corpus (*ḫamṭu*).

The nominalized phrase has, as a rule, a head or antecedent on which it depends, e.g., lú "person", níĝ "thing", u$_4$ "day, time", mu "year", etc.; but often the antecedent has to be supplied, because it is not explicitly expressed.

It seems most practical to arrange the material by the case in which the nominalized phrase occurs, usually indicated by a case particle following the nominalizer [a], though we shall not provide examples for every case.

12.16.1. *The nominalized phrase is in the absolutive (or "casus pendens"), unmarked (-Ø)*

níĝ Ki-en-gi-ra ba-a-gu(-ul)-la kur-ra ga-àm-mi-íb-gu-ul "what has been destroyed in Sumer, I will destroy in the foreign land" Šulgi D 219; cf. line 335: níĝ Ki-en-gi-ra ba-a-gu-ul-la kur-ra ì-mi-in-gu-ul.

The head of the phrase is níĝ, "thing, what", and the nominalized phrase is, morpho-syntactically, in apposition to, or an adjective added to, níĝ.

^{d}E$_4$-nun-na . . . a-gin$_7$ ba-e-ne-diri-ga "the Enūna . . . among whom you (= Inana) are so much superior" Ninmešara 115.

Note: The phrase is to be understood as a vocative which is unmarked.

. . . dam-šè ha-tuku bí-in-du$_{11}$-ga PN$_1$ PN$_2$ nam-érim-àm "PN$_1$ (and) PN$_2$ swore that (PN$_3$) declared: 'I will take (PN$_4$ . . .) as a wife'" NG no. 15:6–9; cf. ibid. nos. 16:6–11, 17:7–10, etc., for similar statements made under oath.

Note: It is interesting to note that the quotation of direct speech is not made with the addition of the quotation particle [(e)še], but with nominalized [bi-n-dug] "he declared".

Note: Here, a deposition is confirmed, under oath, by witnesses. nam-érim-àm literally means "it is an evil (which should befall me [= the oath-taking party] in case of perjury)". It is used for an oath concerning something that already happened ("assertory oath"), as against the oath taken as a promise way that one would do or not do—or refrain from—something ("promissory oath").

PN_1 PN_2-na-an-na lú nu-ù-da-nú-a nam-érim-àm "PN_1 swore that apart from PN_2 nobody slept with me" NG no. 24:9'–12' (for = nanna see 13.3).

The syntactical relation between the nominalized statement and the following nam-érim-àm is difficult to establish. One might say the nominalized phrase is in a casus pendens.

See Falkenstein 1956, 63 ff. for the different formulations of "assertorischer Eid" and "promissorischer Eid".

12.16.2. *The nominalized phrase is in the genitive*

diĝir-Gù-dé-a . . . lú E-an-na in-r̂ú-a-kam [i-n-r̂u-a-(a)k-am] "it is the (personal) god of Gudea . . . the one who built the Eana" Gudea Stat. C i 2–5.

ur-saĝ-ug_5-ga ì-me-ša-ke_4-éš [i-me-(e)š-a-(a)k-eš] "because they (= the aforementioned mythological beings) are warriors (once) slain (by Ninĝirsu)" Gudea Cyl. A xxvi 15.

Note: [imešak] is a free standing genitive to which the adverbiative ending [eš] has been added. We cannot give an answer to how [imešakeš] was distinguished from a construction mu . . . -a-šè (see 12.16.5), i.e., *mu . . . ì-me-éš-a-šè.

enim-ama-ne-ne nu-ub-kúr-ne-a [nu-b-kur-(e)ne-a-a(k)] mu-lugal-bi in-pà-dè-eš "they invoked the royal name that they would not change the (word =) disposition of their mother" NG no. 99:44–46.

Note: In this and in many parallel cases it is not certain whether the nominalized phrase should really be understood as standing in the genitive, resumed by the -bi of mu-lugal-bi, or whether it stands in the absolutive, as a "casus pendens".

12.16.3. *The nominalized phrase is in the locative*

u_4 ^{d}Nin-ĝír-su-ke_4 šà-ge ba-pà-da-a [ba-n-pad-a-a] "when Ninĝirsu had (called him in the heart =) chosen him" En. I 2 i 7–ii 1.

The nominalized phrase is in the locative, and there is no genitival (regens-rectum) relation between the head (u_4) of the phrase and the phrase itself. Therefore, the phrase can only be defined—morpho-syntactically—as an apposition or an adjective joined to u_4. If we see the phrase as an apposition the head (u_4) would virtually be in the locative, too, with the locative case particle deleted following a rule that in a sequence of parallel syntactical members only the last one will be marked by a case particle: u_4(-da) . . . -a. Cf. the sequence an ki-a "in heaven (and) on earth" where the locative after an (*an-na = [an-a]) has been deleted: an//ki-a.

If, on the other hand, we see the relation between head (u_4) and phrase as a connection of substantive (u_4) + adjective (nominalized phrase), there is no need to postulate the deletion of a case particle after u_4.

By the time of the Ur III dynasty, the separate notation of nominalizer [a] and locative case particle [a] often coalesced so that a single written [a] may stand for both. But note still Hammu-rapi bí-in-du_{11}-ga-a RIME 4, 335 no. 2:20.

The u_4 . . . -a construction is extremely popular. In Akkadian it has an exact parallel in the sequence *inu/inūma* . . . Moreover, the sometimes very elaborate construction u_4 . . . (1) . . . -a, (2) . . . -a, (3) . . . -a (etc.) u_4-ba . . . "when . . ., (at that day =) then . . ." (e.g., En. I 20 i 9–iii 2) has its counterpart in Akkadian *inu* . . . *inūmišu* . . . "when . . ., then . . .", e.g., Hammu-rapi RIME 4, 335 no. 2:1–25//1–28.

mu balaĝ ušumgal-kalam-ma ba-dím-ma [ba-dim-a-a] "the year (when) the harp (called) 'Dragon of the Land' was fashioned", year name Gudea of Lagaš 3; see Edzard 1997, 27.

The construction of the year date formulae exactly follows the pattern u_4 . . . -a (see before). The nominalized phrase is in the locative and so is—virtually—the head mu.

However, as against the u_4 . . . -a construction, the mu . . . -a construction was often reduced to a formula where [a] has been deleted after the verbal form, e.g., mu Lugal-Ba-gára é-a ba!-ku_4 "the year (when) the Lord of Bagara entered (his) house" Gudea year 16; see Edzard 1997, 27. The head mu here behaves like a subjunction.

bar še-bi nu-da-sù-sù-da-ka [nu-n-da-n-su(d)sud-a-(a)k-a] "because he (= Ur-LUM-ma of Umma) no longer was willing to (lengthen, extend =) restore that grain (with =) to him" Ent. 28–29 A ii 27.

Note: The syntagma is bar-Noun-ak-a, lit. "at the side of Noun" with the noun here represented by a verbal phrase + nominalizing [a], which we have to understand as "because of . . ."; see PSD B 109 f. bar C, esp. p. 110: 3.

12.16.4. *The nominalized phrase is in the ablative*

ba-dú-ud-dè-en-na-ta [ba-dud-en-a-ta] ninta-kal-ga-me-en "I am a mighty king since I was born" Šulgi A 2.

Ba-gára . . . im-ti-a-ta "after he had come close to the Bagara (sanctuary)" Gudea Cyl. A ii 7.

^{d}Nin-a-zu-ù . . . šùd-da mi-ni-in-pà-pà-da-ta "after Nin-azu . . . had pronounced many blessings thereon" Šulgi X 126.

di šu la-ba-an-ti-en-za-na [la-ba-n(i)-ti-enzen-a] enim-šè la-ba-dúr-ru-ne-en-za-na-ta [la-ba-durun-enzen-a-ta] "because you (pl.) did not accept the verdict (and) did not abide by the word" Enki-hegal/Enkitalu 191 (see Karahashi 2000, 169 no. 12a).

eĝer ba-ùr-ra-ta "after (the flood) had swept thereover" SKL 40.

12.16.5. *The nominalized phrase is in the terminative*

mu ĝeš-nú-PN ba-an-zuh-a-šè "because he had stolen PN's bed" NG no. 203:3–4.

Note: mu "name" and the following nominalized phrase may be defined—morpho-syntactically—as a head noun with an apposition, both standing in the same case, but with the case particle deleted after the head noun: mu[-šè] . . . -a-šè. See the discussion in 12.16.5 locative under u_4 . . . -a.

mu PN-e mu-lugal pà-da du_{11}-ga-na ba-ni(-n)-ge-na-šè PN_2 PN_3 ba-an-tuku "because PN_1 had (confirmed on his saying =) admitted that (the royal name had been invoked =) an oath (invoking) the king had been sworn, PN_3 married PN_2" NG no. 14:18–21.

Sumerian mu . . . -a-šè constructions correspond to Akkadian subordinate clauses with *aššum* "because".

12.16.6. *The nominalized phrase is in the equative*

lugal-ra . . . e_4 mu-na-a-tu_5-a-gin_7 [mu-na-V-tu-a-gin] "as I (= Inana) bathed for the king" Šulgi X 14–15; see 16, and cf. lines 19, 21, 24, etc.

Note: The comparative function of -gin_7 "in the same way as . . .", "like . . ." here coalesced with a temporal function.

Cf. Lugal 390–392, 419–422, 483, 617.

12.16.7. *Nominalized phrase with a possessive particle*

u_4 An-né kur-kur-ra saĝ-ki ba-da-an-gíd-da-ba [ba-bda-n-gid-a-b(i)-a] "when An had frowned upon all the lands" LamSumUr 22; see ibid. 23–26.

Note: We have to do with an extension of the u_4 . . . -a construction (see 12.16.3). The locative supposed to follow the nominalized verbal form has been shifted after the possessive particle -bi.

^{d}En-líl lú-nam-tar-tar-re-dè a-na bí-in-AG-a-ba ^{d}En-líl-le Elam^{ki} . . . kur-ta im-ta-an-è "what Enlil who makes inescapable decisions actually did is that he, Enlil, brought the Elamites . . . down against us from their highlands" LamSumUr 165 f.

[ana binAGaba] lit. is "in its 'what-he-did thereby'".

Note: lú here functions as a 'relative pronoun'; hardly "in order to decide the fate of mankind" (Michalowski's translation), because lú "person" must be kept separate from (nam-)lú-u_{18}-lu [(nam)lulu] "man(kind)".

CHAPTER THIRTEEN

POST-NOMINAL AND/OR POST-VERBAL PARTICLES OTHER THAN CASE PARTICLES (5.4)

This heading is a catch-all for different kinds of particles, both nominal and nominal/verbal (general), lacking a collective denominator. We kept them apart from the (nominal) case particles in spite of Attinger 1993, 260 "les postpositions 'isolantes'" (Krecher's term).

The particles described here cannot even be said to follow a common morpho-syntactical behaviour pattern, because some of them may be affixed directly to a noun, pronoun, or finite verbal form ([(e)še], [ĝešen], [nanna]), and some to a nominalized verbal form ([ĝešen], [ri]), while [šuba] stands apart in that it follows a noun standing in a dimensional case (but also may be the head of a copula).

The matter is in need of more thorough treatment.

13.1. The particle [(e)še]

Sumerian has a suffixed quotation particle corresponding to Akkadian *-mi*. [(e)še] is a particle which may be added to both nouns and verbs (see 4.1). It is first found in the Gudea corpus, spelled éše(ŠÈ); -ši occurs in Ur III, and OB and later texts (including the lexical evidence) have -e-še.

e-še: *mi-i* KI.TA ("mi, suffixed") NBGT I 461 (MSL 4, 147); II 13 (ibid. 149).

lú an-gin$_7$ ri-ba ki-gin$_7$ ri-ba-éše "the person who, as you said, was as enormous as the skies, enormous as the earth" Gudea Cyl. A v 13 (see ibid. 15).

Note: Instead of éše, -šè was read until Thomsen 1984, 102, and it was interpreted as the terminative case particle ("concerning . . .").

Ur-ni$_9$-ĝar-ra Ab-ba-sa$_6$-ga-a kù in-da-tuku-ši mu-lugal . . . ga-ab-su bí-in-dug$_4$ "A declared: 'name of the king, I will repay it by . . .', having said (-ši) that (U. has silver with him =) he owes U. silver" TCL 2,2557:1–6.

ĝeš-nú-ĝu$_{10}$ gub-ba-ab-zé-en ga-ba-nú-e-še "'set up my bed, I want to sleep' I said" Schooldays 15; see ibid. 26, 29, . . . 41.

The origin and etymology of [(e)še] are unknown; there can hardly be a connection with the adverbiative particle (see 11).

See Falkenstein 1952, 113–130, who still thought of [eše] as a "Potentialis- und Irrealissuffix".

13.2. [ĝešen] ([ĝišen])

The suffixed particle [ĝešen] ([ĝišen]) is rarely attested in context and, therefore, its function may only be described in a preliminary way.

me-en-dè-ĝeš-en, me-en-zé-en-ĝeš-en, e-ne-ne-ĝeš-en = *nīnu-man, attunu-man, šunu-man* "were it we, you (pl.), they" OBGT I 460–462 (MSL 4, 52).

ĝeš-en = ma-an (KI.TA) (i.e., used as a suffix) NBGT I 460 (MSL 4, 147).

Both AHw. (following GAG § 152d) and CAD M/1, 202, define Akkadian *man* as a particle denoting the irrealis mood; this would also suit the Sumerian context of [ĝešen].

It is not yet possible to propose an etymology for [ĝešen] ga-nam ga-ug$_5$-g(a)-en-dè-en [ga-ug-enden] ĝeš-en ga-an-gu$_7$, ga-nam ga-ti-le-en-dè-en [ga-til-enden] ĝeš-en ga-bí-íb-ĝar "well, we might die (Akkad. sg.), (so) let me eat (it all); (or) well, we might live (Akkad. sg.), (so) let me store (food)" BWL 244 f.: 42–45.

Note: ĝeš-en is on both occasions written at the beginning of a new line, as if it were a separate word. This, however, must be a misunderstanding, since the Babylonian grammarians defined [ĝešen] as a suffix (KI.TA), see above.

á mu-e-da-áĝ-ĝeš-še-en á-áĝ-ĝá ma-ab-šúm-mu-un-e-še "if I would tell you to do something you would say '(how come) you are giving me orders'" Father and Son 43 f.

igi-r̂ú-r̂ú-a na-an-gig-ga-ĝeš-še-en ki-ad-da-ĝá mu-e-(var. ì-)kiĝ-ĝá-ĝeš-še-en ĝá-e mu-zu-šè gi$_6$-an-bar$_7$(NE)-ba ù-du$_{10}$ nu-mu-e-da-ku-ku-u[n] ". . . because of you I am unable to sleep and rest at day or at night" Father and Son 119–121.

13.3. The suffixed particle [nanna]

In addition to the syntagma -X-da nu-me-a "not being with X" = "without X" (see 5.4.2.6.a), another Sumerian expression rendering the idea of "without" is suffixed -[nanna]. It occurs with pronouns, nouns, and nominalized verbal forms.

me-en-dè-na-an-na	=	*ša lā n[iāti]*	"without us"
me-en-zé-en-na-an-na	=	*ša lā [kunūti]*	"without you"
e-ne-ne-na-an-na	=	*ša lā [šunūti]*	"without them"
		OBGT I 488–490 (MSL 4, 53)	

It is not yet possible to propose an etymology for the particle [nanna], but it would not be to bold to propose that the initial element [n(a)-] is related with the [n] of negative [nu] or prohibitive [na].

PN-na-an-na lú nu-ù-da-nú-a . . . (see 12.16.1).

dub-lá-mah u_4-ul-lí-a-ta ki-šu-tag šuku-UD šub-ba ì-me-a-na-an-na é-bi nu-r̂ú-àm "apart from the D. (where) from ancient days offerings (and) . . . which had been neglected had not been there (and) (apart from) that house which had not been built (Amar-Suena did build . . .)" RIME 3/2, 254, Amar-Suena 9:3–8.

13.4. The particle [šuba]

šub-ba [šuba] is originally either a *ḫamṭu* participle of šub "to throw, leave (behind), neglect": "left neglected", or an imperative: "leave (it)" (suggestion of J. N. Postgate). In the latter case, šub-ba would closely follow Akkadian *ezib/ezub*. [šuba] secondarily became a particle expressing the idea "apart from". [šuba] is not, however, directly suffixed (see note below), thus not strictly fulfilling the features of the particles collected under 13.

me-en-dè-a šub-ba	=	*ez[ib niāti]*	"left apart from us"
šub-ba-me-en-zé-en	=	*ezi[b kunūti]*	"you (pl.) are set apart"
e-ne-ne-a šub-ba	=	*ezi[b šunūti]*	"left apart from them"
šub-ba-me-en-da-nam	=	*ezi[b niātima]*	"it is we who are set apart"
šub-ba-me-en-za-nam	=	*ezi[b kunūtima]*	"it is you (pl.) who are set apart"
e-ne-ne-a šub-ba-kam	=	*ezi[b šunūtima]*	"it is of being left apart from them"

OBGT I 491–496 (MSL 4, 53)

Note: In none of the six occurrences does [šuba] function as an immediately suffixed particle. It is only the Akkadian translations that treat [šuba] on the same level as [ĝešen] (13.2) or [nanna] (13.3). [šuba] cannot even be defined as a suffixed particle, because it may also stand as the head of a phrase containing a copula.

For more lexical evidence see CAD E 429 ezib (prep.) lex. sect.

mu ^{d}Ba-ú nin-ĝá-ka-e(!) šub-ba é-^{d}Nanna-kam ⌜ĝarza⌝ ki-gub-ba nu-tuku-a = *aššum* Bau *bēltia ezub ina bīt Suen parṣa u mazzāzam lā išûma* "that apart from that which relates to my mistress Bau, I have no office (or) position in the house of the Moongod" (transl. of CAD E 429) PBS 1/2, 135: 13–15 (see Falkenstein 1952, 122; van Dijk 1953, 128).

Note: [šuba] here, as in some of the lexical entries quoted above governs a dimensional case: [mu-Bau ninĝ(u)-ak-a-e(!)].

13.5. The suffixed particle [ri]

-ri occurs after nominalized verbal forms ending in -a. Krecher 1965 defined it as an "isolierende Postposition", i.e., an affixed particle highlighting the meaning of the verbal form. Attinger 1993, 260, who preliminarily adopted Krecher's term, showed that -ri may stand in variation with ablative -ta "after".

Note: It is unlikely that the respective particle [ri] should be identical in meaning and function with the deictic particle [ri], treated above, 7.4. For lexical occurrences of the latter see OBGT I 785–786, and 789–791 (MSL 4, 58) and OBGT XIV 4–5 (ibid. 122), and see above, 7.4.

mu-5-àm mu-10-àm ba-e-zal-la-ri "after five, ten years had passed" GEN 40 = 83 = 127; see Enmerkar 430 and Green 1978, 145.

šà-zu im-mi-ib-du$_{11}$-ga-ri//šà-zu mi-ni-ib-du$_{11}$-ga-ta "after your heart spoke about it" Attinger 1993, 260.

All of Krecher's (1965) and Green's (1978, 145) examples favour an ablative interpretation of suffixed [ri].

If that be the case, the choice of -ri rather than -ta may have been a matter of style rather than grammar.

At any rate, more research is needed.

CHAPTER FOURTEEN

CONJUNCTIONS AND SUBJUNCTIONS

Sumerian as an agglutinative language has few conjunctions or subjunctions, and some of them are actually loans from Akkadian. In fact, Sumerian has no original word for "and". As for subjunctions, their number is restricted, too, because what is expressed by a conjunction in a non-agglutinative language such as Semitic or Indo-European is mostly represented by a nominalized verbal form plus a dimensional particle in Sumerian, i.e., Kiš . . . im-ug_5-ga-ta "after Kiš . . . had been killed" (Curse of Akkade 2) where the nominalized verbal form [im-ug-a] is put in the ablative, with [ta], in order to denote temporal distance.

In the following, conjunctions and, specially, subjunctions are treated without assigning them to strict grammatical categories, because they are essentially atypical for Sumerian.

14.1. Conjunctions

14.1.1. *[u]*

Sumerian borrowed Semitic [wa] "and" in its Akkadian form *ù* [u]. Akkadian [u] has not so far been the subject of a detailed study, nor has Sumerian [u]. [u] occurs much less in Akkadian than it does in its cognate Semitic languages, partly because it was replaced—for linking sentences—by [ma]. Therefore, Sumerian ù can hardly be expected to occur more frequently.

Note: *wa* (or *ù*) is still much more frequent in the Ebla (24th cent. B.C.) variant of Old Akkadian.

The allegedly oldest occurrences of ù in pre-Sargonic Sumerian (cf. Thomsen 1984, 16 and 83) are actually found in Akkadian contexts (Ebla and Abu Ṣalābīḫ): IAS no. 326//ARET 2 no. 6). It should be stressed, however, that the Ebla scribe used *ù* instead of the *wa* (PI) otherwise preferred for "and" in literary Ebla-Akkadian texts. The scribe may, therefore, have used Ù as a Sumerogram which would, at least indirectly, attest to ù as an Akkadian loan in pre-Sargonic Sumerian. The question needs more attention.

ù "and, and also" definitively gained currency in Sumerian by the time of Ur III, becoming as Sumerian as, more recently, Arabic *wa* "and" became Turkish in the form of *ve*.

ù frequently occurs connecting two personal names (e.g., NG no. 7:17–18, and see Sollberger 1966, 182 s.v. u 1:2–4), but it is not used in the enumeration of the names of judges or witnesses. By Ur III times, PN_1 ù PN_2 practically replaced former PN_1 PN_2-bi(-da) (see 4.2.(7) and 5.4.2.6).

Moreover, ù may connect PN and a pronoun, two nouns, or two verbal forms (see Sollberger 1966 ibid. 1.27).

ù eĝer-ab-ba-ne-ne ì-ba-e-ne "and they will also divide the estate of their father" NG no. 7:20.

The relation of sentence-connecting ù to the more traditional asyndetic construction is in need of further elucidation, especially with regard to diachrony.

14.1.2. *[ma]*

By the OB period, apart from *ù* Akkadian connective *-ma* has also been borrowed.

dub-ĝu$_{10}$ ì-ȓú ì-[sar] ì-til-ma mu-gub-ba-ĝu$_{10}$ ma-an-gub-bu-uš "I set up my tablet, [wrote] (it), finished (it), and then they put before me (my standing lines =) the model lines (to be copied by me)" Schooldays 5–6.

Cf. A. Falkenstein, WO 1/3 (1948) 176.

14.2. Subjunctions

14.2.1. *[uda]*

[uda] is spelled ù-da or u$_4$-da in Pre-Sargonic Lagaš inscriptions. If the etymology of the subjunction were actually the locative of the word u$_4$(-d) "day", i.e. u$_4$-da "at the day; today", the word would have become a subjunction secondarily. It would be difficult to explain, however, why in that case a variant ù-da should have occurred which is graphically more complex.

[uda] introduces a clause with the verb in conjugation pattern 1 (intransitive) or 2a (transitive) (see 12.7), both translated by us as present tense. Such a clause is followed by a second clause equally with the verb in pattern 1 or 2a. The whole complex may be interpreted as a conditional sentence construction consisting of a protasis ("if A") and an apodosis ("then B").

u_4-da ka-ka-na níg-érim ba-ĝá-ĝá ^{ĝeš}gag ka-ka-na šè-gaz "if she (the seller) (puts evil in her mouth =) behaves dishonestly/treacherously a wooden peg will be driven into her" SR no. 43 vi 1–2.

Note: The exact meaning of the sanction is unknown.

ù-da (var. u_4-da) mu-šè-sa_{10}-sa_{10} [mûše-sasa-(e)n] kù šà-ĝá a-sa_6-ga lá-ma "if you (want to) sell it to me, pay me silver (which is pleasant for my heart =) which I find appropriate" Ukg. 4–5 xi 7–10//xi 38–xii 3.

Note: Thomsen 1984, 85, offers two OB occurrences of u_4-da for "when", "if"; for both, however, a translation "today" would fit, especially so in EnmEns. 26 where the verb following u_4-da is in conjugation pattern 2b (preterite).

14.2.2. *[tukumbi]*

[tukumbi] "if" graphically is one of the most elaborate "dirig" compounds in the spelling of Sumerian words. Apart from final -bi, it is usually written with four elements: ŠU.GAR.TUR.LÁ, whose origin has not yet been explained.

tu-ku-um-bi ŠU.GAR.TUR.LÁ-bi = *šu-um-mu* Diri V 120 see CAD Š/3, 275 *šumma* lex. sect.

tukum alone occurs in èn tukum-šè "how long still; until when?" (note LamSumUr 451) which is formed after more frequent èn-šè (*adi mati*) "until when?".

tukum, instead of tukum-bi, is found in tukum še ì-ĝál, RA-na-an-šúm-mu, tukum na-ĝál, é-ZAR-ta, ha-mu-na-ra-pà-dè "if there is barley, let him give it to him; if there is not, let him find it for him from the ..." Sollberger 1966 no. 367 r. 2'–6'.

Note: tukum alone may just be a scribal idiosyncrasy (note, too, the unusual RA-, instead of *ha-, in 3') because otherwise the corpus of Ur III letters regularly has tukum-bi (see Sollberger 1966 p. 181).

Beginning with the Code of Ur-Namma (Ur III), tukum-bi regularly introduces conditional sentences. The verb of the protasis is in conjugation pattern 1 (intransitive) or 2 b (transitive preterite), exactly corresponding to the preterite (more rarely perfect) found with Akkadian *šumma* "if", clearly another Sumero-Akkadian areal feature.

tukum-bi lú-ù saĝ ĝeš bí-in-ra lú-bi ì-gaz-e-dam "if a person commits a murder that person will have to be killed" Ur-Namma Code C 52–54 (§1), see Wilcke 2002, 311.

14.2.3. *[ena]*

en-na is parallel to Akkadian *adi* in its dual functions of (a) a subjunction and (b) a preposition.

There is no strict rule observable for the morphological behaviour of the verb dependent on the subjunction.

(1) en-na + finite verbal form: en-na àm-du igi-ĝu$_{10}$-šè enim-bi a-bala-e "until he will have come here (and) the respective matter will have been brought to me" Sollberger 1966 no. 125:8–9; see ibid. no. 68:4 (i-im-du).

(2) en-na + nominalized verbal form: gu$_4$ . . . en-na ab-lah$_5$-a "oxen . . . (up to =) as many as could be brought" Ur-Namma A 87. éren en-na ba-ug$_5$-ga "soldiers (up to =) . . . as many as have died" ibid. 139.

Note: Susa var. has in-na ba-⌜šub⌝-e; see Flückiger-Hawker 1999, 125.

(3) en-na + nominalized verbal form with terminative case particle: PN$_1$ ù PN$_2$ en-na igi-ĝu$_{10}$ -šè di in-da-an-du$_{11}$-ga-aš [i-n-da-n-dug-a-š(e)] "until PN$_1$ will have had (his) lawsuit with PN$_2$ in my presence" Sollberger 1966 no. 113: 3–5,
en-na na-an-ga-ti-la-aš ARN 7:8–11, see above 12.12.2.5.
en-na may be used with a noun, thus virtually functioning as a preposition: en-na sukud-řá-bi "(the walls) to their highest point" Curse Akk. 227.
Since the etymology of [en] in en-na (or of [ena] as such) is unknown, it is difficult to describe the difference (if any) between [ena] "until" and en/èn-šè "until when, how long?".

14.2.4. *[mu]*

mu "year" in Sumerian year formulae may, from Gudea of Lagaš onward, be followed by a finite, not nominalized, verbal form. In such a case, mu may be taken as a subjunction; see above 12.16.3 end.

14.2.5. *[iginzu]*

igi-zu, i-gi_4 -in-zu (and other variant spellings, see Wilcke 1968, 229) "as if" mainly introduces hypothetical comparisons.

alam igi-zu [d]Nin-ĝír-su-ka-kam "a statue, as if it were one of Ningirsu" Gudea Stat. B vii 58–59.

Note: See (Th. Jacobsen, apud) Wilcke 1968, 232, and correct Edzard 1997, 36.

[d]ur_9 šu àm-kar-kar-re, i-gi_4-in-zu ní-te-a-ni-šè, lugal-a-ni-šè-àm "the donkey stallion runs along as if it were for himself, (but) it is for his master" UET 6, 275; see J. Bauer, Fs. W. W. Hallo (1993) 39.

Note: The etymology of [iginzu] is still unknown, as Wilcke's discussion of alleged "the eye noticed" makes clear (Wilcke 1968, 238 f.).

C. Wilcke, Das modale Adverb I-GI_4-IN-ZU im Sumerischen, JNES 27 (1968) 229–242, with additions added to offprint; Attinger 1993, 170.

CHAPTER FIFTEEN

EXCLAMATIONS

"Exclamations" should be understood as a catch-all term for calls, interjections, or even such expressions as "yes" or "no".

Although exclamations are, strictly speaking, part of the lexicon rather than of grammar, we will still briefly quote the most important ones. The exact meaning of an exclamation being highly dependent on its cultural context, it is difficult today to arrive at a strict definition (and delimitation from related terms). Therefore, many translations have to be taken as approximations only.

The following list of transliterated terms is arranged alphabetically.

15.1. [A]

For a "woe", "ouch", see Krecher 1966, 145.

a gú-ĝu$_{10}$ . . . a-nir im-ĝá-ĝá-ne "ouch, my neck, . . . they are wailing" GEN 155.

15.2. [ALALA]

a-la-la, exclamation of a positive character, also used as a work cry. See PSD A/1, 100.

Note: [l] in exclamations (see also 15.6) is a universal phenomenon. Cf. only Classical Greek ἀλαλά, Hebrew hallelūyā, Spanish olè, French hélas, olàlà, German hallo, halali; ululation, etc., whatever the etymology of the individual expression.

15.3. [ALULU]

a-lu-lu "woe", see PSD A/1, 107.

15.4. [ALLILI]

al-li-li(-àm-ma), interjection of unclear meaning, found in context with a-ù-àm-ma (see 15.5) and ù-li-li (15.13).

S. N. Kramer, Or. 54 (1985) 120 i 23–24, and p. 128; see PSD A/3, 153.

15.5. [AUA]

a-ù-a, a-ù-u$_8^!$-a, a-ù-àm-ma are exclamations partly of a lamenting, partly of a soothing character; see PSD A/1, 199, a-u$_3$-a A, and cf. above, 15.4, and below, 15.12.

15.6. [ELLU, ELALA, ILU, ILULAMMA]

e-el-lu, el-lu, el-lú, e-el-lum, e-la-lu, i-li(-a), i-lu-lam-ma, etc. Krecher 1966, 148, with fn. 433, collected references to exclamations all based on the voiced lateral [l]; see note to 15.2.

15.7. [GANA]

ga-na is an encouraging, often self-encouraging, exclamation, "come on now", "let's get moving", etc. The first syllable [ga] is most probably identical with the modal cohortative indicator [ga] (see 12.11.3).

ga-na ga-na-ab-du$_{11}$ "come on then, I will have to tell it to her" Gudea Cyl. A iii 22 f.

15.8. [HEAM]

hé-àm "let (it) be", i.e., the copula (3rd sg.) prefixed by the modal precative indicator [he] (see 12.11.5), has become the Sumerian term for "yes" (Akkadian *annu(m)*).

For hé-àm du$_{11}$(-g)/e "to assent, to say 'yes'" see Attinger 1993, 552 f. with bibl.

Another (more emphatic?) assertion is na-nam; see 12.11.10.

15.9. [INU]

in-nu "no" most probably may be explained as the negative indicator [nu] (see 12.11.2) prefixed by indicator [i/e] (see 12.9); [nu] would in this case have been treated as a verbal base.

in-nu ní te-ba-ab in-nu téš tuku-ba-ab "no, be respectful to them (= the words I recited to you), no, be ashamed to oppose them" Enkita and Enki-hegal 102 (see Wilcke 1969, 82 fn. 76).

15.10. [I UTU]

i ^{d}Utu "woe, O Sungod" is found in contexts where someone desperately turns for help to the Sun-god as the supreme god of justice.

lú-bi ì ^{d}Utu ì-e "that person will cry 'woe, O Sungod'" Ukg. 6 ii 14'.

Strangely enough, the expression is found, thereafter, only as a noun, i ^{d}Utu "complaint". It may not even be excluded that the above quoted Ukg. passage has already to be understood as "that person will lay a complaint".

níg-érim i ^{d}Utu ĝìri bí(-n)-ús "(Gudea) (set (his) foot on the neck of =) eliminated evil (and) complaint" Gudea Cyl. B xviii 11.

i- ^{d}Utu was eventually understood a genitival compound: lú-i-^{d}Utu-ka [lu-i-Utu-(a)k-a(k)] "person of complaint" = "oppressor" as in Ur-Namma C 35 (together with ní-zuh "thief".).

15.11. [MEL(I)EA]

me-li-e-a (pronounced as three or four syllables?) "alas", = Akkadian *inimma, inimmu* (CAD I s.v.). No etymology available for the expression in either language. me-li-e-a may stand at the beginning or the end of a phrase.

me-li-e-a me-a tuš-ù-dè-en me-a gub-bu-dè-en "woe is me, where shall I sit down, where shall I stand?" Ur Lament 294, and see 295, 304, etc.

enim-du$_{11}$-ga-še-ša$_{4}$-ĝu$_{10}$ me-li-e-a: *inimmu amat iqbû ušadmimanni* "the bitter word pronounced for me, alas" (Akkadian "alas, the word he said has made me moan"), see CAD I 148 *inimma* bil. sect.

15.12. [UA]

The great variety of spellings for [ua] "woe" has been collected by Krecher, 1966, 114 f.: ù-a, ú-a, u_5-a, ù-u_8-a, etc. While [ua] is essentially a sound of lamentation (with its labial element comparable to Latin vae, English woe, German o weh, Yiddish auvay, etc.), it also occurs as a soothing sound in [ua aua].

ù-a erim$_6$-ma-ĝu$_{10}$ "alas for my treasure house" VS 1, 25 ii 6 f. (Krecher 1966, 54).

u_5-a a-ù-a "sleep baby", beginning of the Sumerian lullaby (see Attinger 1993, 49 s.v. "Lullaby").

The different sounds which probably lie behind the different notation of the two [u] sounds as u_5 and ù, cannot be reconstructed.

Note: B. Landsberger, MSL 2 (1951) 29 f., tentatively suggested for u_8 "ein langgedehntes offenes o" (as in English paw, law).

The onomatopoeia of [ua aua] in lullabies may easily be rendered by corresponding soothing sounds in other languages, such as, e.g., Russian bayubayubayubáy or German eiapopeia.

15.13. [ULILI]

munus-ù-li-li = *zammirtu* "ulili woman" (Akkadian "songstress") Lu III ii 16 (MSL 12, 124).

Note: The lexical context has to do with singing and performance, but the exact meaning of [ulili] cannot be reconstructed.

CHAPTER SIXTEEN

EMESAL

Emesal (eme-sal) is a sociolinguistic variety of Sumerian attested for the speech of women or goddesses and of the "cantor" (gala). The pronunciation is supported by the Akkadian loanword *ummisallu* (AHw. s.v.; see also *emesallu*, CAD E). The meaning of the term is not completely clear; maybe "thin, fine tongue" (sal = *raqqu*) referred to a highpitched voice; cf. Russian *tonkij golos* "thin (high-pitched) voice"; see also Krecher 1967b, 87 fn. 1).

Note: The fact that the "cantor" used a form of speech otherwise attested for female persons has caused much speculation: Was the gala a eunuch or an effeminate male? See the discussion in Schretter 1990, 124–36. It is, however, well known that the modern counter-tenor or even altus is sung by sexually normal male persons.

Emesal is first attested in the early OB period. It is found in a one-to-one relation with eme-gi_7(-r) in phonology, morphology, vocabulary, and syntax. The main difference between the standard form of Sumerian (eme-gi_7(-r)) and emesal regards sounds and lexicon.

Emesal is spelled phonetically (e.g., zé-eb [zeb] = dùg "good, sweet") or semi-phonetically (e.g., ^{d}Mu-ul-líl [Mullil] = Enlil where the second element líl is never given as *li-il). It is quite probable that also traditional eme-gi_7(-r) spelling could be read in emesal when required by context.

Only a few examples out of the very ample evidence for emesal will be offered here, the whole material having been collected by Krecher 1967b and Schretter 1990, with special attention to the phonetic evidence.

eme-gi_7(-r)	eme-sal	
a-ga	a-ba	"back, rear"
dùg	zé-eb	"good, sweet"
ga-	da-	(modal indicator: cohortative)
enim	e-ne-èĝ	"word"
nir-ĝál	še-er-ma-al	"person of authority"
diĝir	dìm-me-er	"deity"

lú	mu-lu	"person"
nin, ereš	ga-ša-an, gašan	"lady"
en	ù-mu-un, umun	"lord"
túm	ir	"to bring"
a-na-àm	ta-àm	"what (is it)?"
ma-an-šúm	ĝá-ba-zé-em	"he gave me"
im-ma-da-te	in-ga-da-te	"he approached me"

Apart from heteronymy (e.g., [lu] : [mulu], [nin] : [gašan]) there are consonantal and vocalic correspondences (e.g., [g] : [b], [g] : [d], [ĝ] : [m], [g] : [z], [u] : [e]). In spite of parallel occurrences of some of those correspondences, emesal forms are not predictable for us. The two verbal forms quoted last show that also the string of prefixed morphemes may have been affected by emesal variation.

Apart from the usage of emesal in literary texts, individual emesal words and name variants are also found in lexical lists (see Schretter 1990, 17–30). A special "Emesal Vocabulary" of post-OB date has been edited in MSL 4 (1956) 3–44. It consists of three "Tablets" the first of which contains divine names and the second and third offer nouns, a few verbal bases and verbal forms as well as a very restricted number of pronouns and numerals.

Krecher 1967b; Schretter 1990 (see also the review of J. Black, OLZ 87 [1992] 382–85); Langenmayr 1992.

CHAPTER SEVENTEEN

THE SUMERO-AKKADIAN LINGUISTIC AREA

Sumerian and Akkadian coexisted in a region of about the size of modern Belgium during most of the 3rd millennium B.C. and during the first quarter of the 2nd millennium. Many speakers of the two languages then lived in closest proximity. The final result of mutual contacts was—apart from extensive borrowing of vocabulary—a considerable divergence of Akkadian from the traditional "Semitic" language type; and—on the other hand—non-Sumerian, "Semitic", traits in Sumerian. These have often been interpreted as faulty treatment of "classical" Sumerian by scribes who—allegedly—no longer would have been used to, and aware of, the typical grammatical categories of Sumerian. Consequently, some scholars have maintained that Sumerian had already ceased to be a living spoken language as early as the time of the Third Dynasty of Ur.

But what actually happened was the building up of a "linguistic area" or "convergence area" where "speakers can switch from one code to another with a minimum of additional learning" (Gumperz/ Wilson 1971, 154). Seen in such a context, many features of both Sumerian and Akkadian may be easily explained.

17.1.

The following diagram tries to demonstrate what happens when languages A and B enter such a "convergence area". A here stands for Sumerian and B for Akkadian. The example illustrated is the common Semitic conjunction [wa], borrowed by Sumerian as [u] (ù).

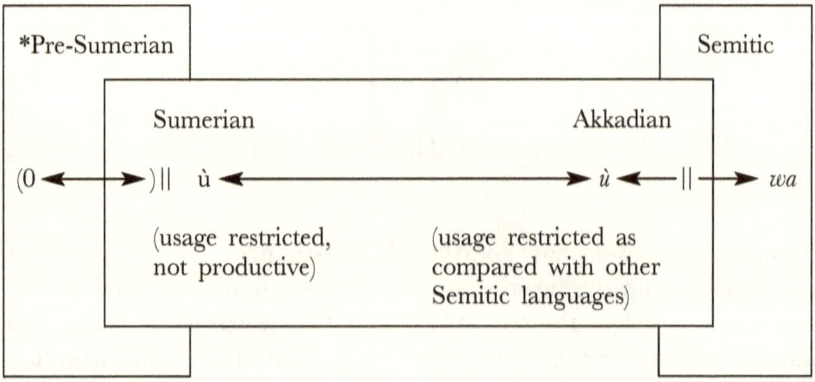

Note: Common Semitic *wa* "and", "and also", often used as a "sentence opener" (Satzweiser, see Richter 1970, 39.84), is still attested in its full set of functions in Ebla Akkadian. In Mesopotamian proper, its usage is restricted, and as a connector of phrases it has mainly been replaced by enclitic *-ma*. Akkadian *wa* in its (pronunciation and) spelling *ù* has been borrowed into Sumerian where it is mainly used to connect nouns (see 14.1.1). Sumerian itself lacks a connecting particle "and". The relatively rare usage of ù in Sumerian then most probably had its reverse effect on Akkadian where *ù* is of limited application as compared to the usage of *wa* in the other Semitic languages. This, then, may be called a real areal feature.

We will enumerate a number of other such features attesting to the Sumero-Akkadian "convergence area".

17.2.

The subject-object-verb (SOV) word order is common to both Sumerian and Mesopotamian Akkadian as against more traditional Eblaite Akkadian where we often encounter VOS (cf. Edzard 1984, 115 f.). The older V(O)S order is still found—as an 'archaism'—in Ur III and OB personal names, e.g., *iddin-Sin* "the Moongod gave (the child)". When, however, the Akkadian verbal form of a PN is set in the ventive, the word order S(O)V prevails: *Sin-iddinam* "the Moongod gave me (the child)".

The SOV word order is also maintained in Akkadian when the subject is extended by the addition of a relative clause, this leading to veritable "Schachtelsatz" constructions (see Poebel 1947, 23–42). The same holds for the insertion of infinitive constructions which stand between S and V. Therefore, most probably Akkadian word order was influenced by Sumerian.

17.3. Ventive

The formation of the Akkadian ventive, permeating the whole verbal system except for the non-finite forms, has not developed on its own. The ventive : non-ventive dichotomy of the finite verbal system of Sumerian has left its impact on neighbouring Akkadian where a post-verbal morpheme [an], inherited from common Semitic affirmative [an], was given a new function (cf. Pedersén 1989, 433–36). The personal names Nanna-manšum "the Moongod gave (the child) to me" and Sin-iddinam (ditto) may be translated back and forth in word order (SV) and morpheme by morpheme.

Note: Common Semitic [an] became [am] in Akkadian in word-final position only, e.g., *iddin-am*. Otherwise [an] maintained its identity except that the [n] was assimilated to a following consonant: *iddin-a*N*-kum* → *iddinakkum* "he gave to you", etc.

17.4. Loss of Sumerian [H] and of Akkadian [h], [ḥ], and [ʿ]

It may be assumed that the reduction of the Akkadian consonantal phoneme inventory, as inherited from common Semitic, was due to Sumerian substratum. By Ur III times at the latest, [h], [ḥ], and [ʿ] can no longer be substantiated for Akkadian phonology.

Dead loss in Hilgert 2002.

One cannot, on the other hand, escape the conclusion that Sumerian originally had an unvoiced laryngeal phoneme which we tentatively transliterated as [H] (see 3.1.2, p. 20). So if phoneme reduction in Akkadian is being considered as due to Sumerian substratum, loss of [H] on the Sumerian side would be said to follow a similar tendency. Nothing could be more eloquent for an areal situation.

17.5. Phraseology of Sumerian and Akkadian has much in common

gú šub "to throw the neck" = *aḫam nadûm* "to throw the arm" = "to be neglectful".—ĝéštu gub "to set the ear" = *uznam šakānum* (ditto) = "to be attentive".—igi ĝar "to set the eye" = *pānam šakānum* "to set the face" = "to prepare to (. . .)".—a-šà è "to bring out =) rent a field" = *eqlam šūṣûm* (ditto).—nam-X AG = *X-ūtam epēšum* "to exercise the X-ship" = "to follow a profession, trade".—šà-šè gíd "to draw to the heart" = "to consider carefully" = *ana libbim šadādum* (ditto).—enim-ma tuš "to (sit to the word =) obey" = *ana awāti wašābum* (ditto).—ù-ma-a-du_{11} "would you please say" (polite imperative, see 12.12.1.2) = *qibima* "say and . . .".

17.6. Application of the Akkadian stative conjugation pattern to substantives

In Akkadian, the conjugation pattern *ṣabtāku, ṣabtāta* "I am, you are holding" may also be applied to substantives: *belēku, šarrāta* "I am lord", "you are king". The pattern as such has its counterpart in the "perfect" of, e.g., Hebrew, Arabic, or Ethiopic, where it is restricted to verbs. The application to substantives in Akkadian is most probably due to influence of the Sumerian copula (me, see 12.7.1.1) which is mainly used with substantives: dub-sar-me-en "I am/you are a scribe".

Note: Application of the Sumerian copula has not, however, been completely reflected in Akkadian. So, e.g., ki-áĝ-ĝá-$ĝu_{10}$-me-en "you are my beloved" has no such Akkadian correspondence as **narāmtī-āti*.

17.7. Case system

There is a conspicuous phonetic similarity between Sumerian [(e)š(e)], mark of the terminative case particle (5.4.2.8), and the ending of the Akkadian terminative-adverbial [iš]. Although there can be no doubt of the Semitic background of Akkadian [iš], the fact that the Akkadian case was maintained throughout the millennia may be due to the parallel existence of a case with comparable function(s) in Sumerian.

Pedersén 1989, 430–33.

Note: The theory of an original ergativity of Semitic (cf. Diakonoff 1965, 1988; Kienast 2001, 179; see also p. 141) rests on the misinterpretation of the Akkadian locative-adverbial case in *-um*, seemingly identical with the nominative in *-um*. The two authors did not consider the important evidence of the construct state used for Akkadian nominative and locative-adverbial. In the first case *-um* is eliminated or replaced by a Stützvokal: *bēlum* → *bēl, wardum* → *warad, napištum* → *napišt(i)*; in the second case, *-um* (or more recent *-u*) is maintained in the construct state: *ṣillum Sin* "in the shade of the Moongod", or the [m] is assimilated to a following consonant: *ṣiluššu* "in his shade". So, the two cases have to be strictly kept apart.

17.8. NAM- AND -ŪTUM

Sumerian and Akkadian both have a nominal device to express the abstract of title, profession, or adjective: nam-lugal = *šarrūtum* "all that has to do with a ruler" = "king-ship". Both in Sumerian and Akkadian, the respective pattern is fully productive.

17.9. THE PLURAL OF ADJECTIVES

In Akkadian, a restricted number of adjectives (mostly indicating some kind of dimension) form a plural where the middle radical of the root is lengthened: *rabûm* "big" → *rabbûtum, arkum* "long" → *arrakūtum, ṣeḫrum* "small" → *ṣeḫḫerūtum*, etc.; see Reiner 1966, 64. One may easily compare this type of 'internal' plural with the reduplicated Sumerian adjectives which, following a substantive, indicate plural (5.3.7, and see 4.1.1.b), e.g., diĝir-gal-gal-(e-ne) = *ilū rabbûtum* "the great gods".

Note: Both AHw. and CAD R offer an entry *rabbû* (sg.), conceding, however, that it mainly occurs in the plural.

17.10. VERBAL MOOD

Akkadian has a set of verbal moods which it is easier to compare to the system of Sumerian moods (cf. chart on p. 112 f.) than to the moods known from other Semitic languages. To quote but one example: There is a complete correspondence between Sumerian positive affirmative 1, occurring in the 1st and 3rd p. and built on the (*ḫamṭu*) conjugation patterns 1 or 2b (see 12.11.7) and the Akkadian positive affirmative 1: *lū aprus, lū iprus*, equally occurring in the 1st and 3rd p. and built on the preterite (*iprus*) conjugation pattern.

For more details see Edzard 1973, 121–141, specially pp. 140 f.

Note: Edzard's article has a considerable number of misprints because the author had no opportunity to read and return proofs.

17.11. Mutual borrowing of lexical items in Sumerian and Akkadian

This topic, worth a whole book, can only be dealt with here very briefly. It should also be kept in mind that (mutual) lexical borrowing may be—but is not necessarily—a symptom of an areal situation.

The CAD volumes A, B, D, E, G, H, I/J, K, L, M, N, Q, R, S, Ṣ, Š, and Z (with P, T, Ṭ, and U/W still missing) include ca. 13.630 Akkadian lemmata. Of these, about 980 are Sumerian loanwords (ca. 320 of which are only attested in lexical lists). This count yields a little above 7% of Sumerian loanwords in the Akkadian vocabulary.

Note: The above figures have been added from the author's CAD reviews in ZA 53 (1959) to 90 (2000) (see M. Krebernik/M. P. Streck, ZA 91 [2001] 13–20). In spite of the author's own skepticism on the exactitude of these figures, they have never so far been challenged.

Unfortunately, no corresponding data may so far be offered for Akkadian loanwords in Sumerian because Sumerian lexicography is still in its infancy.

Note: PSD B was published in 1984 whereas PSD A (1992 ff.) is still incomplete. The following data of PSD B, while not negligible, are in no way eligible for a projection on the situation of Akkadian loanwords in Sumerian in general. There are only about 13 words of Akkadian origin among ca. 350 entries in PSD B; of these 13, 5 occur only in lexical lists. This count yields 3,7% of Akkadian loanwords for Sumerian words beginning with the letter B. We must repeat that the figure can in no way be regarded as representative for the vocabulary as a whole.

CHAPTER EIGHTEEN

SUMMARY—AND WHAT IS STILL MISSING?

The present grammar, in its essential aspects, is traditionally descriptive. It is not under the obligation of a more recent method—generative, structural, or transformational. It is far from perfect as, e.g., in contrast to A. Falkenstein's monumental "Gudea" grammar (1949, 1950), it lacks a section—or chapters—on syntax, the stepchild of more recent grammars. However, quite a few features that would traditionally figure in a "syntax" (the description of how parts of speech as well as phrases are "set together", but also of the way by which parts of speech and phrases are morphologically marked for their functions), have been included in the above chapters: e.g., functions and morpho-syntactical behaviour of the case particles (5.4), the system of the modal and connecting indicators (12.11, 12.12), the vast complex of the non-finite verbal forms (12.14), or the nominalisation of finite verbal forms (12.16).

On the other hand, the author may much too often have left the impression of Sumerian as one uniform block instead of a living being with a marked diachronic evolution. At any rate, a historical grammar of Sumerian still has to be written.

Thirdly, the author has endeavoured, as often as possible, not to describe Sumerian as a completely isolated body, but in connection with Akkadian, the language of those inhabitants of Mesopotamia who were the immediate neighbours of the Sumerians for a whole millennium or even longer.

The author will not enumerate here topics that would have merited inclusion in a grammar of Sumerian, such as, e.g., word formation and nominal compounds, morphological variation (both nominal and verbal) in different manuscripts of a given line of a literary composition, or literary style in general. There is no end of addenda—and corrigenda.

Finally, according to the witty remark of the late I. M. Diakonoff that there are as many kinds of Sumerian as there are authors of Sumerian grammars, I freely admit the highly subjective character of my own effort.

BIBLIOGRAPHY

Note: Bibliographical items that have been quoted above unabridged are not repeated here.

B. Alster 1974: The Instructions of Suruppak. A Sumerian Proverb Collection (= Mesopotamia 2).

id. 1991–93: The Sumerian Folktale of the Three Ox-Drivers of Adab, JCS 43–45, 27–38.

J. Aro 1961: Die akkadischen Infinitivkonstruktionen (= StudOr. 26).

P. Attinger 1993: Eléments de linguistique sumérienne. La construction de du_{11}/e/di "dire" (= OBO Sonderband).

id. 1995: Les préfixes absolutifs de la première et de la deuxième personne singulier dans les formes *marû* ergatives, ZA 75, 161–78.

J. Bauer 1993: Ein sumerisches Sprichwort, in: (ed. M. E. Cohen et al.) Fs. W. W. Hallo, 39–41.

J. Black 1984: Sumerian Grammar in Babylonian Theory (= StudPohl SM 12); id. ^{2}1991.

id. 2003: (in press) (on Sumerian adjectives) in: (ed. K. Maekawa) Fs. M. Yoshikawa.

A. Cavigneaux 1978: L'essence divine, JCS 30, 177–85.

M. Civil 1974 see W. Heimpel 1974 and J. N. Postgate 1974.

id., 1976: Lexicography, in: (ed. St. Lieberman) Fs. Th. Jacobsen (= AS 20) 123–57.

M. E. Cohen 1975: ur.sag.me.šár.ur_4. A Širnamšubba of Ninurta, WO 8, 22–36.

F. d'Agostino 1990: Il sistema verbale sumerico nei testi lessicali di Ebla (= StudSem. NS 7).

W. Deeter 1963: Armenisch und die kaukasischen Sprachen, HdOr. 1. Abt. Bd. 7, 1–79.

A. Deimel 1924: sumerische Grammatik (= Or. SP 9–13); id. ^{2}1939.

I. M. Diakonoff 1983: Towards a History of Mathematical Speculation, JAOS 103, 83–93.

J. J. A. van Dijk 1953: La sagesse suméro-accadienne. Recherches sur les genres littéraires des textes sapientiaux.

R. M. W. Dixon 1994: Ergativity.

D. O. Edzard 1967: Das sumerische Verbalmorphem /ed/ in den alt- und neusumerischen Texten, HSAO 1, 29–62.

id. 1970: Die *bukānum*-Formel der altbabylonischen Kaufverträge und ihre sumerische Entsprechung, ZA 60, 8–53.

id. 1971: *ḫamṭu, marû* und freie Reduplikation beim sumerischen Verbum, ZA 61, 208–32.

id. 1972: (as 1971) ZA 62, 1–34.

id. 1973: Die Modi beim älteren akkadischen Verbum, Or. 42, 121–41.

id. 1976a: (as 1971) ZA 66, 45–61.

id. 1976b: Zum sumerischen Eid, AS 20 (Fs. Th. Jacobsen), 63–98.

id. 1976c: "Du hast mir gegeben", "ich habe dir gegeben". Über das sumerische Verbum sum, WO 8, 159–77.

id. 1980: Sumerisch 1 bis 10 in Ebla, StudEb. 3, 122–27.

id. 1984: Zur Syntax der Ebla-Texte, in: (ed. P. Fronzaroli) Studies on the Language of Ebla (= QuadSem. 13) 101–16.

id. 1990: Gilgameš und Huwawa A. I. Teil, ZA 80, 165–203.

id. 1991: Gilgameš und Huwawa A. II. Teil, ZA 81, 160–233.
id. 1995: The Sumerian Language, in: (ed. J. M. Sasson) CANE IV 2107–16.
id. 1997: Gudea and His Dynasty (= RIME 3/1).
id. 2003a: Zum sumerischen Verbalpräfix a(l), in: (ed. W. Sallaberger et al.) Fs. C. Wilcke, 87–98.
id. 2003b: Sumerisch 1 bis 120, in: (ed. Y. Sefati) Fs. J. Klein.
id. 2003c: Wann ist Sumerisch als gesprochene Sprache ausgestorben, in: (ed. K. Maekawa) Fs. M. Yoshikawa.
A. Falkenstein 1939: Untersuchungen zur sumerischen Grammatik 1. Der Plural des Kohortativs; 2. Das richtungsanzeigende Infix -ra-, ZA 45, 169–94.
id. 1949–1950: Grammatik der Sprache Gudeas von Lagaš. I. Schrift- und Formenlehre. II. Syntax (= AnOr. 28–29).
id. 1952: Das Petentialis- und Irrealissufix -e-še des Sumerischen, Indogerm. Forschungen 66, 113–30.
id. 1956: NG I.
id. 1959a: Das Sumerische (= HdOr. I/2/1–2/1).
id. 1959b: Untersuchungen zur sumerischen Grammatik 5. Zum Akzent des Sumerischen, ZA 53, 98–105.
G. Farber-Flügge 1973: Der Mythos "Inanna und Enki" unter besonderer Berücksichtigung der me (= StudPohl 10).
D. A. Foxvog 1974: apud Heimpel 1974.
id. 1975: The Sumerian Ergative Construction, Or. 44, 395–425.
I. J. Gelb ²1961: Old Akkadian Writing and Grammar (= MAD 3).
Y. Gong 2000: Die Namen der Keilschriftzeichen (= AOAT 268).
G. B. Gragg 1968: The Syntax of the Copula, in: (ed. J. W. M. Verhaar) The Verb 'Be' and its Synonyms 3 (= Foundations of Languages, Suppl. Series 8).
id. 1973: Sumerian Dimensional Infixes (= AOAT 5).
M. Green 1978: The Eridu Lament, JCS 30, 127–67, esp. pp. 145 f. for -ri.
J. J. Gumperz/R. Wilson 1971: Convergence and Creolization. A Case for the Indo-Aryan/Dravidian Border in India, in: (ed. D. Hymes), Pidginization and Creolization, 151–67, esp. p. 154.
W. Heimpel 1974: The Structure of the Sumerian Prefix Chain (ms.).
M. Hilgert 2002: Akkadisch in der Ur III-Zeit (= IMGULA 5).
B. Hruška 1969: Das spätbabylonische Lehrgedicht "Inannas Erhöhung", ArOr. 37, 473–521.
Th. Jacobsen 1956: Introduction to the Chicago Grammatical Texts, MSL 4, 1*–50*.
id. 1965: About the Sumerian Verb, in: (ed. H.G. Güterbock/Th. Jacobsen) Fs. B. Landsberger (= AS 16) 71–101); reprinted in Jacobsen 1970, 245–70 + 430–66.
id. 1970: (ed. W. L. Moran) Toward the Image of Tammuz and other Essays on Mesopotamian History and Religion (= HSS 21).
id. 1988: The Sumerian Verbal Core, ZA 78, 161–220; the reader is warned for a number of regrettable misprints.
B. Jagersma 1999: apud Zólyomi 1999.
M. Jaques n.d. [1999]: Le vocabulaire des sentiments dans les textes sumériens (= thèse de doctorat, Université de Genève).
R. Jestin 1943: Le verbe sumérien (I).
id. 1946: Le verbe sumérien (II).
id. 1951: Abrégé de grammaire sumérienne.
T. B. Jones/J. W. Snyder 1961: Sumerian Economic Texts from the Third Dynasty.
I. T. Kaneva 1996: Šumerskij jazyk.
F. Karahashi 2000: Sumerian Compound Verbs with Body-part Terms (diss. Univ. of Chicago).
D. Katz 1993: Gilgamesh and Akka.

B. Kienast 1980: Probleme der sumerischen Grammatik 4. Bemerkungen zu *ḫamṭu* und *marû* im Sumerischen, ZA 70, 1–35.
J. Klein 1981. Three Šulgi Hymns. Sumerian Royal Hymns Glorifying King Šulgi of Ur.
id. 1993: The Suffix of Determination /a/, ASJ 15, 81–98.
S. N. Kramer 1936: The Sumerian Prefix Forms be- and bi- in the Time of the Earlier Princes of Lagaš (= AS 8).
M. Krebernik 1983: Zu Syllabar und Orthographie der lexikalischen Texte aus Ebla II, ZA 73, 1–47.
id. 1998: Die Texte aus Fāra und Tell Abū Ṣalābīḫ, in: (ed. P. Attinger/M. Wäfler) Mespotamien. Späturuk-Zeit und Frühdynastische Zeit (= OBO 160/1), 237–427.
J. Krecher 1965: Zur sumerischen Grammatik 1. Isolierende Postpositionen, ZA 57, 12–29.
id. 1966: Sumerische Kultlyrik.
id. 1967a: Die pluralischen Verben für "gehen" und "stehen" im Sumerischen, WO 4, 1–11.
id. 1967b: Zum Emesal-Dialekt des Sumerischen, HSAO 1, 87–110.
id. 1978: Die Form und der Gebrauch der nominalen Verbalformen und die Determination im Sumerischen, Or. 47, 376–403.
id. 1985: Die /m/-Präfixe des sumerischen Verbums, Or. 54, 133–81.
id. 1987: Morphemeless Syntax in Sumerian as Seen on the Background of Word-Composition in Chukchee, ASJ 9, 67–88.
id. 1993: Über einige 'zusammengesetze Verben' im Sumerischen, in: (ed. A. F. Rainey et al.) Mem. R. Kutscher, 107–118.
id. 1995: Die *marû*-Formen des sumerischen Verbums (= AOAT 240) 141–200.
W. G. Lambert 1991: The Reference of *ḫamṭu* and *marû* in Lexical Lists, ZA 81, 7–9.
B. Landsberger 1944: Die Anfänge der Zivilisation in Mesopotamien (Ankara Üniv. Dil ve Tarih-Coğrafya Fak. Dergisi II/3, 431–37); see also (transl. and edited by M. de J. Ellis) The Beginnings of Civilisation in Mesopotamia (1974), Monographs of the Ancient Near East 1/2, 8–12.
A. Langenmayr 1992: Sprachpsychologische Untersuchung zur sumerischen "Frauensprache", ZA 82, 208–11.
H. Limet 1968: L'anthroponymie sumérienne dans les documents de la 3e dynastie d'Ur.
P. Michalowski 1980: Sumerian as an Ergative Language, I, JCS 32, 86–103.
id. 1898: The Lamentation over the Destruction of Sumer and Ur (= MesCiv. 1).
id. 1993: Letters from Early Mesopotamia.
O. Pedersén 1989: Some Morphological Aspects of Sumerian and Akkadian Linguistic Area, in: (ed. H. Behrens et al.) Fs. Å. W. Sjöberg, 429–38.
A. Poebel 1923: Grundzüge der sumerischen Grammatik.
id. 1931: The Sumerian Prefix Forms e- and i- in the Time of the Earlier Princes of Lagaš (= AS 2).
id. 1939: Studies in Akkadian Grammar (= AS 9).
id. 1947: Miscellaneous Studies (= AS 14), esp. pp. 23–42: The "Schachtelsatz" Construction of the Narâm-Sîn Text RA XVI 157 f.
J. N. Postgate 1974: Two Points of Grammar in Gudea, JCS 26, 16–54.
M. A. Powell 1971: Sumerian Numeration and Metrology (= diss. Univ. of Minnesota).
id. 1989: Maße und Gewichte, RIA VII (1987–90) 457–517.
W. Richter 1970: Exegese als Literaturwissenschaft. Entwurf einer alttestamentlichen Literaturtheorie und Methodologie.
E. Reiner 1966: A Linguistic Analysis of Akkadian.

W. H. Ph. Römer 1965: Sumerische "Königshymnen" der Isin-Zeit.

id: 1969: Einige Beobachtungen zur Göttin Nini(n)sina . . ., in: (ed. W. Röllig) Fs. W. von Soden (= AOAT 1). 279–305.

id. 1976: Kleine Beiträge zur Grammatik des Sumerischen 1. Das modale grammatische Element nu-uš-, in: (ed. B. L. Eichler et al.) Fs. S. N. Kramer (= AOAT 25) 371–78.

id. 1980: Das sumerische Kurzepos "Bilgameš und Akka" (= AOAT 2009/1).

id. 1982: Einführung in die Sumerologie (esp. pp. 27–97, "Einiges zur Sprache").

G. Rubio 1999: On the alleged 'Pre-Sumerian' substratum, JCS 51, 1–16.

W. Sallaberger 1993: Der kultische Kalender der Ur III-Zeit (= UAVA 7/1 und 7/2).

A. Salonen 1968: Agricultura Mesomotamica.

R. Scholtz 1934: Die Struktur der sumerischen engeren Verbalpräfixe (Konjugationspräfixe) speziell dargelegt an der I. und II. Form (E- und Mu-Konjugation) (= MVAG 39/2).

M. Schretter 1990: Emesal-Studien.

Y. Sefati 1998: Love Songs in Sumerian Literature. Critical Edition of the Dumuzi-Inanna Songs.

A. Shaffer 1963: Sumerian Sources of Tablet XII of the Epic of Gilgameš (= Ph.D. diss. Philadelphia).

Å. W. Sjöberg 1975: in-nin šà-gur$_4$-ra. A Hymn to the Goddess Inanna by the en-Priestess Enḫeduanna, ZA 65, 161–253.

E. Sollberger 1952: Le système verbal dans les inscriptions "royales" présargoniques de Lagaš.

id. 1961: Le syllabaire présargonique de Lagaš, ZA 54, 1–50.

id. 1966: The Business Administration Correspondence under the kings of Ur (= TCS 1).

H. Steible 1982: Die altsumerischen Bau- und Weihinschriften I. II (= FAOS 5/ I–II).

G. Steiner: Intransitiv-passivische und aktivische Verbalauffassung, ZDMG 126, 230–80.

id. 1981: *Ḫamṭu* und *Marû* als verbale Kategorien im Sumerischen und im Akkadischen, RA 75, 1–14.

P. Steinkeller 1979: Notes on Sumerian Plural Verbs, Or. 48, 54–67.

M. P. Streck 2000: Das amurritische Onomastikon der altbabylonischen Zeit I, Die Amurriter. Die onomastische Forschung. Orthographie und Phonologie. Normalmorphologie (= AOAT 271/1).

V. V. Struve 1984: (ed. G. Kh. Kaplan) Onomastika rannedinastičeskogo Lagaša.

M.-L. Thomsen 1984: The Sumerian Language. An Introduction to its History and Grammatical Structure (= Mesopotamia 10); ^{3}2001, 3rd unchanged and unextended edition.

H. Vanstiphout 1985: On the Verbal Prefix /i/ in Standard Sumerian, RA 79, 1–15.

Aa. Westenholz 1991: The Phoneme /o/ in Akkadian, ZA 81, 10–19.

C. Wilcke 1969: Das Lugalbandaepos.

id. 1968: Das modale Adverb I-GI$_4$-IN-ZU im Sumerischen, JNES 27, 229–42.

id. 1988: Anmerkungen zum 'Konjugationspräfix' /i/- und zur These vom "silbischen Charakter der sumrischen Morpheme" anhand neusumerischer Verbalformen beginnend mit ì-, íb-, ì-im- und ì-in-, ZA 78, 1–48.

id. 1990: Orthographie, Grammatik und literarische Form. Beobachtungen zu der Vaseninschrift Lugalzaggesis (SAKI 152–156), in: (ed. Tz. Abusch et al.) Fs. W. L. Moran, 455–504.

id. 2002: Der Kodex Urnammu (CU): Versuch einer Rekonstruktion, in: (ed. Tz. Abusch) Mem. Th. Jacobsen, 291–333.

id. 2003: (in print) (the verb si sá), in: (ed. K. Maekawa) Fs. M. Yoshikawa.
C. Woods 2003: (in print) (Sumerian demonstratives), in: (ed. K. Maekawa) Fs. M. Yoshikawa.
Yang Zhi 1989: Sargonic Inscriptions from Adab (= The Institute for the History of Ancient Civilizations. Periodic Publications of Ancient Civilizations 1).
M. Yoshikawa 1968a: On the Grammatical Function of -e- of the Sumerian Verbal Suffix -e-dè/-e-da(m), JNES 27, 251–61.
id. 1968b: The Marû and Ḫamṭu Aspects in the Sumerian Verbal System, Or. 37, 401–16.
id. 1979: The Sumerian Verbal Prefixes mu-, i- and Topicality, Or. 48, 185–206.
id. 1981: Plural Expressions in Sumerian Verbs, ASJ 3, 111–24.
id. 1993a: Spatial Deictic System in Sumerian, ASJ 15, 185–92.
id. 1993b: Studies in the Sumerian Verbal System (= ASJ SS 1), a reprint of 24 articles published between 1968 and 1993.
A. Zgoll 2003: . . ., in: (ed. K. Maekawa) Fs. M. Yoshikawa.
G. Zólyomi 1999: Directive infix and oblique object in Sumerian: An account on the history of their relationship, Or. 68, 215–53.

INDEX

[a] (exclamation) 167
a > i (e.g., dab_5 > díb) diachronically 14
ablative(-instrumental) (case) 33 f., 41 f.
absolutive (case) 33–35
achevé (verbal aspect) 73
adjectives 25, 47–48
adverbiative 26, 42
adverbs 26 f., 69
affirmative 1 (verbal mood) 117 f.
affirmative 2 (verbal mood) 119 f.
affirmative 3 (verbal mood) 120
a(l)- (prefixed verbal indicator) 111 f.
[alala] (exclamation) 167
[allili] (exclamation) 167
[alulu] (exclamation) 167
Anatolia 4
"and" (lack of) 41
areal situation (Sumero-Akkadian) 4 f., 173 ff.
[aua] (exclamation) 167

b (variant of verbal indicator [bi]) 100 f.
B = base
B-[Ø] (verb) 130–132
[ba] (non-ventive directional indicator) 94 f.
B-[a] 132 f., 137 f.
B-[ada] (verb) 134 f., 136 f.
[bara] (modal verbal indicator: vetitive) 117
[bara] (modal verbal indicator: negative affirmative) 118
base (verb) 71 and passim
Basque (prefix chains) 72
B-B-[Ø] (verb) 130 f.
[bda] (non-ventive directional indicator) 96
B-[ed] 130, 134
B-[eda] 134–136
B-[ede] 134–136
[bi] (demonstrative) 50
[bi] (non-ventive directional indicator) 98–101
-bi(-da) "and" 41
*[bra] 22
[bši] (non-ventive directional indicator) 98
[bta] (non-ventive directional indicator) 97

cardinal numbers 61–66
case 33–45
Caucasus 4
causative 101
causative (Akkadian) 98 f.
circumpositional syntagma 56
class (person, non-person) 1, 24
clusters (syllabic) 22
cognates of Sumerian (alleged) 2 f.
cohortative (verbal mood) 115 f.
comitative (case) 33 f., 40 f.
compounds (nominal) 2
compound verbs 142–150
conjugated participle 137–142
conjugation 81
conjugation patterns 81–88
conjugation pattern 1 (intransitive and passive) 81–83
conjugation pattern 2a (transitive) 83–87
conjugation pattern 2b (transitive) 87–90
conjunctions 27, 161–162
conjunctions and subjunctions 161–165
connecting indicators (verb) 112, 121–127
consonants 7–8, 14–21
copula 55, 82–83
cuneograms, classification of 8–10

dative (case) 33 f., 40
dedli 31 f.
deli 62, 141 f.
demonstrative particles 49–51
demonstrative pronouns 57
determination (of nouns) 49–51
determinatives 9 f.
dili see deli
dimensional indicators (verb) 92–109
diphthongs 13 f.

directive (case) 33 f., 43 f.
distribution 41 f., 67
dug$_4$/e/di 76 f.

e/i (difficulty to distinguish them) 14
[e] (prefixed verbal indicator) 109–111
-e (demonstrative?) 50
Ebla glosses 4
[ed] 74, 82
[eda] (non-ventive dimensional indicator) 96
[elala] (exclamation) 168
Elamite 3
[ellu] (exclamation) 168
eme-gi$_7$(-r) 1
eme-Ki-en-gi-ra 1
Emesal 66
  (numerals) 171 f.
[ena] (subjunction) 164
[enea] (non-ventive dimensional indicator) 95 f.
[eneši] (non-ventive dimensional indicator) 98
equative (case) 33 f., 44
ergative (case) 33 f., 35 f., 90 f.
ergativity 1 f., 35 f.
[era] (non-ventive dimensional indicator) 94
[eri] (non-ventive dimensional indicator) 99
[eš] (adverbiative) 26, 42
[eši] (non-ventive dimensional indicator) 97
exclamations 27, 167–170
exclusive 30

finite verb 71
focus 2
fractions 67
free genitive 38 f.
"frozen" morpheme 2
frustrative (verbal mood) 120 f.

ĝ 17
[ga] (modal verbal indicator: cohortative) 115
[gana] (exclamation) 168
Gatumdu 4
"-gé" 36
[ge] (modal verbal indicator: cohortative) 115
ĝen/du (irregular behaviour in non-finite verb) 140 f.
genitive (case) 33 f., 36–39
Georgian (stops) 16
Girsu/Lagaš 4
grids (for verbal bases) 71 f., 74–78
[gu(mu)] (modal verbal indicator: cohortative) 115

H (Sumerian consonantal phoneme) 19 f., 50, 175
-H 40
ḫ 20
[ha] (modal verbal indicator: precative) 116 f.
[ha] (modal verbal indicator: affirmative 1) 117 f.
ḫamṭu 71 ff. passim
ḫamṭu participle 47, 132 f.
[he] (modal verbal indicator: precative) 116 f.
[he] (modal verbal indicator: affirmative 1) 116 f.
[heam] (exclamation, "yes") 27, 168
heteronymy (verbal base) 71
hi-a 32
Hiatustilger (r) 94, 99
[hu(mu)] (modal verbal indicator: precative) 116 f.
[hu(mu)] (modal verbal indicator: affirmative 1) 117 f.
Hurrian 4

[i] (prefixed verbal indicator) 109–111
[ilu] (exclamation) 168
[ilulamma] (exclamation) 168
[(i)mmeri] (ventive verbal indicator) 108
imperative 127–130
  extended i. 129 f.
  polite i. 122 f.
  unextended i. 128 f.
imperfective (verbal aspect) 74
inachevé (verbal aspect) 74
inalterable (class of verbs) 75
inclusive 30
indefinite pronoun (?) 59
indicative (verbal mood) 113
infinitive (Akkadian) 71
[(i)nga] (connective verbal indicator) 123–127
interrogative pronouns 57 f.
"intransitive" 36
[inu] "no" (exclamation) 169
inverted genitive construction 31

Iran 4
[i Utu] (exclamation) 169

ke_4 36
KID 36

l_1, l_2 17 f.
lexical lists 2, 23 f., 26
linear script (Elamite) 3
linguistic affiliation (of Sumerian) 2 f.
linguistic area (Sumero-Akkadian) 4 f., 25, 173–178
linguistic environment (of Sumerian) 3–4
liquids 17 f.
loan-words (Sumerian in Akkadian) 7, 16, 37
locative (case) 33 f., 39, 44
locative 2 see [ni]
logograms 8

[ma] (ventive dimensional indicator) 103
-ma (conjunction, borrowed from Akkadian) 162
marû 73 f.
[mda] (ventive dimensional indicator) 105
[me] 1st p. pronoun) 55 f.
[me] (ventive dimensional indicator) 108
[mea] (ventive dimensional indicator) 104
measures (terminology) 67
[mel(i)ea] (exclamation) 169
mes-Ane-pada construction 133
[mini] (ventive dimensional indicator) 108
[mma] (ventive dimensional indicator) 104
[mmara] (ventive dimensional indicator) 106
[mmeri] (ventive dimensional indicator) 107 f.
[mmi] (ventive dimensional indicator) 107 f.
[mmini] (ventive dimensional indicator) 109
modal indicators (verb) 113–121
"monosyllabic myth" 4
[mši] (ventive dimensional indicator) 107
[mta] (ventive dimensional indicator) 106
[mu] (= mu-V-) (ventive dimensional indicator) 107
[mu] ("year", as subjunction) 164
[muda] (ventive dimensional indicator) 105
[mueda] (ventive dimensional indicator) 105
[mueda(?)] (ventive dimensional indicator) 105
[muera] (ventive dimensional indicator) 103
[muεši] (ventive dimensional indicator) 107
[muna] (ventive dimensional indicator) 103 f.
[munda] (ventive dimensional indicator) 105
[mune] (ventive dimensional indicator) 108
[muni] (ventive dimensional indicator) 107
[munši] (ventive dimensional indicator) 107
[muri] (ventive dimensional indicator) 107
[muši] (ventive dimensional indicator) 106

[n] (variant of [ni], locative 2) 98
[na] (non-ventive dimensional indicator) 94
[na] (modal verbal indicator: affirmative 2) 119 f.
[na] (modal verbal indicator: prohibitive) 118 f.
[nam] (nominal prefix) 25
Nanše 4
nasals (consonants) 16 f.
[nda] (non-ventive dimensional indicator) 96
[ne(n)] (demonstrative) 49 f., 57
[(e)ne] (non-ventive dimensional indicator) 101
[(e)nea] (non-ventive dimensional indicator) 95 f.
[(e)neda] (non-ventive dimensional indicator) 96
negative affirmative (verbal mood) 118
negative precative see vetitive
negative verbal indicators 113–118
[(e)neši] (non-ventive dimensional indicator) 98
[ni] (non-ventive dimensional indicator: locative 2) 98 f., 102

[ni] (non-ventive dimensional indicator: 3rd p. sg. person class) 99
"no" 27, 169
nominalization (of finite verbal forms) 150–155
non-finite verb 71
non-finite verbal forms 130–142
non-ventive dimensional indicators 93 (grid) 94–102
[nši] (non-ventive dimensional indicator) 98
[nta] (non-ventive dimensional indicator) 97
[nu] (modal indicator: negative indicative, negation of non-finite verbal forms) 113–115
"nuclear" writing 11
number 2, 24, 31–33
numerals 26, 61–67
[nuš] (modal verbal indicator: frustrative) 120 f.

o (in Sumerian) 7
o (in Akkadian) 7, 13
ordinal numbers 66 f.

particles 23
parts of speech 23–27
passive 95
perfective (verbal aspect) 74
person 30 f.
personal pronouns 55 f.
phonetic indicators 8
phonology 13–21
  vowels 13–14
  consonants 14–21
plural bases (verb) 74, 78
polite imperative 122 f.
possession 24, 29–31, 56 f.
possessive pronouns 56 f.
post-nominal and/or post-verbal particles other than case particles 157–160
Präsens-Futur 73
Präteritum 73
precative (verbal mood) 116 f.
prohibitive (verbal mood) 118 f.
pronominal conjugation 137–142
pronouns 25 f., 55–59
pronouns (alleged) 58 f.
prospective (connective verbal indicator) 121–123
Proto-Ea 8
"Proto-Elamite" script 3
quadruplication (of verbal base) 81
quotation particle 157 f.

r̂ 18 f.
[ra] (non-ventive dimensional indicator) 97, 109
redundancy of spelled consonants 10, 35
reduplication 24 f.
  r. (number) 31
  r. of adjectives 25, 31, 48
  r. of verbal base 75 f., 79–81
  pseudo r. of verbal base 75
reflexive pronoun (?) 58
[(e)ri] (non-ventive dimensional indicator) 99

Sanskrit (stops) 16
secondary construction (verb) 74
sequence (of post-nominal particles) 53
sexagesimal system 26, 61–66
sibilants 20 f.
sign names (Akkadian) 7, 14
specification (of nouns) 49–51
spelling of Sumerian 8–11
spelling variants 7
"split ergativity" 2, 90 f.
'Sprachgruppe' 3
standard construction (verb) 74
stops 8, 14–16
subjunctions 27, 162–165
subordinate temporal clause 42 f.
substantivation 25
  see also nominalization
substantives 24
substratum (pre-Sumerian, alleged) 4
Sumero-Akkadian linguistic area 4 f., 173–178
syllabaries 11
syllabic spelling (in Akkadian, to identify Sumerian) 7
syllable-closing consonants (spelling of) 11
syllable structure 22
syllabograms 8
[ša] (modal verbal particle: affirmative 3) 120
[še] (demonstrative) 51
[ši] (modal verbal particle: affirmative 3) 120
[(e)ši] (non-ventive dimensional indicator) 97

[šu(mu)] (modal verbal particle: affirmative 3) 120
šu ti/te(-ĝ) (behaviour of the "object") 145 f.

[ta] (non-ventive verbal indicator) 109
Tepe Yaḥyā 3
terminative (case) 33 f., 42 f.
ternary system (of numerals) 66
"transitive" 36
triplication (of verbal base) 81
[tukumbi] 163 f.

[u] (verbal connective indicator, prospective 121–123
see also polite imperative
[u] (conjunction) 161 f.
[ua] (exclamation) 170
[uda] (subjunction) 162 f.
[ulili] (exclamation) 170
ur_5 (demonstrative) 55, 57
-ūtu (Akkadian) 25

ventive (Sumerian) 92
ventive (Akkadian) 92
ventive dimensional indicators 93
(grid) 103–109
verb 26, 71–155
verbalizer (in compound verbs) 143, 148 f.
vetitive (verbal mood) 117
vocative (case) 35
"vowel harmony" 99 f., 110
vowels 7, 13 f.
phonemes 7
quality 7, 13 f.
quantity 7

"without" 41
"word" 23
word order (S–O–V) 2

"yes" 27, 168

zero 87

www.ingramcontent.com/pod-product-compliance
Lightning Source LLC
Chambersburg PA
CBHW030343240426
43661CB00052B/1731